1/92

The Path We Tread
(Second Edition)

The Path We Tread
Blacks in Nursing, 1854-1990

Second Edition

Mary Elizabeth Carnegie,
DPA, RN, FAAN
Editor Emerita, *Nursing Research*

Foreword by
Josephine A. Dolan,
RN, MS, PdD
Professor Emerita and Special Lecturer
University of Connecticut
Storrs, Connecticut

ISBN 0-88737-534-0

This book was set in Baskerville by Harper Graphics. Rachel Schaperow was the editor and designer. St Mary's Press was the printer and binder. The cover was designed by Lillian Welsh.

Printed in the United States of America

To my late cousin, Iola Melbrook,
who through the years had been supportive of me
in all my endeavors

Foreword

Despite the rapidly expanding professional role of nursing, the need to reflect on the people and events that formed the basis of our rich historical heritage demands our reflection and appreciation. It is with pride that one observes the current resurgence of interest in the documented history of our profession, as well as the emergence of significant historical research. One area that has needed strengthening has been research and delineation of the accomplishments of our black nurse leaders. *The Path We Tread* provides a valuable contribution to the dearth of those historical data.

Dr. Mary Elizabeth Carnegie is eminently qualified to have undertaken the research and writing of this historical publication. The author's education, the positions of great responsibility she has held especially in the key editorial roles of our leading nursing journals *(American Journal of Nursing, Nursing Outlook*, and *Nursing Research)* have brought her in touch with events and those who are molding our professional achievements. Carnegie's own contributions to our professional enrichment have been praised and honors have been showered upon her. Among these tributes, the Nursing Archives at Hampton University has been named in her honor. Carnegie has held many board offices in association with institutions of higher learning, as well as in professional associations, such as the past presidency of the American Academy of Nursing.

In this book, the long and constant struggle to gain a rightful position in the health care system for black nurses has been identified by Carnegie. Through her efforts, a gold mine of information and illustrations not available previously have been vividly portrayed.

The Path We Tread should highlight an awakening of interest in the historical evolution of black nurses, and the impact of their leadership should be understood. Pride in their achievements and their education should be elicited on the part of all nurses. All black nurses should glow with pride and gratitude to those who have achieved and to Carnegie, who brings it forth for all to view.

Josephine A. Dolan, RN, MS, PdD

Preface to First Edition

Black nurses, like blacks in many other professions, have had a long and difficult history. Whereas many books have been written about blacks in this country, no comprehensive history of black nursing exists under one cover. Furthermore, most books on black history have excluded the nursing profession.

Despite there being many general books on the history of nursing, until recently only a few have mentioned or devoted more than a sentence or two to black nurses and their contributions to health care. The one typical sentence found in nursing history texts is, "Mary Mahoney was the first trained black nurse in America, having been graduated from the New England Hospital for Women and Children in 1879." All nursing history books, for example, refer to Florence Nightingale, the founder of modern nursing, and her work in the Crimean War, but omit the fact that a black woman nursed along with her. Another example of how black nursing history has been ignored: All history books credit the University of Minnesota as having established the first nursing program in a university setting in 1909, but Howard University, a black school in Washington, D.C., had established one 16 years before, in 1893.

In 1980, the U.S. registered nurse population was estimated to be 1,662,382. Of this number, 60,845, or 3.7 percent were black (*Facts About Nursing*, 1983). In the four years since 1980, graduates of the 1,422 basic nursing programs have added to this pool. These nurses, both black and white, have been deprived of historical data on the heritage of their profession, and thus their education has been incomplete. A book on black nursing history is not only timely, but also highly relevant to professional education in contemporary society.

The Path We Tread is organized into six chapters, the content of which spans 131 years—from 1854 to 1984. No attempt has been made to interpret the facts presented or to make philosophical projections.

The first chapter, "Answering the Call," is about black nurses in the early wars. It begins with the Crimean War in which Mary Seacole, a black woman from Jamaica, is depicted as having served as a nurse on the battlefield along with Florence Nightingale. Of the many women and men who served as nurses during the Civil War (also called the War Between the States), the work of three black women is referred to: Sojourner Truth, Harriet Tubman, and Susie King Taylor. During the Spanish-American War in 1898, blacks served as contract nurses, an outstanding one being Namahyoke Sockum Curtis who was given a government pension for her services and was buried in Arlington National Cemetery, along with other famous war dead.

In collecting data on black men and women who served as nurses during the Civil and Spanish-American Wars, extensive use was made of the National Archives in Washington, D.C. Records of those blacks who nursed in the Civil War were kept in a separate journal, which facilitated the research. Information on all nurses who served in the Spanish-American War was recorded on alphabetically arranged personnel data cards which had an item requesting the person to indicate his or her "color." The responses to this question included "light," "dark," "medium," "fair," "black" (only one), "blond," "brunette," "colored," "light skinned," "brownish," "mulatto," and "octoroon"; a few did not answer the question. Because both black and white people commonly refer to themselves as "fair," "light," and "dark," it was difficult to determine race; therefore, other demographic information was considered, such as place of birth, address, school of nursing attended, and the like.

The second chapter, "The Foundation Is Laid," is devoted to formal education programs—basic and advanced. The basic programs at historically black institutions are divided into diploma, baccalaureate, and associate degree, with two tables—one listing diploma programs that existed from 1886, the other listing baccalaureate and associate degree programs at historically black colleges and universities as of 1984. The advanced programs include two in public health nursing and two in nurse-midwifery that were conducted in the South exclusively for black registered nurses and three master's programs that are offered at historically black institutions of higher education.

The third chapter, "From Dreams to Achievements," describes the Cadet Nurse Corps that was in operation during World War II and explores three special education projects: one to recruit minorities for all types of nursing programs; one to help recruit and retain disadvantaged students in baccalaureate programs; and one to increase the number of doctorally prepared nurses from ethnic/racial minority populations.

The fourth chapter, "Struggle for Recognition," is devoted to those national nursing organizations that have or have had relevance for black nurses, including those established by and for black nurses themselves. Special attention is given to the role of the National Association of Colored Graduate Nurses in its fight for integration of the black nurse in the American Nurses' Association and into the mainstream of professional nursing. Included, also, are biographical sketches of each of the black regular and honorary fellows of the American Academy of Nursing.

The fifth chapter, "Stony the Road," highlights black nurses who pioneered in the profession in the late 19th and early 20th centuries, paving the way for black nurses of today.

The final chapter, "So Proudly We Hail," deals with black nurses in the federal government—the military, the U.S. Public Health Service, and the Veterans Administration.

The terms *Negro* and *colored* have been used when appropriate to maintain the historical perspective of the resources used.

Mary Elizabeth Carnegie, DPA, RN, FAAN
1984

Preface to Second Edition

The first edition of this book spanned 131 years—from 1854 through 1984. This second edition extends the time frame through 1990, noting the progress made by black nurses.

The popularity of the first edition has convinced me that black nurses take pride in their heritage and accomplishments, and nonblack nurses have learned about the contributions of black nurses to health care in this country. It shows how black nurses have had to work, sometimes desperately, to create, against tremendous odds, a place in the mainstream of the profession.

The first chapter, "Answering the Call," an account of the contributions of black women who nursed in the early wars—the Crimean War, the Civil War, and the Spanish-American War, has only a few additions. Included in the new material is a reference to James Derham, a black man who earned enough money working as a nurse to buy his freedom from slavery. He later became a prominent physician in Philadelphia, recognized by the well-known Dr. Benjamin Rusk.

The second chapter, "The Foundation Is Laid," is devoted to basic and advanced programs in nursing. This chapter lists an additional 15 black diploma programs, bringing the total to 90 that existed between 1886 and 1982. Nursing programs at historically black colleges and universities are identified: baccalaureate—23; associate degree—six; master's degree—four.

The third chapter, "From Dreams to Achievements," presents special educational projects. A new component to the American Nurses' Association Minority Fellowship Program—one which focuses on leadership training for minority women nurses who have earned doctorates—is described in this chapter.

The number of professional nursing organizations, discussed in Chapter 4, "Struggle for Recognition," has increased from 12 in the first edition to 24, including two regional bodies. This large increase is due not only to the growing number of new organizations that have or have had blacks in leadership roles, but to old, well-established ones that have or have had elected or appointed black officials since the first edition went to press. Included, also, are biographical sketches of the 38 black nurses who have been inducted into the American Academy of Nursing, an increase of ten.

Nothing was added to the fifth chapter, "Stony the Road," because of its nature—biographical sketches of the black pioneers in nursing, all of whom are deceased.

The last chapter, "So Proudly We Hail," devoted to blacks in the federal government—the military, the Public Health Service, and the Veterans Administration—has a number of changes that are due primarily to the reorganization of the Public Health Service and the identification of more black nurses in key positions.

The chronology has been broadened to include not only additional nursing events, but those events that have relevance for blacks in nursing (e.g., the 1954 Supreme Court Decision ending segregation in public schools.)

Because members of other disciplines and those teaching or engaged in research on women have used the book as a resource, the bibliography has been broadened to include more sources related to the content.

My thanks goes to the many readers and to those faculty in schools of nursing who have adopted the book as a text in their courses on issues and trends.

The acknowledgment section has been enlarged to express special appreciation to Memphis State University in Tennessee and Indiana University in Indianapolis for providing staff and other resources needed to complete this second edition.

Mary Elizabeth Carnegie, DPA, RN, FAAN
1990

Acknowledgments

Acknowledgment is made to the following individuals, associations, and institutions for generously contributing their knowledge, making suggestions, giving encouragement and support, and providing resources for the preparation of this book: The American Nurses' Association: The *American Nurse*, Hattie Bessent, Director, Minority Fellowship Programs, Margaret Carroll; The American Academy of Nursing: Bette Mitchell; The American Journal of Nursing Company: Cosy Brown, Mary Mallison, Thelma Schorr; Bennett College Library Historical Collection, Greensboro, North Carolina; Priscilla Butts; Chi Eta Phi Sorority; Josephine Dolan; John Hope Franklin; Guilford County Health Department, Greensboro, North Carolina; Hampton University M. Elizabeth Carnegie Nursing Archives, Patricia Sloan, director; Fred Hinson; Jesse J. Johnson; Maternity Center Association, Ruth Lubic; Mamie Montague; Helen S. Miller; Missouri Nurses' Association; Moorland-Spingarn Research Center, Howard University, Washington, D.C.; Beatrice Murray; Nancy Noel; National League for Nursing: Katherine Brim; National Student Nurses' Association: B.J. Nerone, Robert Piemonte, Mary Ann Tuft; National Archives and Records Service: Robert Clarke, Chief, Navy and Old Army Branch, Charles A. Shaughnessy, archivist; North Carolina Nurses' Association; Pennsylvania Nurses' Association: Donna Fealtman, Executive Secretary; Rosetta Sands, Dean, Tuskegee Institute School of Nursing; Schomburg Center for Research in Black Culture, New York Public Library; Women's Research and Resource

Center, Spelman College, Atlanta, Georgia; State Boards of Nursing; Della Sullins; United Nations Archives; U.S. Air Force Nurse Corps: Brigadier General Diann Hale, Chief; U.S. Navy Nurse Corps: Commodore Mary J. Nielubowicz, Director; U.S. Army Center of Military History: Major Mary E.V. Frank, ANC, Army Nurse Corps Historian, Charles W. Ellsworth, Jr., archivist; University of North Carolina at Greensboro: Eloise R. Lewis, Dean, School of Nursing, Catherine Turner, Marian Davis Whiteside; U.S. Public Health Service: Faye Abdellah, Joyce Elmore (special thanks for providing many photographs and background material), Helen Foerst, Doris Mosley, Mary S. Harper, Dan J. Rondeau, Mary S. Hill, Division of Nursing, Dorothy L. Moore, Jennie Hunt, Howard Drew, Susan Sparks, National Library of Medicine, Lula Whitlock, Shallie Marshall, Doris Bloch; Veterans Administration: Vernice Ferguson; Virginia Commonwealth University, Medical College of Virginia: Jodie L. Koste, archivist, Coralease B. Wallace, Special Collections and Archives; David T. Miller, Nursing Editor, J.B. Lippincott Company, who worked with me closely throughout the production of the first edition, and for his encouragement, enthusiasm, and support; Rosemary McCarthy; Linda Harvey, Hollis Burke Frissell Library, Tuskegee University, Tuskegee, Alabama; Joyce Prestwidge; Lillian Stokes, for reading final copy of the second edition; Paulette Johnson, National Institutes of Health; Jacqueline Patton, my research assistant for the second edition, who worked with me tirelessly and enthusiastically; Frances Craig, Secretary, Loewenberg School of Nursing, Memphis State University, Tennessee; and Linda Martin, Secretary, Indiana University School of Nursing, Indianapolis. A special thanks to Norma Long, Dean, Memphis State University School of Nursing, Memphis, Tennessee, and Constance Baker, Dean, Indiana University School of Nursing, Indianapolis, for providing me with the personnel and resources to conduct the research necessary for the preparation of the second edition.

M.E.C.

Contents

Abbreviations xx

1. Answering the Call 1

The Crimean War 2
The Civil War 5
The Spanish-American War 12

2. The Foundation Is Laid 19

Black Basic Programs 22
Advanced Programs 38

3. From Dreams to Achievements 47

Cadet Nurse Corps 48
Breakthrough 53
Sealantic 57
ANA Minority Fellowship Programs 61

4. Struggle for Recognition 71

The National League for Nursing 71
The American Nurses' Association 74

The National Association of Colored Graduate Nurses 92
The American Red Cross Nursing Service 100
The National Organization for Public Health Nursing 103
The American Public Health Association 105
Sigma Theta Tau International 106
Chi Eta Phi 108
The American Journal of Nursing Company 110
The National Student Nurses' Association 111
Nurses' Educational Funds 112
The American Nurses' Foundation 113
The American Association of Colleges of Nursing 115
The National Black Nurses' Association 117
The American Association for the History of Nursing 119
The Society for Nursing History 121
The Association of Black Nursing Faculty in Higher
        Education 122
The American Academy of Nursing 124
Regional Nursing Organizations 170
Selected Specialty Organizations 172

5. Stony the Road 177

6. So Proudly We Hail 195

The Military 195
The U.S. Public Health Service 217
The Veterans Administration 252

Bibliography 261

Appendices 267

A. Black Deans and Directors of Baccalaureate
        and Higher Degree Programs in Nursing,
        December 31, 1990 267
B. Charter Members, National Association of Colored
        Graduate Nurses 270
C. Mary Mahoney Award Recipients, 1936–1990 271
D. Charter Members, Chi Eta Phi Sorority 273
E. Honorary Members, Chi Eta Phi Sorority 274
F. Charter Members, National Black Nurses'
        Association 275

Chronology 277

Index 291

Abbreviations

AAANA	American Academy of Ambulatory Nursing Administration
AACN	American Association of Colleges of Nursing
AAF	Army Air Forces
AAIN	American Association of Industrial Nurses
ABNF	Association of Black Nursing Faculty in Higher Education
ACSN	Association of Collegiate Schools of Nursing
ADAMHA	Alcohol, Drug Abuse, and Mental Health Administration
AETC	AIDS Education and Training Centers
AHCPR	Agency for Health Care Policy and Research
AID	Agency for International Development
ANA	American Nurses' Association
ANF	American Nurses' Foundation
APHA	American Public Health Association
ATSDR	Agency for Toxic Substances and Disease Registry
CBIC	Certification Board of Infection Control
CDC	Centers for Disease Control
CFP	Clinical Fellowship Program
COAR	Commission on Organizational Assessment and Renewal
DAR	Daughters of the American Revolution
DHEW	Department of Health, Education, and Welfare
DHHS	Department of Health and Human Services

EAP	Extramural Associates Program
ECA	Economic Cooperation Administration
FDA	Food and Drug Administration
FOA	Foreign Operations Administration
FSNA	Florida State Nurses' Association
GEB	General Education Board
HRSA	Health Resources & Services Administration
ICA	International Cooperation Administration
ICN	International Council of Nurses
IHS	Indian Health Service
MARNA	Mid-Atlantic Regional Nursing Association
MCA	Maternity Center Association
MCHB	Maternal and Child Health Bureau
MFP	Minority Fellowship Programs
MSA	Mutual Security Agency
NAACP	National Association for the Advancement of Colored People
NACGN	National Association of Colored Graduate Nurses
NBNA	National Black Nurses' Association
NCNR	National Center for Nursing Research
NEF	Nurses' Educational Funds
NHSC	National Health Service Corps
NIH	National Institutes of Health
NIMH	National Institute of Mental Health
NLN	National League for Nursing
NLNE	National League of Nursing Education
NLM	National Library of Medicine
NNCWS	National Nursing Council for War Service
NOLF	National Organization Liaison Forum
NOPHN	National Organization for Public Health Nursing
NSNA	National Student Nurses' Association
OASH	Office of the Assistant Secretary for Health
ODWIN	Opening the Doors Wider in Nursing
PHS	Public Health Service
SREB	Southern Regional Education Board
STEM	Special Technical Economic Mission
UNRRA	United States Relief and Rehabilitation Administration
USPHS	United States Public Health Service
VA	Veterans Administration
WHO	World Health Organization

Chapter 1

Answering the Call

Long before nurses were trained to care for the sick, many women—black and white—volunteered their services during crises. Black men were also nurses. A case in point: working as a nurse in New Orleans in 1783, James Derham was able to save enough money to buy his freedom from slavery. Within six years, he had become an outstanding physician. After he moved to Philadelphia, he won the highest respect from his colleagues in the medical profession, especially that of the eminent Benjamin Rusk (Quarles, 1969). Derham has been credited with having been the first black physician in America (Lincoln, 1967).

Historically, nursing was a role assigned to black women. During the time of slavery, for example, black women were expected to take care of the sick in the families that owned them, breast-feed the white babies, and care for their own families and fellow slaves. Although the term *nurse* was not applied to them, their activities were clearly within the definition of nursing. Thus, in situations of great crisis, it was "natural" for many black women with such practical experience to volunteer as nurses.

This chapter is limited to the stories of five black women who served as nurses in three wars: Mary Seacole, who nursed along with Florence Nightingale in the Crimean War; Sojourner Truth, Harriet Tubman, and Susie King Taylor who nursed in the Civil War, or War Between the States; and Namahyoke Sockum Curtis, who served under contract with the federal government in the Spanish-American War.

1

THE CRIMEAN WAR

In the Crimean War (1853–1856), Great Britain, France, and Turkey fought against Russia for control of access to the Mediterranean from the Black Sea. The immediate causes of the war were more complicated than this, but of a pattern familiar enough today—the "protection of oppressed minorities" in the target country and reprisals for the death of nationals in religious riots. The war on land was fought in three main theaters: the Danube Valley, Asia Minor, and the Crimea (Blake, 1971).

Russia and France had members of religious orders to care for their armies, but England had only untrained men to care for the sick and wounded. Ugly rumors of deplorable medical and sanitary neglect and mismanagement of casualties began to reach England. A famous letter from Sir Sidney Herbert, secretary of state for war, to Florence Nightingale, printed in the *Daily News* on October 28, 1854, contained a plea for Nightingale to supervise the military hospitals in Turkey:

> There is but one person in England that I know who would be capable of organizing and superintending such a scheme . . . . My question simply is, Would you listen to the request to go out and supervise the whole thing? You would of course have plenary authority over all the nurses, and operation [cooperation] from the medical staff, and you would also have an unlimited power of drawing on the Government for whatever you think requisite for the success of your mission . . . . I must not conceal from you that I think upon your decision will depend the ultimate success or failure of the plan. Your own personal qualities, your knowledge and your power of administration, and among greater things your rank and position in Society give you advantages in such a work which no other person possesses . . . . [Cook, 1913, p. 153]

On October 21, 1854, Nightingale set out for the Crimea with 38 women volunteers to serve as nurses, among whom were Roman Catholic and Anglican sisters and lay nurses. She and her band were assigned to the base hospital at Scutari, across the strait from Constantinople (Dolan, 1968).

There may have been other black women who nursed in the Crimean War, but the services of only one, Mary Seacole, have been documented in the literature.

Mary Seacole

Mary Grant Seacole (1805–1881) (Fig. 1–1) learned the caring and healing arts from her mother, who, in her native Jamaica, British West Indies,

Figure 1–1 Mary Grant Seacole, black nurse in the Crimean War. (Courtesy Moorland-Spingarn Research Center, Howard University)

was nicknamed "the Doctress" because of her ministrations to the sick in her lodging house in Kingston. There she nursed many of the British army officers and their families from Up-Park Camp. As a person with no formal training in nursing (none existed at that time), Mary Seacole served in Panama and Cuba during cholera and yellow fever epidemics. In order to learn more about the effects of the disease, she performed a postmortem examination on an infant who had died of cholera in Panama (Burnett, 1981).

When Seacole learned that hostilities had broken out in the Crimea, she wrote the British government asking to be allowed to join Nightingale in the Crimea as a nurse, but her request was denied. She was especially concerned when she learned that many of the regiments she had known in Jamaica were being sent to this area where disease killed more soldiers than did wounds. She was convinced that her knowledge of tropical diseases was vital to Britain's war effort. So, at her own expense, Seacole sailed to England with a letter of introduction to Nightingale, but her attempts to join the group of recruited nurses were blocked because of her color. She presented personal credentials written by army doctors as evidence of her impeccable qualifications. When her services were rejected, she appealed to the War Office. Mrs. Sidney Herbert, wife of the secretary of war, petitioned on her behalf, but the Crimean Fund would not reverse its decision. Undaunted, Seacole purchased stores and traveled 3,000 miles to the Crimea. There she built and opened a lodging house on the road between Balaklava and Sebastopol for the comfort of the troops, naming it "The British Hotel." On the lower floor was a restaurant and bar; the upper floor was arranged like a hospital ward with her supply of medicines, many of which she concocted herself and used to nurse the sick among the officers (Alexander & Dewjee, 1981).

Seacole still had the faint hope of securing a position as an army nurse, but when she met with Nightingale, the response was the same—no vacancies. However, each night at 7:00, after having worked in her provisions store on the outskirts of the camp, she made her way to the hospital and worked as a volunteer side by side with Nightingale. Seacole attended not only the British casualties, but French, Sardinian, and Russian soldiers as well. She saved the lives of countless soldiers wounded during the Crimean War and thousands of other with cholera, yellow fever, malaria, diarrhea, and a host of other ailments.

Although her services in the Crimea went unheralded by the British government, Seacole had won the admiration, respect, and love of many of the English people. Public resentment brought attention to those whose prejudice had prevented her official enlistment (King, 1974). At the end of the war, all England was ringing with her fame. A contemporary London *Times* correspondent, William Howard Russell, bore testament to her services: "trust that England will not forget one who has nursed her sick . . ." (Swaby, 1979, p. 9). Long after the war ended, the government bestowed a medal upon her for services rendered the sick and injured.

In the Institute of Jamaica is a terra-cotta bust of Seacole modeled by Count Gleichen, a nephew of Queen Victoria; and two of her Crimean War medals. Seacole had nursed Gleichen in her canteen-hotel-hospital during the Crimean War (Rogers, 1947).

On the campus of the University of the West Indies is Mary Seacole Hall. In 1954, the nurses of Jamaica named their headquarters Mary Seacole House. The building was opened in 1960, and a life-sized bust was placed in the foyer where it stands today. The bust was reproduced by a Jamaican sculptor, Curtis Johnston, from the original in the institute. At the Kingston Public Hospital is Mary Seacole Ward. All these tributes have been made in a conscious attempt to perpetuate the name of a great Jamaican and an even greater nurse, one who the Cubans called, "The Yellow Woman from Jamaica with the Cholera Medicine," and the Crimean soldiers, "The Florence Nightingale of Jamaica."

The British Commonwealth Nurses War Memorial Fund and the Lignum Vitae Club, an organization of Jamaican women in London, provided funds to restore Seacole's grave (Swaby, 1979). On November 20, 1973, there was a ceremony of reconservation of the grave of a nurse who had served in the Crimean War, who had returned to England, who had received rapturous acclaim, but who, after her death on May 14, 1881, had been totally forgotten in England—although not in her own country. According to her wish, Seacole was buried in the Catholic portion of the cemetery at Kensal Green, London, where her restored headstone today says simply, in letters of gold and blue, "Here lies Mary Seacole (1805–1881) of Kingston, Jamaica, a notable nurse who cared for the sick and wounded in the West Indies, Panama, and on the battlefield of the Crimea, 1854–1856" (Gordon, 1975).

THE CIVIL WAR

The Civil War (1861–1865) has been called the second American Revolution, the War of the Rebellion, the War Between the States, the War for Southern Independence, the Rich Man's War and the Poor Man's Fight, the War to Save the Union, and the War for Freedom. It was also called a struggle between national sovereignty and states' rights. It has been referred to as a contest between profiteers, northern and southern. We know it was a revolution in which slaves and owners were freed, for both were enslaved by the system of forced labor. James Ford Rhodes, Civil War historian, stated in 1913, "Of the American Civil War it may safely be asserted that there was a single cause, slavery" (Wesley & Romero, 1967, p. 2).

> Slavery was the underlying cause of the War, despite the economic and political questions which were involved. The North contended that its fight was to preserve the Union, while the South rested its defense on states' rights. Each section declined to recognize slavery publicly as a cause of the War—until the issuance of the Emancipation Proclamation. [Wesley & Romero, 1967, p. xi]

When the Civil War began with the Confederate attack on Fort Sumter, South Carolina, April 17, 1861, there were no formally trained nurses in the country. However, thousands of men and women from the North and South volunteered almost immediately for nursing assignments in field hospitals and on hospital transports.

On June 8, 1861, Dorothea Lynde Dix, a school teacher from New England, already well known as a humanitarian on behalf of the mentally ill, and a group of women friends journeyed to Washington, D.C., and offered to assist the War Department by providing care for sick and wounded soldiers. On June 10, 1861, Dix was appointed by Secretary of War Simon Cameron to superintend the women nurses. This was a post of honor, but one that carried no official status and no salary. Dix's wide-ranging authority, dated April 12, 1861, theoretically gave her the power to organize hospitals for the care of the sick and wounded soldiers; to appoint nurses; and to receive, control, and disburse special supplies donated by individuals or associations for distribution among the troops (Brockett & Vaughan, 1867). Many nursed all through the war without official recognition or financial compensation; those who had been regularly appointed received $12 a month from the government, or 40¢ a day and rations (Piemonte & Gurney, 1987).

No accurate records of the appointment of nurses, their number, where they served, or the number who died, can be found. However, the records show that women serving in hospitals during the Civil War were

> . . . regularly appointed nurses, about 3,214; Sisters of Charity, number not known; women of middle age and no training acting as cooks, etc.; women who gave time without pay; women accompanying regiments; wives, etc; and colored women . . . [Stimson & Thompson, 1928].

In the National Archives in Washington, D.C., are 20 journals containing information about contract nurses in the Civil War, one of which is devoted to colored nurses. According to these records kept on nurses at 11 hospitals in three states, 181 colored nurses—men and women—served between July 16, 1863, and June 14, 1864: Convalescent Hospital, Baltimore, Maryland—16; Contraband Hospital, Portsmouth, Virginia—14; Flag of Truce Boat, from Fort Monroe, Virginia—three; Contraband Small Pox Hospital, New Bern, North Carolina—44; Jarvis USG Hospital, Baltimore, Maryland—46; Chesapeake Hospital, Virginia—21; Green Heights Hospital, Virginia—one; McKims Mansion Hospital, near Alexandria, Virginia—three; and Patterson Park, U.S. General Hospital, Baltimore—seven (Colored Nurses, 1863–64).

The stories of three black women who played significant roles as nurses in the Civil War—Sojourner Truth, Harriet Tubman, and Susie King Taylor—are presented here, although they were not contract nurses.

Sojourner Truth

Born a slave in New York, where slavery had been officially recognized as legal since 1684, and freed by the New York State Emancipation Act of 1827, Sojourner Truth (1797–1883) (Fig. 1–2) was not only a famous abolitionist and underground railroad agent, itinerant preacher, lec-

Figure 1–2   Sojourner Truth visits President Abraham Lincoln, 1864. (Courtesy U.S. Army Center of Military History)

turer, women's rights worker, and humanitarian, but also a nurse during the Civil War and immediately thereafter. When she gained her freedom in 1827, she changed her name from Isabella to Sojourner Truth to reveal the nature of her mission —"Sojourner" because she would travel and "Truth" because she would tell the truth about slavery wherever she went (Wesley & Romero, 1967).

Of the slaves who were freed in New York on July 4, 1827, Truth was destined to be the most remarkable. An abolitionist and an advocate of women's rights, she remained a lifelong illiterate, but made a deep impression by her commanding figure. With a hopeful heart and an unshakable confidence in ultimate justice and the goodness of God, she bore pity rather than bitterness toward the slaveholders (Quarles, 1969).

The newly freed slaves—many sick, decrepit, mentally ravaged, and destitute—poured into Washington, D.C., from the South during and after the war (slavery had been abolished in Washington in 1862) with the hope that their needs would be provided for. Because of this problem, the War Department of the United States decided to establish the Freedmen's Bureau and to create an emergency facility. Started by the concerned citizens, the endeavor was quickly ratified by an act of the 38th Congress, dated March 3, 1865, "to Establish a Bureau for the Relief of Freedmen and Refugees."

Truth worked as a nurse/counselor for the Freedmen's Relief Association during Reconstruction in the Washington area, helping freed men who had migrated from the South find homes and employment in northern states. Many of her activities were sanctioned by President Lincoln, whom she visited in 1864, traveling from Battle Creek, Michigan, to do so. Lincoln is reported to have told her during their meeting that he had heard of her activities before being elected president. He autographed her book of names of interesting people she had met, writing, "For Aunty Sojourner Truth, October 29, 1864, A. Lincoln" (Wesley & Romero, 1967).

While in Washington, Truth spent much time in Freedmen's Village providing care to patients in the hospital. She organized a corps of women to clean Freedmen's Hospital because she contended that the sick can never be made well in dirty surroundings. Truth also visited Congress to urge that funds be provided to train nurses and doctors. In 1986, as part of the Black Heritage series, the commemorative Sojourner Truth postage stamp was issued.

Harriet Tubman

Harriet Ross Tubman (1820–1913) (Fig. 1–3), a woman of unusual capabilities and great courage, was born to slave parents in Bucktown, Dorchester County, Maryland. In addition to being an abolitionist, she had the unofficial title, "Conductor of the Underground Railroad." Before and during the Civil War, she made 19 secret trips below the Mason and Dixon Line, leading more than 300 slaves north to freedom. To join her rescue party meant to remain with it, for she threatened to kill anyone who attempted to turn back.

Tubman also volunteered her services as a nurse. By 1858, she was known in abolitionist circles in England, Ireland, Scotland, Liberia, and Canada and had received financial aid from Great Britain and Canada.

During the Civil War, Tubman served as a nurse in the Sea Islands off the coast of South Carolina, caring for the sick and wounded without regard to color. She also held the position of matron or nurse at the

Figure 1–3   Harriet Tubman, abolitionist and nurse in the Civil War.

Colored Hospital, Fort Monroe, Virginia (Bradford, 1961). Acting Assistant Surgeon General Henry K. Durrant was so moved by her warmth and generous attitude that he wrote a note, addressing it, "To Whom It May Concern," commending her for "kindness and attention to the sick and suffering" (Wesley & Romero, 1967, p. 107).

Citing her for outstanding work as a nurse, a Union general urged Congress to award Tubman a pension. Like all Civil War nurses, she received it nearly 30 years after the close of the war, by an act of Congress (27 Stat. 348). However, unlike the white Civil War nurses, whose pensions were only $12 a month, Tubman, along with a select few, was awarded $20 a month for the remainder of her life. In addition to her husband's pension, which she received, she was compensated by Congress for her work as a spy and a scout for the Union Army.

In 1914, a bronze plaque containing a portrait of Tubman and an inscription was erected next to the entrance of the Cayuga County Courthouse in Auburn, New York. On February 1, 1978, the U.S. government honored Tubman with a commemorative postage stamp, the first in the Black History Heritage USA series. The fact that Tubman was chosen to inaugurate this new series, in recognition of the contributions of black Americans to the growth and development of the United States, is of great importance. Even though she was only 5 feet tall, the stamp depicts a strong face matched by her great physical strength, endurance, and a commanding presence. Unable to read or write, she developed remarkable skill planning activities as a fugitive slave, while avoiding arrest as she acted upon her single driving passion—freedom for herself and others.

The original artwork of the Tubman commemorative stamp was presented to Hampton University for placement in the M. Elizabeth Carnegie Nursing Archives during a ceremony at the university on April 15, 1978 (Fig. 1–4). The program was co-sponsored by the American Nurses' Association (ANA), and Joyce Elmore, director of ANA's Department of Nursing Education, described the impact that Tubman's nursing practice had on both the military and civilian population. Earlier that year, NBC Television Network had aired a two-part special program on the life of this famous black Civil War nurse and freedom fighter, "A Woman Called Moses," in which Cicely Tyson portrayed Tubman.

The House of Representatives passed and cleared S. J. Resolution 257, to designate March 10, 1990, as "Harriet Tubman Day." The resolution included a description of her service "in the Civil War as a soldier, spy, nurse, scout, and cook, and as leader in working with newly freed slaves . . . whose courageous and dedicated pursuit of the promise of American ideals and common principles of humanity continues to serve and inspire all people who cherish freedom—died at her home in Auburn, New York, on March 10, 1913. . ." (Congressional Record, 1990, p. H672).

Susie King Taylor

Susie King Taylor (1848–1912) (Fig. 1–5) was born into slavery on the Isle of Wight in Liberty County, about 35 miles from Savannah, Georgia. When she was only 14 years old and had learned surreptitiously to read and write, a Union officer placed her in charge of a school for black refugee children at Fort Pulaski, after it fell to the Union army. Wife of a noncommissioned officer in Company E of the First South Carolina Volunteers, Taylor was employed as a laundress for the company, but served as both teacher and nurse in her free time. When the hospital needed additional competent women to nurse the growing number of wounded Union troops, she quickly volunteered her services (Wesley & Romero, 1967).

At Beaufort, South Carolina, during the summer of 1863, Taylor met Clara Barton, a former New England school teacher, later to be the great "moving spirit" in the founding of the American Red Cross. Taylor frequently accompanied Barton, who treated her very cordially, on rounds in the hospitals at the front (Roberts, 1954).

Figure 1–4   Art work of the Harriet Tubman postage stamp presented to Hampton University for placement in the Mary Elizabeth Carnegie Nursing Archives, 1978. Pictured with the Harriet Tubman stamp artwork at the ceremonies at Hampton University are, from left to right, Mary Elizabeth Carnegie, initiator of the School of Nursing at Hampton University; Fostine G. Riddick Roach, Dean, Hampton University School of Nursing; Mabel K. Staupers, former Executive Secretary and last President, National Association of Colored Graduate Nurses; and Carl Hill, President, Hampton University.

Figure 1–5   Susie King Taylor served as both teacher and nurse in the Civil War.

As the Civil War continued in the South, Taylor assumed duties as a volunteer nurse on the battlefront, and for four years and three months she witnessed horror, pain, suffering, and death. During her service with the Union, she received no pay, and later, because she was not classified as an official army nurse, she received no pension or government recognition, although her services were witnessed and had been documented. (It should be noted that only contract nurses, regardless of color, received a pension.)

On April 9, 1865, Confederate General Robert E. Lee surrendered to General Ulysses S. Grant at Appomattox Court House in Virginia, ending the Civil War.

In 1902, Taylor published her book, *Reminiscences of My Life in Camp*. In it, she refers to having cooked, carried out physicians' orders, and taught. "I taught," she said, "a great many of the comrades in Company E to read and write. . . . Nearly all were anxious to learn" (Taylor, 1902).

In 1914, a large bronze statue, "a tribute of honor and gratitude" to Civil War nurses, was erected in the rotunda of the State Capitol Building, Boston, Massachusetts, by the Massachusetts Daughters of Veterans Organization. The statue depicts a woman caring for a wounded Union army soldier. The inscription on the base of the statue reads: "To the Army Nurses from 1861 to 1865, Angels of Mercy and Life Amid Scenes of Conflict and Death" (Piemonte & Gurney, 1987).

THE SPANISH-AMERICAN WAR

Shortly after the Civil War ended in 1865, Cuba, then a Spanish colony, began experiencing unrest among the populace. Repression and rigid control of every aspect of life in Cuba had inspired numerous revolts against Spain, and between 1868 and 1878 there was a full-blown uprising. Toward the end of the century, the Cubans had become determined to have their independence. By that time, the United States had begun to assume a role in world affairs, considering itself the guardian of civilization in the New World (Franklin, 1967).

In January 1898, the American battleship USS *Maine* was ordered to Havana to protect American life and property and to demonstrate to Spain that the United States was willing to take action. On February 15, an explosion of undetermined origin sank the *Maine* in the Havana harbor, killing over 250 officers and men, including 30 black sailors (Stillman, 1968). This incident set off a train of events that culminated in war two months later. On April 24, Spain declared war on the United States; the next day, the United States declared war on Spain, and hostilities continued until August 12, 1898, when the armistice protocol was signed.

The American and Spanish peace commissioners met in Paris, and on December 10, 1898, the Treaty of Paris was signed. The treaty provided that Spain was to relinquish all claim to sovereignty over Cuba. In lieu of a war indemnity, Spain ceded to the United States the island of Puerto Rico and the other Spanish insular possessions in the West Indies. Upon the payment of $20 million by the United States, Spain was to relinquish the Philippines to the victor (Franklin, 1967).

At the onset of the Spanish-American War, the surgeon general requested and promptly received congressional authority to appoint women nurses under contract at the rate of $30 a month and a daily ration. Three days after the United States declared war on Spain, Anita Newcomb McGee, a medical doctor who was also vice president of the National Society of the Daughters of the American Revolution (DAR), approached the assistant surgeon general of the army with a plan to provide nurses for the army (McGee, 1898). McGee's plan was accepted, and she was placed in charge of selecting graduate nurses for the army. She also suggested that the DAR act as an application review board for military nursing services. Thus, the DAR Hospital Corps was founded, with McGee as its director (Shields, 1981).

The epidemics of typhoid fever, malaria, and yellow fever, which were rampant during the Spanish-American War, killed many more American soldiers than did Spanish bullets. Although there were 400 training schools for nurses and more than 2,000 trained nurses in the country, there were difficulties in recruiting a sufficient number of trained nurses. During the summer of 1898, some 1,200 nurses were contracted to care for patients in the general and field hospitals in the United States and Cuba (Flanagan, 1976).

As in the Civil War, black women served. One such woman was Namahyoke Sockum Curtis (1871–1935), who played a leadership role, although she was not a trained nurse.

Namahyoke Curtis

When yellow fever appeared among troops in Santiago, McGee contacted Namahyoke Curtis (Fig. 1–6), wife of Austin M. Curtis, surgeon-in-chief at Freedmen's Hospital in Washington, D.C. Curtis, who had had yellow fever herself and was thus immune to it, was sent on July 13 under contract by the surgeon general of the army to New Orleans, Louisiana, and cities in Alabama and Florida to secure the services of blacks, both male and female, who were immune to yellow fever. Curtis was able to

Figure 1–6   Namahyoke
Sockum Curtis, contract
nurse during the Spanish-
American War. (Courtesy
Moorland-Spingarn Re-
search Center, Howard
University)

register 32 immune blacks to work as nurses (Kalisch & Kalisch, 1978).
According to Stimson et al. (1937), 80 colored women served as nurses
during the Spanish-American War.

Curtis also served under Clara Barton, head of the American Red
Cross, during the Galveston flood in Texas in 1900. During the San
Francisco earthquake in 1906, she carried a commission from William
H. Taft, then secretary of war. Because of her wartime service, she
received a government pension. At her death on November 25, 1935,
Curtis was buried in Arlington National Cemetery with the nation's military dead. A newspaper article dated November 26, 1935, recorded
that, "Her work with the nurses during the Spanish-American War won
her high official commendation."

According to the records of Tuskegee University, a black school in
Alabama, five of its nursing graduates served in the camps during the
war (Washington, 1910). Personnel data cards in the National Archives
in Washington, D.C., show that other black trained nurses had served:
two 1898 graduates of Freedmen's Hospital—Sarah Jane Ennies Brooks
and Lillian May Sumley; Nellie Singleton, an 1898 graduate of Provident
in Chicago; Sarah L. Stowall, an 1897 graduate of Massachusetts General

Hospital in Boston; and May Williams, who indicated that she was a graduate of Phillis Wheatley Training School, 1896, and Charity Hospital in New Orleans. One black man who volunteered as a contract nurse indicated that he was a dentist by profession.

Although the Spanish-American War was of short duration, it gave the army nurses ample time to become indispensable to the service. It was the distinguished service of contract nurses during and following the war in the United States, Cuba, Puerto Rico, the Philippines, Hawaii, China, and briefly in Japan, and on the hospital ship *Relief*, that paved the way for a permanent nurse corps in the army, established on February 2, 1901 (Shields, 1981).

On May 22, 1902, a monument to the Spanish-American War nurses who gave their lives in 1898 was dedicated in the nurses' section of Arlington National Cemetery (Fig. 1–7). The memorial was given by surviving Spanish-American War nurses who paid tribute "To Our Comrades" (Shields, 1981).

Figure 1–7   Memorial to the Spanish-American War nurses at Arlington National Cemetery. (Courtesy U.S. Army Center of Military History)

SUMMARY

Between 1853 and 1898, three wars were fought in which it is known that black women, most of whom were untrained, served as nurses: the Crimean War, the Civil War, and the Spanish-American War. Although there may have been other black nurses in the Crimean War, Mary Seacole is the only one documented in the literature.

Serving in the Civil War were Sojourner Truth, Harriet Tubman, and Susie King Taylor. These women's stories are only illustrations of the contributions made by many in the course of the war. Throughout the South, on untold battlefields and in many camps, black women worked with the Union army as spies, scouts, nurses, and teachers. They served in their way, as did their menfolk, to show the willingness of blacks to sacrifice for freedom (Wesley & Romero, 1967).

The only black woman cited by name in the literature for service in the Spanish-American War is Namahyoke Sockum Curtis, an untrained contract nurse, who not only received a pension from the War Department but, when she died in 1935, was buried in Arlington National Cemetery with other famous war dead. Of the 80 black women who served as nurses in the Spanish-American War, 32 (mostly untrained, but immune to yellow fever) were recruited by Curtis.

REFERENCES

Alexander, A., & Dewjee, A. (1981). Mary Seacole. *History Today, 31*, 45.

Blake, R.L.V.F. (1971). *The Crimean War*. London: Leo Cooper.

Bradford, S. (1961). *The Moses of her people*. New York: Corinth Books.

Brockett, L.P., & Vaughan, M.C. (1867). *Women's work in the Civil War: A record of heroism, patriotism, and patience*. Philadelphia: Seigler, McCurdy.

Burnett, S.M. (1981). Jamaica: Professional progress, case for all are goals. *American Journal of Nursing, 81*, 13–14.

Colored Nurses—Contract Nurses, 1863–64. Record Group 94, Entry 591. Washington, D.C.: National Archives.

Congressional Record. (1990). Proceedings and Debates of the 101st Congress Second Session, Vol. 136, No. 22. Washington, D.C.: Government Printing Office.

Cook, E. (1913). *The life of Florence Nightingale* (Vol. 19). London: Macmillan.

Dolan, J. (1968). *History of nursing* (12th ed.). Philadelphia: W.B. Saunders.

Flanagan, L. (1976). *The story of the American Nurses' Association*. Kansas City: American Nurses' Association.

Franklin, J.H. (1967). *From slavery to freedom* (3rd ed.). New York: Alfred Knopf.

Gordon, J.E. (1975). Mary Seacole—a forgotten nurse heroine of the Crimea. *Midwife, Health Visitor & Community Nurses, 11*, 47–50.

Kalisch, P., & Kalisch, B. (1978). *The advance of American nursing*. Boston: Little, Brown.

King, A. (1974, April). Mary Seacole, Part II, the Crimea. *Essence*. pp. 68, 94.

Lincoln, C.E. (1967). *The Negro pilgrimage in America*. New York: Bantam Books.

McGee Journal. (1898). Washington, D.C.: The National Archives.

Piemonte, R.V., & Gurney, C. (1987). *Highlights in the history of the Army Nurse Corps*. Washington, D.C.: U.S. Army Center of Military History.

Quarles, B. (1969). *The Negro in the making of America*. New York: Collier Books.

Roberts, M.M. (1954). *American nursing: History and interpretation*. New York: Macmillan.

Rogers, J.A. (1947). *World's great men of color: 3000 B.C. to 1946 A.D.* (Vol. II). New York: Author.

Shields, E.A. (1981). *Highlights in the history of the Army Nurse Corps*. Washington, D.C.: Government Printing Office.

Stillman, R.J. (1968). *Integration of the Negro in the U.S. armed forces*. New York: Praeger.

Stimson, J.D., & Thompson, E.C.S. (1928, January–February). Women nurses with the union forces during the Civil War. *The Military Surgeon*, *62*, 208–230.

Swaby, G. (circa 1979). The story of Mary Seacole. *The Profession of Nursing*, 19–20.

Taylor, S.K. (1902). *Reminiscences of my life in camp*. Boston: Author.

Washington, B.T. (1910). Training colored nurses at Tuskegee. *American Journal of Nursing*, *10*, 167–171.

Wesley, C., & Romero, P. (1967). *Negro Americans in the Civil War*. New York: Publishers Co.

Chapter 2

The Foundation Is Laid

This chapter is devoted to the history of basic and advanced nursing programs at historically black institutions. Basic programs include those awarding the diploma and baccalaureate and associate degrees; advanced programs include two nondegree programs—one in public health nursing, the other in nurse-midwifery—and four master's degree programs. The master's program at Meharry Medical College, Nashville, Tennessee, reported in the first edition, was short lived, opening in 1982 and closing in 1985.

When the early schools of nursing were established in the United States, quota systems restricted the admission of black students. The New England Hospital for Women and Children in Boston, Massachusetts, founded by a group of women physicians, was incorporated on March 18, 1863, with a charter calling for the admission of one Negro and one Jew to each nursing class. The purposes of the hospital were (1) to provide for women medical aid of competent physicians of their own sex; (2) to assist educated women in the practical study of medicine; (3) to train nurses for the care of the sick; and (4) to prove to the world that a woman could be a good physician and a skillful surgeon (Annual Report for 1878). Although the first formal program in nursing at the hospital was not begun until 1872, nursing students were accepted as early as 1866, receiving only six months of training. Those who completed the course were given neither a diploma nor a certificate. Later, the course was increased to one year, and to 16 months by 1878 (Chayer, 1954).

On March 23, 1878, the first black student, Mary Eliza Mahoney (Fig. 2–1) was admitted to the 16-month course at the New England Hospital for Women and Children; she was graduated on August 1, 1879. Of a class of 42, Mahoney was one of the four students who successfully

Figure 2–1   Mary Eliza Mahoney, America's first trained
black nurse.

completed the course. The opportunity given to Mahoney was also extended to a few other blacks. Before the school closed in 1951, six other
known blacks had completed the program: Lavinia Holloway, Josephine
Braxton, Kittie Toliver, Ann Dillit, Roxie Dentz Smith, and Laura Morrison Bayne. Throughout her life, Mahoney, America's first black trained
nurse, gave unselfishly of herself in professional and community affairs.
In 1920, the Nineteenth Amendment to the Constitution was ratified to
enfranchise women. At the time Mahoney cast her vote, she was 76 years
old.

In 1926, Mahoney died at the age of nearly 81. A hallmark of her
more than 40 years of service included the furthering of intergroup
relations. Among her many honors conferred posthumously was the
Mary Mahoney Award established in 1936 by the National Association
of Colored Graduate Nurses (NACGN) for presentation to a person(s)
for outstanding contributions in the area of intergroup relations. The

first recipient of the Mary Mahoney Award was Adah B. Thoms, a black nurse who devoted her time and energies during 1917 and 1918 to gaining admittance for black nurses to the American Red Cross, which would make them eligible for service in the U.S. Army Nurse Corps. Since 1952, the Mary Mahoney Award has been given by the American Nurses' Association (ANA) at each biennial convention. In 1970, the city of Boston honored Mahoney by naming the Area 2 Family Life Center in Roxbury the Mary Eliza Mahoney Family Life Center.

In 1973, Chi Eta Phi, a national black sorority, and ANA restored Mahoney's grave in Woodlawn Cemetery, Everett, Massachusetts, and a granite monument bearing a sculpture of her head was erected. In 1976, along with 14 other outstanding nurses, Mahoney was admitted to the ANA Hall of Fame. In September 1984, nurses from across the nation traveled over the Labor Day weekend to join Chi Eta Phi Sorority and ANA as they made the first national pilgrimage to the gravesite of Mahoney, where a service of commemoration was held. This service was repeated in June 1990 during the ANA convention, which was held in Boston (Fig. 2–2). The Community Health Project, Inc., a nonprofit corporation funded by the Department of Health, Education, and Wel-

Figure 2–2   Mary Morris (second from left), Supreme Basileus, Chi Eta Phi Sorority, and Dr. Lucille Joel (right), president of the American Nurses' Association, conduct a memorial ceremony at Mary Mahoney's gravesite. (Courtesy, *The American Nurse*)

fare (DHEW), has established a center in her memory. It is located in Oklahoma and provides health care services to isolated communities (Grippando, 1983).

Only two other black women in this country had been honored with a gravesite ceremony—in Battle Creek, Michigan, Sojourner Truth, an abolitionist and Civil War nurse, and Mary McLeod Bethune, a renowned educator, who was interred in Daytona, Florida, where she had founded a black school, Bethune-Cookman College, which currently has a baccalaureate program in nursing. Bethune, founder of the National Council of Negro Women and the first black woman to receive a major appointment from the U.S. government, directed the Division of Negro Education during the life of the National Youth Administration, one of the federal agencies of the Great Depression, and gave practical assistance and effectively promoted the aspirations of the NACGN.

In addition to those black nurses who completed the course of study at the New England Hospital for Women and Children, a few other black women were graduated, along with whites, from other schools— New York Infirmary in New York City and Washington General Hospital and Asylum Training School for Nurses in the District of Columbia were among them. Martha Franklin from Connecticut, who was to found the NACGN, completed the course in 1897 at the Women's Hospital in Philadelphia, which had been established in 1861 by a group of Quaker women of Philadelphia who announced their intention of opening a school "for training of a superior class of young women" (Jamieson & Sewall, 1944). Franklin was the second and last black nurse to be graduated from the Women's Hospital. The first one, Anne Reeves, was graduated in April 1888 (West, 1931).

Gertrude Voorhees graduated from Blockley Hospital Training School (renamed Philadelphia General). Rose Snowden finished the course of study at Jefferson Polyclinic in Chicago. Sarah L. Stowall, who served as a contract nurse during the Spanish-American War, indicated on her personnel data card that she had been graduated from McLean Hospital School of Nursing in 1896 and Massachusetts General Hospital, Boston, in 1897 (Personnel Data Cards, 1898). Three black women graduated from the nursing program at Berea College in Kentucky in 1902: Sarah Belle Jerman, Mary Eliza Merritt, and Margaret Jones (Peck & Pride, 1982). Mossell (1908, p. 178) reports, "It is also said that Johns Hopkins [in Baltimore] has twenty-four Afro-American women graduates."

BLACK BASIC PROGRAMS

By the early part of the 20th century, America had started developing rigid patterns of segregation and discrimination in all sections of the country. Nursing, along with other kinds of education, was affected. Black codes were set up in the South by law and in the North by custom. In 1904, a bill was passed in Kentucky declaring it "unlawful for any person, corporation, or association of persons to maintain or operate any college, school, or institution where persons of the white and Negro races are both received as pupils for instruction" (Peck & Smith, 1982, p. 51).

Hospitals and nursing schools followed the segregated pattern, which forced the establishment of hospitals and schools of nursing for blacks.

Diploma

Like the typical nursing school that emerged in this country in the late 1800s, most of those established exclusively for blacks had their origins in hospitals and led to a diploma. The few nursing schools established outside of the hospital also led to a diploma.

Founded in 1881, the Atlanta Baptist Female Seminary (renamed Spelman College in 1924 after Lucy Henry Spelman, the mother-in-law of John D. Rockefeller) was the first college for black women in the country. Spelman College grew from a school started in the basement of Friendship Baptist Church, a Negro church. The founders were two New England white women, Sophia B. Packard and Harriet E. Giles, who, deploring the lack of educational opportunities for black women, went to the South during the post-Civil War period to establish a school for young black women who had been freed from the bondage of slavery. John D. Rockefeller had given a large grant to the school.

Feeling the need to open to Negro women a wide field of honorable, lucrative, and helpful employment, as part of the missionary course, a two-year nursing program leading to a diploma was added at Spelman in March 1886 (*Spelman Messenger*, 1908). This was the first nursing program exclusively for blacks in the country. In 1901, Dr. Malcolm MacVicar raised funds and built the 31-bed MacVicar Hospital on the campus of Spelman Seminary as a department of the school for the benefit of black women and children (*Spelman Messenger*, 1914). The hospital also served as a practice facility for the nursing students. Before then, clinical practice had been limited to the school's infirmary (Fig. 2–3). The program, which had expanded to three years, was closed in 1928 so that students could be exposed to more extensive clinical experiences available in larger institutions. During its lifetime, Spelman had graduated 117 nurses.

Howard University was conceived in 1866 by members of the Missionary Society of the Congregational Church of Washington, D.C. The original educational objectives were to provide instruction for "colored men for the ministry; later, for the education of teachers and preachers;

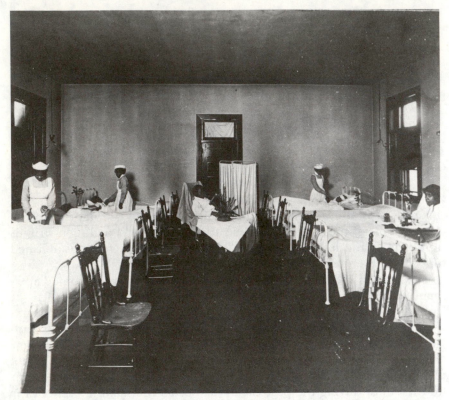

Figure 2–3   Early nursing students at Spelman College gaining clinical experience in the school's infirmary. (Courtesy, Spelman College)

finally, for the preparation of anyone who might contemplate any vocation or profession whatever" (Dyson, 1921, p. 9). The university was formally approved by President Andrew Johnson on March 2, 1867.

By 1893, the School of Medicine at Howard University had decided to train nurses in theory and practice and so established an 18-month program. The students enrolled in this program gained clinical experience at Freedmen's Hospital. As of July 1, 1894, 75 nursing students were in attendance. Seven of the women who were admitted in 1893 graduated in 1895. The diplomas were signed by the medical faculty and the officials of the university. Although this first program at Howard University was short-lived—discontinued when Freedmen's Hospital School of Nursing assumed responsibility for the nurse training program in 1894—it is significant to note that it did exist, with the unique feature of having been established under the aegis of a university. Two factors may have been responsible for the demise of the Howard University program: economic conditions that followed the panic of 1873, which created budgetary problems for all colleges and universities, and the general consensus that higher education for women was neither necessary nor practical (Davis, 1976).

Like most nursing schools in the beginning, black schools were established by hospitals because of the need to have patients receive nursing care at no, or little, cost to the hospital. Formal education for nurses was not the primary goal. Unlike most diploma schools in this country, when Lincoln School for Nurses in New York was established in 1898, it was operated independently of the hospital—one of the principles upon which the Nightingale system was based. Lincoln was supported by a group of white philanthropists. The school's major purpose was to train black women to care for the black sick people. During its lifetime of 64 years, this nationally accredited school graduated 1,864 nurses. Its sphere of influence was both national and international, with students coming from just about every state in the Union and 16 foreign countries, including Canada, Bermuda, the British West Indies, British Guiana, the Bahamas, Haiti, Panama, Liberia, and Nigeria. Before Lincoln closed in 1961, the charter had been changed to permit the admission of white students. Esther Eshelman, who graduated in 1957, was the only white student to receive a diploma from Lincoln.

In the North, for the most part, schools of nursing were segregated. Only 39 of the 1,708 schools of nursing existing in the North in 1928 had a policy to admit blacks. Because blacks were denied admission to most of the white schools in the North, schools were created just for blacks. Provident Hospital School of Nursing in Chicago was established in 1891 by a black physician, Daniel Hale Williams, because a black woman, Emma Reynolds from Kansas City, had been denied admission to every school of nursing in Chicago.

Between 1891 and 1924, eleven nursing schools for blacks were established in five northern states: Illinois, Kansas, Pennsylvania, New York, and Michigan (Table 2–1). However, the vast majority of blacks attended only six of these schools: Provident in Chicago, Lincoln and Harlem in New York, Douglass in Kansas City, and Mercy and Douglass in Philadelphia. In 1949, Mercy and Douglass merged, becoming Mercy-Douglass Hospital School of Nursing.

Both Lincoln and Harlem were controlled and administered by whites in the beginning; both had black directors before they closed: Ivy N. Tinkler at Lincoln and Alida Dailey at Harlem, followed by Edith Benoit. From their inception, Provident and Mercy-Douglass were administered and controlled by blacks. From the beginning, Provident had an interracial board and treated patients regardless of race, creed, or nationality. By 1893, Provident Hospital had gained fame when Dr. Daniel Hale Williams, its founder, performed the first recorded operation on the human heart. In later years, the Julius Rosenwald Fund made possible many improvements in the school of nursing (Staupers, 1961).

In the South, a typical pattern emerged: the dual system, in keeping with the doctrine of "separate but equal" as an outcome of the *Plessy* v. *Ferguson* Supreme Court Decision of 1896. This decision supported the constitutionality of a Louisiana law requiring separate but equal facilities for whites and blacks in railroad cars. As a result, schools of nursing were established in all-black institutions—hospitals and colleges. Some white hospitals conducted two programs—one for whites and one for blacks. Theory was usually given by the same white faculty in separate classrooms; practice was also gained separately—for black students in separate buildings, wings, or wards for black patients. Separate, yes, but in no way equal!

In 1924, the Hospital Library and Service Bureau conducted a survey of the black schools of nursing in the country to determine management of these schools—control of budget, amount of white cooperation, number of students, number of instructors, entrance requirements, length

Table 2–1
Diploma Nursing Programs for Blacks, 1886–1982

Institution	Location	Year Established	Year Closed
Alabama			
Tuskegee University	Tuskegee	1892	1948*
Hale Infirmary	Montgomery	1917	1932
Fraternal Hospital	Montgomery	1919	1941
Tuggle Institute	Birmingham	1925	1930
Burwell Hospital	Selma	1927	1933
Stillman College	Tuscaloosa	1930	1948
Tennessee Coal & Iron	Birmingham	U	1931
Arkansas			
United Friends	Little Rock	1918	1932
Bush Memorial (Royal Circle)	Little Rock	1918	1933
Great Southern Fraternal	Little Rock	1921	1930
District of Columbia			
Howard University	Washington	1893	1895
Freedmen's Hospital	Washington	1894	1973
Florida			
Brewster Hospital	Jacksonville	1902	1954
Brewster Hospital	Jacksonville	1961 (reopened)	1963
Daytona Hospital	Daytona Beach	1922	1939
Florida A & M University	Tallahassee	1925	1936*

Table 2–1 (continued)
Diploma Nursing Programs for Blacks, 1886–1982

Institution	Location	Year Established	Year Closed
Georgia			
Spelman College	Atlanta	1886	1928
Lamar Wing, University Hospital	Augusta	1894	1957
Lamar Wing, University Hospital	Augusta	1960 (reopened)	1965
Charity Hospital	Savannah	1901	U
Lula Grove Hospital	Atlanta	1913	U
Grady Hospital	Atlanta	1917	1982
John Archbold	Thomasville	1925	U
Morris Brown College	Atlanta	Circa 1930	U
City Hospital	Columbus	U	U
McKane Hospital	Savannah	U	U
Illinois			
Provident Hospital	Chicago	1891	1966
New Home Sanitorium	Jacksonville	1922	1930
Hinsdale Sanitarium and Hospital	Hinsdale	1922	1969
Kansas			
Douglass	Kansas City	1898	1937
Protective Home & Mitchell Hospital	Leavenworth	1909	1911
Kentucky			
Citizens National Hospital	Louisville	1888	1912
Red Cross Hospital	Louisville	1898	1938
Louisiana			
Flint Goodrige Hospital	New Orleans	1896	1934
Providence Sanitarium	New Orleans	1907	1917
Maryland			
Provident	Baltimore	1895	1976
Crownsville State Hospital	Crownsville	1917	1930
Maryland Tuberculosis Sanitorium	Henryton	1926	1962
Michigan			
Battle Creek Sanitarium	Battle Creek	1910	1934
Dunbar Memorial Hospital	Detroit	1924	1931
Mississippi			
Mississippi Baptist Hospital	Jackson	1911	1960
Missouri			
University Medical College	Kansas City	1895	1897
Provident Hospital	St. Louis	1899	U
Kansas City General Hospital, No. 2	Kansas City	1911	1973
Wheatley-Provident Hospital	Kansas City	1914	1934
Homer G. Phillips Hospital	St. Louis	1919	1968
People's Hospital	St. Louis	1921	1928
St. Mary's Infirmary	St. Louis	1933	1958
Perry Sanitorium	Kansas City	1910	1929
New York			
Lincoln School for Nurses	New York	1898	1961
Harlem Hospital	New York	1923	1977

Table 2–1 (continued)
Diploma Nursing Programs for Blacks, 1886–1982

North Carolina

Good Samaritan Hospital	Charlotte	1891	1960
St. Agnes Hospital	Raleigh	1896	1959
Lincoln Hospital	Durham	1902	1971
Community Hospital	Wilmington	1920	1936
Community Hospital	Wilmington	1940 (reopened)	1966
Negro Division, State Sanitorium	Sanitorium	1926	1953
L. Richardson Memorial Hospital	Greensboro	1927	1953
Kate Bitting Reynolds Hospital	Winston-Salem	1938	1971

Pennsylvania

Douglass Hospital	Philadelphia	1895	1923
Mercy Hospital	Philadelphia	1907	1949
Mercy-Douglass Hospital	Philadelphia	1949	1960

South Carolina

Hospital and Training School for Nurses	Charleston	1897	1959
Good Samaritan Waverly	Columbia	1910	1953
Benedict College	Columbia	1917	U
Waverly Fraternal	Columbia	1924	U
Columbia Hospital	Columbia	1935	1965

Tennessee

Meharry Medical College	Nashville	1900	1947*
University of West Tennessee	Memphis	1900	1923
Mercy Hospital	Nashville	1900	U
Terrell Memorial Hospital	Memphis	1907	U
Collins Chapel Hospital	Memphis	1907	1940
Negro Baptist Hospital	Memphis	1912	U
Millie Hale Hospital	Nashville	1916	1928
Mercy Hospital	Memphis	1918	U
Royal Circle Hospital	Nashville	1921	U
City of Memphis Hospitals	Memphis	1956	1968

Texas

Prairie View A & M University	Prairie View	1918	1952*
Negro Baptist Hospital	Fort Worth	1919	1930
Houston Negro Hospital	Houston	1927	1933
Houston Negro Hospital	Houston	1943 (reopened)	1944

Virginia

Dixie Hospital	Hampton	1891	1956
Richmond Hospital	Richmond	Circa 1899	Circa 1923
Burrell Hospital	Roanoke	1915	1933
Piedmont Sanitarium	Burkeville	1918	1960
Whittaker Memorial Hospital	Newport News	Circa 1918	Circa 1930
St. Philip Hospital	Richmond	1920	1962

West Virginia

Lomax Sanitarium	Bluefield	1906	1928
Brown Hospital	Bluefield	1919	1937
Barnette Hospital	Huntington	Circa 1920	1930

U - Unknown
* - Converted to baccalaureate program

of course, working hours per week, division of service, postgraduate courses, housing, and recreation. Regarding the quality of these schools, one white director of a southern school commented:

> The type of training the average colored nurse receives in this part of the country is far inferior to that given to white nurses. Even the best training for colored nurses hardly approximates the poorest training given to white nurses. From another standpoint, their educational background is not so good .... ["Educational Facilities," 1925]

In 1917, Julius Rosenwald, a Jewish immigrant and president of Sears Roebuck and Company, created the Julius Rosenwald Fund as a philanthropic corporation to promote better black education and American race relations (Kessel, 1989). In 1928, the fund was reorganized and modeled after the Rockefeller Foundation and management was turned over to a professional staff. The fund continued to work on behalf of blacks, developing programs in medical economics, fellowships for the professions, library service, social studies, general education, and race relations (Jones, 1981). By the time of his death in 1932, Rosenwald had contributed over $4 million to the building of more than 5,000 Rosenwald schools.

Under the aegis of the Rosenwald Fund, Nina D. Gage, a highly respected nurse educator, and Alma C. Haupt, associate director, National Organization for Public Health Nursing, made a survey in 1932 of black schools of nursing in six southern states: Alabama, Georgia, Louisiana, Mississippi, Tennessee, and Texas. They reported:

> The schools of nursing themselves are of many varieties—some so poor as to make one question how they can possibly meet the standards of a State Board of Nurse Examiners .... In ... one, two shabby houses were used as a hospital of 35 beds and a nurses' home for 12 students. A colored nurse is superintendent of nurses and the sole member of the faculty. A three-year course is given, every subject being taught by the one nurse .... No public health subjects are included in the curriculum ... but the students are frequently sent out to homes as private duty nurses, and the wages thus earned help to run the hospital. [Gage & Haupt, 1932, p. 678]

Twelve years after the Gage and Haupt survey, Estelle Massey Riddle Osborne, consultant for the National Nursing Council for War Service, and Rita E. Miller Dargan, part-time consultant for the U.S. Public Health Service, made a survey at the request of Surgeon General Parran to determine the status of black nursing schools in the country and to elicit trends relating to the employment and professional participation of black nurses. They found that conditions in the schools, especially in the South, had not changed to any great extent. They also reported that in Negro nursing schools having white directors, with the exception of one, the interest and knowledge of these directors in the broader aspects of Negro life ranged from apparent indifference to hostility. These attitudes, they said, were definitely reflected in the programs for the nurses and the communities' reaction to the group (Newell, 1951).

Although Osborne and Dargan made specific recommendations for upgrading the educational situation in the poorer schools, no formal steps were taken at that time to implement the recommendations (Newell, 1951). It should be noted that not all black schools were poor in quality. Many were excellent, meeting all national standards. The 1949 interim classification of state-approved schools offering basic programs, based on data voluntarily submitted by 1,156 schools in the United States, Hawaii, and Puerto Rico, consisted of two groups. Group I included the upper 25 percent of all basic programs; group II included the middle 50 percent. Of the 29 black schools in existence at that time, 16 were included in groups I and II—nine in group I and seven in group II. Of the nine in group I, six were baccalaureate programs and three were diploma programs. Of the seven in group II, only one was a baccalaureate program, whereas the other six were diploma programs (West & Hawkins, 1950).

After the midcentury, the number of black diploma programs steadily decreased. From 1886 to 1982, when the last black diploma program closed, 90 black diploma programs in 86 institutions (four hospitals had had two programs over the years, i.e., they closed, reopened, and closed again) in 20 states and the District of Columbia had been in existence, graduating the vast majority of black nurses in the country up to that time (Table 2-1). Four diploma schools located in academic institutions were converted in time to baccalaureate programs: Tuskegee University in Alabama (the oldest continuing historically black program in the country); Florida A & M in Tallahassee; Meharry in Nashville, Tennessee; and Prairie View A & M University in Texas.

Tuskegee University, which had had a diploma program since 1892, began a baccalaureate program in 1948. Florida A & M University, whose diploma program had been state-approved since 1925, established a baccalaureate program in 1936. Prairie View A & M University in Texas had had a diploma program since 1918 and initiated a baccalaureate program in 1952. Meharry Medical College, which began its diploma program in 1900, changed to a baccalaureate program in 1947, but closed it in 1962.

After the famous May 17, 1954, Supreme Court Decision on school desegregation (*Brown* v. *the Board of Education of Topeka*), which nullified the *Plessy* v. *Ferguson Decision of 1896*, establishing the separate-but-equal doctrine, all types of educational discrimination were considered, including nursing. The unanimous decision read by Chief Justice Earl B. Warren, asserted that "separate educational facilities are inherently unequal, making racial segregation in public schools unconstitutional." It was also around this time that schools of nursing were being accredited according to national standards, and many schools were forced to close. However, not all of the black schools closed because they did not meet standards, some closed because of financial difficulties.

With integration permitting black students to be admitted to formerly all-white schools—North and South—good black schools often had difficulty attracting the number of qualified students who otherwise might have applied; hence, many closed. It should be noted that not all formerly all-white schools voluntarily opened their doors to black students. For example, Esther McCready, a black resident of Baltimore, brought suit against the University of Maryland School of Nursing because her application for admission had been denied. She had been advised by the officials of the university to apply to an all-black school. McCready instituted legal proceedings in 1950, the result of which was her eventual admission to the University of Maryland School of Nursing by an order of the Maryland Supreme Court.

It is interesting to note that in 1955, when the master's program was being established at the University of Maryland School of Nursing, Dean Florence Gipe contacted this author by telephone to inform her that the decision had been made to include blacks in the enrollment and to request that a qualified black nurse be sent for admission to the program. As a result, Juanita Franklin Wilson who had a diploma from Homer G. Phillips Hospital School of Nursing in St. Louis, Missouri, and a bachelor's degree from Florida A & M College, enrolled and was the first in her class to complete the requirements for a master's degree, with a major in psychiatric nursing. This was an annual request for several years thereafter.

To obtain official data on the diploma programs, boards of nursing in those states with known historically black schools of nursing were contacted by this author. Because registration laws were not in effect until 1903, and only four states had such laws in that year, many records do not exist for schools established before then. In one state, North Carolina, the records had been destroyed by fire; in some, the data were just not available. However, from the data available, a profile emerges in terms of location, administrative control, financial support, length of program, life span of the program, state approval, enrollment, number of graduates, and reasons for closing.

All but six of the schools were located in urban areas. As for administrative control, ten were in colleges and universities, three were under medical schools, and one was independent. Six were supported by the state, five of which were in tuberculosis sanitariums; one was supported with federal funds; and the rest were financed with private funds, mostly by religious organizations, but some by physicians. The programs ranged in length from 18 months to three years, and the life span was from one to 81 years. Most of those existing after state registration laws were passed had state approval. The enrollment was as few as one (in one school), and the number of graduates ranged from one to nearly 2,000. The reasons given for closing were many, among which were financial difficulties; insufficient applicants; integration (i.e., white and black units in the same institution combined to one school or black students were admitted to formerly all-white schools in the same area); student strikes because of poor living and working conditions; and loss of state board approval or national accreditation.

In 1965, the nursing profession took the position that all education for nursing should take place in institutions of higher education and that by 1985 the bachelor's degree would be required for entry into practice (American Nurses' Association, 1965). By that time (1965) 70 of the 90 black diploma programs had closed, and after 1982 there were no black diploma programs left. The black diploma programs served a real purpose, and most of the black nurses who have successfully completed programs in higher education and now occupy top-level positions in the profession are graduates of these schools. Without the existence of these schools, the percentage of black professional nurses in the total nurse population, although low, would have been even lower.

Baccalaureate

Entry of nursing programs to institutions of higher education did not begin until 1899, with the establishment of a course for graduate nurses at Teachers College, Columbia University, New York. This was not at that time a degree-granting program, but the course marked a new recognition that nurses needed advanced education to prepare them for leadership positions in hospitals and schools of nursing. It was also an indication of the acceptance of nursing by the university as an academic discipline.

In 1916, the University of Cincinnati established a five-year program leading to a bachelor's degree in nursing—the first in the country (Roberts, 1954). For many years, the pattern followed had consisted of two years of liberal arts courses and three years of nursing. Six years later, in 1922, Howard University, a black school in Washington, D.C., established a five-year program leading to a bachelor of science degree in nursing in cooperation with Freedmen's Hospital, which was already operating a diploma program. The graduate would then have both the degree from Howard and a diploma from Freedmen's. The plan was to have students spend two years in the College of Liberal Arts and three years in the School of Nursing at Freedmen's. The Nursing Department at Howard was part of the School of Public Health and Hygiene. This program was not popular and because of an insufficient number of applicants, it was discontinued three years later, in 1925.

The oldest continuing baccalaureate nursing program at an historically black institution is at Florida A & M University in Tallahassee. As long ago as 1897, attempts had been made by the first president of the State Normal College for Colored Students (later Florida A & M College and now Florida A & M University) in Tallahassee to convince the Florida legislature of the need for establishing a training program for nurses in Florida to give women "one additional field in which they may develop their capacity, and put money in their purses, while soothing back to health and usefulness the suffering patient." After several unsuccessful attempts, in 1909 the school began offering such training in its Department of Mechanical and Domestic Arts. Finally, on April 11, 1911, the legislature approved the Florida A & M Hospital and Nurse Training program and appropriated funds to construct a 19-bed facility on the campus. The new hospital opened its doors on October 12, 1911.

By 1925, the hospital at Florida A & M had expanded to 25 beds and extended its facilities to serve both white and black patients in Tallahassee and the surrounding areas. The early nursing program was two years long until 1925, when the school was established as a three-year diploma program, completely controlled by the hospital and administered by the medical director, who even signed the diplomas. In 1936, the diploma program was discontinued, and the college began offering a bachelor's degree in nursing (Fig. 2–4). With financial assistance from the General

Figure 2–4   Dr. Eunice Johnson Burgess, one of the first three baccalaureate nursing graduates of Florida A & M, 1941.

Education Board of the Rockefeller Foundation, the program was re-organized in 1945 with appointment of a nurse as dean of the school of nursing (Carnegie, 1948). This school still exists, is now an integral part of the university, and is fully accredited by the National League for Nursing. Other baccalaureate nursing programs at historically black colleges and universities have been developed, making a total in 1990 of 23, located in 16 states and the District of Columbia (Table 2–2).

After Florida A & M converted its diploma program to a baccalaureate program in the 1930s, 23 new baccalaureate programs were established during the next five decades at historically black institutions: in the 1940s—Dillard, Hampton, Meharry (converted from diploma in 1947

Table 2–2
Baccalaureate and Associate Degree Programs at Historically Black Schools, 1990

Institution	Location	Type of Program (AD, Bacc)	Year Established	Accreditation
Alabama				
Tuskegee University	Tuskegee	Bacc	1948	NLN
Arkansas				
University of Arkansas at Pine Bluff	Pine Bluff	Bacc	1976	NLN
Delaware				
Delaware State College	Dover	Bacc	1974	NLN
District of Columbia				
Howard University	Washington	Bacc	1969	NLN
Florida				
Florida A & M University	Tallahassee	Bacc	1936	NLN
Bethune-Cookman College	Daytona Beach	Bacc	1977	State
Georgia				
Albany State College	Albany	Bacc	1961	NLN
Morris Brown College	Atlanta	Bacc	1983	—
Kentucky				
Kentucky State University	Frankfort	AD	1967	NLN
Louisiana				
Dillard University	New Orleans	Bacc	1942	NLN
Grambling University	Grambling	Bacc	1984	State
Southern University	Baton Rouge	Bacc	1986	State

Table 2–2 (continued)
Baccalaureate and Associate Degree Programs at Historically Black Schools, 1990

Institution	Location	Type of Program (AD, Bacc)	Year Established	Accreditation
Maryland				
Coppin State College	Baltimore	Bacc	1974	NLN
Bowie State University	Bowie	Bacc	1979	NLN
Mississippi				
Alcorn State University	Natchez	AD	1963	NLN
		Bacc	1979	NLN
Missouri				
Lincoln University	Jefferson City	AD	1970	NLN
North Carolina				
North Carolina A & T State University	Greensboro	Bacc	1953	NLN
Winston-Salem State University	Winston-Salem	Bacc	1954	NLN
North Carolina Central University	Durham	Bacc	1969	NLN
Oklahoma				
Langston University	Langston	Bacc	1980	NLN
South Carolina				
South Carolina State University	Orangeburg	Bacc	1984	State
Tennessee				
Tennessee State University	Nashville	Bacc	1980	NLN
		AD	1980	NLN
Texas				
Prairie View A & M University	Houston	Bacc	1952	NLN
Virginia				
Hampton University	Hampton	Bacc	1944	NLN
Norfolk State University	Norfolk	AD	1955	NLN
		Bacc	1981	NLN
Virginia State University	Petersburg	Bacc*	1981	State
West Virginia				
Bluefield State College	Bluefield	AD	1967	NLN

Notes: Baccalaureate Program, Howard University, Washington, D.C., 1922–1925; Baccalaureate Program, Meharry Medical College, Nashville, Tennessee, 1947–1962; Associate Degree Program, Mississippi Valley College, Itta Bena, Mississippi, 1964–1979

*Closing

and closed in 1962), and Tuskegee (converted from diploma in 1948); in the 1950s—Prairie View A & M (converted from diploma), North Carolina A & T, and Winston-Salem State College; in the 1960s—Howard, North Carolina Central University, and Albany State; in the 1970s—Coppin, Bethune-Cookman, Alcorn, University of Arkansas at Pine Bluff, Delaware State, Bowie State; and in the 1980s—Tennessee State, Langston, Grambling, Morris Brown, Southern University, South Carolina State, and Norfolk State. The program at Virginia State University in Petersburg is in the process of closing. Black deans and directors of baccalaureate and higher degree programs as of December 31, 1990, are listed in Appendix A.

Associate Degree

The President's Commission on Higher Education's recommendation that all American youth be given tuition-free education stimulated the growth of community and junior colleges in the United States (Brick, 1963).

Associate degree programs, based primarily in community colleges, are the latest type of basic nursing education. This type of program was launched in 1952, and the first nurses were graduated in 1954 after two years of education, with a combination of general and nursing education, including clinical experience, developed in accordance with college policy and the regulations of the state licensing authority. Graduates are prepared to give care to patients as beginning staff nurses and to cooperate and share responsibility for their patients' welfare with other members of the nursing and health staff (Report of the Surgeon General's Consultant Group on Nursing, 1963).

A unique feature of associate degree education in nursing is that "it was the first program to be developed through research, rather than as the result of an historical accident" (Montag, 1980, p. 248). The Division of Nursing Education at Teachers College, Columbia University, New York, initiated and sponsored the Cooperative Research Project in Junior and Community College Education for Nursing under the direction of Mildred Montag as the first major research undertaking of the Institute of Research and Service in Nursing Education at Teachers College. When the project was launched, there was less acceptance than today of the idea that education for nursing should be part of the nation's system of higher education, as recommended by Brown (1948).

The project's study and experimentation extended over five years and involved the cooperation of seven junior and community colleges and one hospital, located in six states. One of the colleges that participated was the Norfolk Division of Virginia State University, a black institution, which entered the project in 1955 (Fig. 2–5). Beginning with these eight programs, the movement has spread so that in 1990, there were 822 programs located in all 50 states, the District of Columbia, Puerto Rico, the Virgin Islands, and Guam. More black students are enrolled in the associate degree program than in any other type. Were it not for the associate degree programs in community colleges, with low cost to the student and flexible standards in terms of age, marital status, and race, many qualified black students would be lost to the field of nursing. Then, too, those junior colleges located in black communities tend to have a higher black enrollment in all areas of study.

In addition to the associate degree program at the Norfolk Division of Virginia State College (established in 1955), six associate degree pro-

Figure 2–5　Dr. Hazle Blakeney, first chairperson of the associate degree nursing program at the Norfolk Division, Virginia State College.

grams were developed at historically black colleges and universities between 1963 and 1980: Alcorn State University, Natchez, Mississippi,
1963; Mississippi Valley College, which existed from 1964 to 1979; Kentucky State University, 1967; Bluefield State College, West Virginia,
1967; Lincoln University, Missouri, 1970; and Tennessee State University, Nashville, 1980 (Table 2-2).

ADVANCED PROGRAMS

As mentioned earlier, advanced education for nurses did not begin until
1899 at Teachers College, Columbia University, New York. Shortly
thereafter, other universities, mostly in the North, began offering advanced courses for nurses. A few black nurses completed these courses,
commonly referred to as "postgraduate" education. However, black nurses
in the South had no such opportunity. To meet this need, several programs were established especially for blacks. Two special courses in public health nursing and two in nurse-midwifery are discussed in this section,
followed by a discussion of the four master's degree programs at historically black institutions.

Public Health Nursing

In 1936, the U.S. Public Health Service, in cooperation with the Medical
College of Virginia in Richmond, established a program in pubic health
nursing for black registered nurses at St. Philip Hospital, the black division of the college, with a white nurse, Lillian Bischoff, as director
(Fig. 2–6). Title VI of the Social Security Act provided scholarship aid
to students selected from 18 cooperating states. The program also at-
tracted black nurses from other countries. The class of 1945, for example, had two foreign students: Mary Little from Liberia, West Africa,
and Bernice Carnegie Redmon from Toronto, Ontario, Canada, who
had completed her basic program the year before at St. Philip.

The program, approved by the National Organization for Public Health
Nursing, which evaluated programs in public health nursing, was at first
one year long, including field experience and leading to a certificate.
Before the program was discontinued in 1956, the curriculum had changed
so that a bachelor's degree in nursing education, with a major in public
health nursing, was offered. Academic courses were taken at Virginia
Union University, a black institution in Richmond, but the degree was

Figure 2–6   The 1943 graduating class, Public Health Nursing Program, St. Philip Hospital School of Nursing, Richmond, Virginia. In the top row, left to right, are Elizabeth Tyler, Savannah Sickles, Louise Blowe, Pansy McFadden Hicks, Ernestine Hill, Mary Cox, Veneley Narcisse. In the second row, left to right, are Thelma Abercrombie, Christine Haith, Lillian Carter Thompson, Sadie Ezelle, Nema Newell. In the first row, left to right, are Lillian Henry, Ione Taylor Carey, Margaret Gilbert, Mozie Lee Thomas. (Courtesy, Archives, Medical College of Virginia)

conferred by the Medical College of Virginia. In the program's 20 years of existence, 57 black nurses were graduated with qualifications for better positions, higher salaries, and the incentive for further education.

Because black registered nurses were denied admission to the public health nursing program at the University of North Carolina at Chapel Hill, a program for black nurses in this specialty leading to a certificate was established in 1946 at North Carolina College (renamed North Carolina Central University) in Durham, with Mary Mills as the first chairperson. Until black faculty could be found, faculty from the University of North Carolina at Chapel Hill conducted classes at the black school. Upon recommendation of the National League for Nursing during an accreditation visit in 1958, and under the leadership of Chairperson

Figure 2–7   Helen S. Miller, Chairperson, Public Health Nursing Program, North Carolina College, Durham, when the generic program was opened.

Helen S. Miller (Fig. 2–7), the program was expanded to permit students to earn a bachelor's degree in public health nursing, while continuing with the program leading to a certificate. By this time, the program at St. Philip in public health nursing had closed, leaving North Carolina College the only school in the South offering public health nursing for black registered nurses. Its enrollment, therefore, consisted of more out-of-state students than those from North Carolina. In 1969, North Carolina College discontinued its specialty program in public health nursing and began offering a generic program for high school graduates and registered nurses leading to a bachelor of science in nursing.

Midwifery

In many countries, midwifery is either a part of the basic nursing curriculum or a postgraduate course for those nurses who wish to become certified in this specialty. Formal training for nurse-midwives in this country did not begin until the early 1930s, with the establishment of the first school at the Maternity Center Association in New York. Need for such a school was recognized when the U.S. Children's Bureau found from its survey that there were at least 45,000 untrained midwives ("grannies") functioning and highlighted the appalling infant mortality rates—124 per 1,000 live births—and the terribly high maternal mortality rates, most coming under the classification of "preventable" (Hogan, 1975).

   In the South, maternal and infant mortality rates were far higher than for the nation as a whole; many needless deaths occurred, particularly in rural districts among families of sharecroppers—both black and white.

Concern about the high infant mortality rates in the rural South led to the beginning of another nurse-midwifery school, this one for black nurses at Tuskegee, Alabama. The first aim of the project was to prepare black nurses in midwifery and then to reduce the number of rural deaths through improved and expanded maternity care and study.

As a demonstration project under the auspices of the Macon County Health Department, the U.S. Children's Bureau, the Julius Rosenwald Fund, Tuskegee University, and the Alabama Department of Health, the Tuskegee Nurse-Midwifery School opened September 15, 1941, with three students: Helen S. Pennington, Salina L. Johnson, and Fannye M. Prentice, who were graduated March 1942. The program was adapted from the curriculum of the Maternity Center Association (MCA) and organized by Margaret Thomas, a member of MCA staff. From 1945 until the school closed, one of its graduates, Claudia Durham (Fig. 2–8), directed the program. After the program was established at Tuskegee, it is reported that black nurses who applied for admission to MCA for training in midwifery were directed to Tuskegee, which had been established for blacks. The association has since had black nurses on its staff. The first to be employed (in 1948) was Dorothy Doyle Harrison, a graduate of Mercy Hospital School of Nursing in Philadelphia.

Figure 2–8 Claudia Durham, last Director, Tuskegee Nurse-Midwifery School.

The course at Tuskegee, for graduates of accredited schools of nursing, was six months long. One-third of the time was spent in theoretical instruction conducted by obstetricians, nurse-midwives, and other specialists. Students were given practical learning experiences in clinics and homes. Each student was required to manage under supervision at least 20 to 30 deliveries and might assist the obstetrician with abnormal deliveries in the hospital. Standing orders were used as approved by consultants from the state health department and the county medical society (Thomas, 1942).

When the school was established, the maternal mortality rate in Macon County was 8.5 per 1,000 live births. In its second year, the service was responsible for the delivery of one-third of all the mothers in the county, with a mortality rate of zero. The infant death rate was 45.9 per 1,000 live births before the opening of the school; by the end of the second year of the demonstration project, it was 14 per 1,000 for women under the care of the nurse-midwives (MCA, 1955). When it closed in 1946, 25 black nurse-midwives had been graduated from the Tuskegee program.

A second nurse-midwifery school for black nurses was established in 1942 in connection with Flint-Goodridge Hospital and Dillard University in New Orleans. Etta Mae Forte Miller, a native of Tuskegee, Alabama, and a certified nurse-midwife from MCA, helped to set up the program at Flint-Goodridge (Carter, 1982). This six-month course was also financed by the U.S. Children's Bureau. After one year, the school closed, having graduated only two black nurse-midwives, who subsequently were employed by the Departments of Health in Louisiana and Mississippi.

The renaissance of nurse-midwifery in the 1970s, coupled with the women's rights movement and increasing interest in nonhospital deliveries, spurred research interest into alternative modes of service as well as continued research into the normal low-risk pregnancy and delivery (Gortner & Nahm, 1977).

Master's Degree Education

Since 1931, when the first black nurse, Estelle Massey Riddle Osborne, with a scholarship from the Rosenwald Fund, earned a master's degree in nursing at Teachers College, Columbia University, New York, many black nurses have earned master's degrees, receiving their education at historically white universities.

Today, master's degree nursing programs exist at four historically black institutions. The first one was established at Hampton University School of Nursing in Hampton, Virginia, followed by Howard University College of Nursing in Washington, D.C.; Albany State College in Georgia; Bowie State University in Maryland. Meharry Medical College Department of Nursing Education in Nashville established a master's program in 1982 but closed it in June 1985.

Hampton University has had a basic baccalaureate nursing program since 1944, the first in the state of Virginia, initiated by Mary Elizabeth Lancaster Carnegie. It was established as a result of the wartime need for nurses for military and civilian service and for black nurses prepared for leadership positions (Lancaster, 1945). In 1976, under the leadership of Fostine G. Riddick Roach (Fig. 2–9), dean of the school at that time, the master's degree program was started, with major courses of study in community health and community mental health nursing. The program has expanded and now includes three specialty areas and two graduate head nurse-practitioner programs. The first master's degree from the program was bestowed in 1978 on Terry Williams Dagrosa of Chesapeake, Virginia, who majored in community health nursing with a functional specialization in education. Her thesis was entitled "Correlation Among Personality Traits which may Facilitate Effective Relief of Chronic Pain by the Transcutaneous Nervous Stimulation Method."

Under the leadership of its first dean, Dr. Anna B. Coles, (Fig. 2–10), the College of Nursing at Howard University in Washington, D.C., has had a baccalaureate nursing program since 1969. This replaced the diploma program at Freedmen's Hospital, which, between 1894 and 1973, had graduated 1,700 nurses. In 1980, the Howard University Board of Trustees approved the establishment of a graduate program leading to the degree of master of science in nursing. At first, the pro-

Figure 2–9 Fostine G. Riddick Roach, Dean, School of Nursing, Hampton University, when master's program was initiated.

Figure 2–10   Dr. Anna B. Coles, Dean, College of Nursing, Howard University, when master's program was initiated.

gram had three major areas of concentration—gerontological nursing, adult health nursing, and family nursing in the urban community. Later, nursing administration and mental health nursing were added to the curriculum as majors.

The graduate program in nursing at Albany State College, Albany, Georgia, under the direction of Dr. Lucille B. Wilson, was approved by the board of regents in August 1988 and admitted its first students that fall. The master's program offers options for two clinical majors: community health nursing and maternal-child health nursing. In conjunction with the development of specialized competencies in one of these two clinical fields, the master's student may select preparation for a career as an administrator or clinical specialist.

The master's degree program in nursing at Bowie State University in Bowie, Maryland, was begun in 1989 under the direction of Dr. Joyce Bowles. The focus is on advanced clinical practice in adult health with emphasis on gerontology and role tracks of nursing administration and nursing education.

SUMMARY

Before and after schools of nursing especially for blacks were established, a few black women entered and completed programs at predominantly white schools, the first being Mary Mahoney, who was graduated from the New England Hospital for Woman and Children in 1879. The first diploma program established for blacks was at Spelman College in Atlanta, Georgia, in 1886, followed by nearly 100 others before the last one at Grady Hospital closed in 1982.

Six years after the University of Cincinnati established the first baccalaureate program in the country in 1916, one was established at a black school, Howard University, but survived only three years—1922 to 1925. Currently (1990) there are 655 baccalaureate programs in the United States, 157 of which are for registered nurses only. Of these, 23 are located at historically black colleges and universities, and all report a mixed racial enrollment.

Associate degree nursing education, the latest type of generic program, began in 1952 as an experimental project. One black school, the Norfolk Division of Virginia State College (now Norfolk State University), participated in the project. Of the 822 associate degree nursing programs today, six are located at historically black institutions.

In the 1930s and 1940s, public health and midwifery programs for registered nurses were established at historically black institutions: St. Philip in Richmond and North Carolina Central University at Durham in the area of public health nursing; and Tuskegee University in Alabama and Flint-Goodridge Hospital/Dillard University in New Orleans in the area of nurse-midwifery.

Ongoing master's degree programs in nursing are located at four black colleges and universities: Hampton University in Virginia; Howard University in Washington, D.C.,; Albany State College in Georgia; and Bowie State University in Maryland. A master's program at Meharry Medical College in Nashville, Tennessee, existed from 1982 to 1985.

REFERENCES

American Nurses' Association. (1965). First position on education for nursing. *American Journal of Nursing, 65*, 106–111.

Annual Report for 1878: New England Hospital for Women and Children, Boston.

Brick, M. (1963). *Forum and focus for the junior college movement*. New York: Teachers College Press.

Brown, E.L. (1948). *Nursing for the future*. New York: Russell Sage Foundation.

Carnegie, M.E. (1948). Nurse training becomes nursing education at Florida A & M College. *Journal of Negro Ed., 17*, 200–204.

Carter, A.J. (1982). Profiles of the Black registered nurse, *ANA Council on Intercultural Nursing Newsletter, 2*, 2–3.

Chayer, M.E. (1954). Mary Eliza Mahoney. *American Journal of Nursing, 54*, 429–431.

Davis, B. (1976). *The origins and growth of three nursing programs at Howard University, 1893–1973*. Unpublished doctoral dissertation, Teachers College, Columbia University, New York.

Dyson, W. (1921). *The founding of Howard University*. Washington, D.C.: Howard University Press.

Educational facilities for colored nurses. (1925). *Trained Nurse and Hospital Review, 74*, 259–262.

Gage, N.D., & Haupt, A.D. (1932). Some observations on Negro nursing in the south. *Public Health Nursing, 24*, 674–680.

Gortner, S., & Nahm, H. (1977). An overview of nursing research in the United States. *Nursing Research, 26*, 10–33.

Grippando, G.M. (1983). *Nursing perspectives and issues*. Albany, New York: Delmar.

Hogan, A. (1975). A tribute to the pioneers. *Journal of Nurse Midwife, 20*, 6–11.

Jamieson, E. M., & Sewall, M. (1944). *Trends in nursing history* (2nd ed.), Philadelphia: W.B. Saunders.

Jones, J. (1981). *Bad blood, the Tuskegee syphilis experiment*. New York: Free Press.

Kessel, F. (1989). Black foundations: Meeting vital needs. *Crisis, 96*, 14–18.

Lancaster (Carnegie), M.E. (1945). How a collegiate nursing program developed in a Negro college. *American Journal of Nursing, 45*, 119.

Maternity Center Association. (1955). *Twenty years of nurse-midwifery, 1933–1953*. A Report. New York: Author.

Montag, M. (1980). Associate degree education in perspective. *Nursing Outlook, 28*, 248–250.

Mossell, N.F. (1908). *The work of the Afro-American woman* (2nd ed,). Philadelphia: George S. Ferguson.

Newell, H. (1951). *The history of the National Nursing Council*. New York: The Council.

Peck, E.S., & Pride, M.W. (1982). *Nurses in times: Developments in nursing education 1898–1981*. Berea College, Berea, Kentucky: Appalachian Fund.

Peck, E.S., & Smith, E.A. (1982). *Berea's first 125 years*. Lexington: University Press of Kentucky.

Personnel Data Cards. (1898). Spanish-American War. Washington, D.C., National Archives.

Report of the Surgeon General's Consultant Group on Nursing. (1963). *Toward quality in nursing: Needs and goals*. Washington D.C.: USHEW.

Roberts, M. (1954). *American nursing: History and interpretation*. New York; Macmillan.

Spelman Messenger. (1908, March). Atlanta: Spelman College.

Spelman Messenger. (1914, February). Atlanta: Spelman College.

Staupers, M.K. (1961). *No time for prejudice*. New York: Macmillan.

Thomas, M.W. (1942). Social priority no. 1, mothers and babies. *Public Health Nursing, 34*, 442–445.

West, R.M. (1931). *History of nursing in Pennsylvania*. Harrisburg: Pennsylvania Nurses Association.

West, M., & Hawkins, C. (1950). *Nursing schools at the midcentury*. New York: National Committee for the Improvement of Nursing Services.

Chapter 3

✤

From Dreams to Achievements

Prior to World War II, the only effort on a national scale to recruit blacks into the nursing profession was made by the NACGN, which had this as one of its objectives. During World War II, a mechanism was set into motion by the federal government to procure additional nursing personnel by financing basic nursing education. This was done through the Cadet Nurse Corps program in which many black nursing schools and students participated.

When the war was over and the Cadet Nurse Corps was terminated, again the only national recruitment program for black nursing students was conducted by NACGN. After NACGN dissolved in January 1951, there was a noticeable decline in the number of black students being admitted to and graduated from nursing programs. The closing of a number of all-black schools, where the vast majority of black students had been enrolled, was a major factor influencing the decline. In the 1950s and 1960s, 15 black schools closed (Carnegie, 1964). There was a noticeable decrease in the registered black nurse population during these years as the number of would-be admissions to the closed black schools was not absorbed by the existing white schools. In fact, in 1969, while blacks made up the largest minority group in the United States (more than 11 percent), the percentage of blacks graduating from schools of nursing leading to registered nurse licensure was only 3.2 percent. This was also the time when integration efforts were stimulated by federal governmental prescriptions. The Civil Rights Act of 1964, supreme court decisions, and executive orders mandated the prohibition of racial segregation in institutions of higher education.

The Nurse Training Act of 1964 and its later revisions provided for special project monies to increase the number of disadvantaged and minority students in schools of nursing. The Higher Education Act of

1965 greatly increased the availability of financial aid to low-income students and provided funds to institutions for special admission and support programs for minority students. These federal acts also stimulated state and local governmental prescriptions for racial integration. In addition, help came from the private sector.

In this chapter, four special projects are discussed—one privately funded and three federally funded. The Sealantic Project for the Disadvantaged received support from a private source. The Cadet Nurse Corps, the Breakthrough to Nursing Project of the National Student Nurses' Association, and the Ethnic/Minority Fellowship Project administered by the ANA were federally funded. The latter is still funded by the federal government.

CADET NURSE CORPS

The creation of the Cadet Nurse Corps played a significant role in procuring nursing personnel during World War II. In 1940, the United States began preparing for the possibility of war. In July of that year, the National Nursing Council on Defense was organized by six national organizations—the American Nurses' Association, the National League of Nursing Education, the Association of Collegiate Schools of Nursing, the National Organization for Public Health Nursing, the American Red Cross Nursing Service, and the National Association of Colored Graduate Nurses—as a means of dealing with problems that might arise in connection with nursing in national defense. One of the main purposes of the council was to serve as a coordinating agency for the participating organizations. It began at once to recruit students and classify graduate nurses as to their availability for military service (Deloughery, 1977).

In the summer of 1941, the U.S. Congress was induced by Frances Payne Bolton, congresswoman from Ohio, to appropriate $1,250,000 for nursing education, and in 1942, $3,500,000. Known as the first Bolton Bill, it provided for (1) refresher courses for graduate nurses, (2) assistance to schools of nursing so that they could increase their enrollments, (3) postgraduate courses, (4) preparation for instructors and other personnel, and (5) training in midwifery and other specialties (Goodnow, 1948).

In 1942, the National Council on Defense became the National Nursing Council for War Service (NNCWS). To increase the number of nurses for military service and at the same time ensure that civilians were cared for, the council planned refresher courses for graduate nurses, pooled teaching staffs, helped to arrange for more centralized schools, and advised on all nursing activities (Goodnow, 1948).

The NNCWS also focused on untapped sources of nursing service—blacks, men, and practical nurses. NACGN worked closely with the council and, in the early days of the war, inquiries about black nurses and opportunities for blacks in schools of nursing were referred by the council to NACGN. NACGN's small staff and limited budget, however, could not carry this increased load. With financial aid from the General Education Board (GEB) of the Rockefeller Foundation, the council elected to set up a black unit on an experimental basis and appointed a black nurse, Estelle Massey Riddle Osborne, to direct it with the title of consultant. The preliminary work was so promising that GEB funds were supplemented by the W.K. Kellogg Foundation and the U.S. Public Health Service (USPHS) and a second black consultant, Alma Vessells John, was integrated into the general program.

The special functions of the two black consultants of NNCWS were (1) to compile data relative to the status and problems of black nurses and (2) to stimulate the progress of black nurses through further integration in the major professional nursing organizations (Roberts, 1954). These two consultants set into motion a series of institutes for nursing school directors, hospital administrators, members of governing boards, and officials responsible for the operation of schools of nursing in black colleges and universities. One very important conference of black college presidents and administrative deans was held at Dillard University in New Orleans in 1944 to develop ways of utilizing educational resources more fully for the preparation of black nurses (Riddle & Nelson, 1945).

In 1943, Bolton put through Congress a second bill, which became Public Law 74, 78th Congress, establishing the U.S. Cadet Nurse Corps under the administration of the USPHS. This had been carefully planned by the NNCWS, aiming to increase as rapidly as possible the number of nurses in the country. The bill passed both houses without a dissenting vote. Lucile Petry Leone was appointed director of the USPHS Division of Nurse Education to administer the Cadet Nurse Corps program. Included on her staff as a part-time consultant was a black nurse, Rita Miller Dargan (Fig. 3–1), on leave from Dillard University in New Orleans where she chaired the Division of Nursing. Dargan's responsibilities were to assist black schools in applying for participation in the Cadet Nurse Corps program, to help black schools qualify for the corps, and to facilitate inclusion of more black students in the program.

A committee on recruitment of nursing students was established by the NNCWS and held its first meeting February 24, 1944 (Fig. 3–2). A cooperative campaign by nurses, hospital administrators, educators, and civic leaders to meet the year's quota of 65,000 new students was mapped out.

Federal funds provided for maintenance of the students in the Cadet Nurse Corps during the first nine months, tuition and fees throughout the program, and necessary expansion of educational and residential

Figure 3–1   Rita Miller Dargan, Consultant, Cadet Nurse Corps.

facilities. Each student was provided school uniforms, the U.S. Cadet Nurse Corps outdoor uniform, and a stipend of $15 a month for the pre-cadet period and $20 a month for the junior cadet period—15 or 20 months. If up to six months were required before the student was eligible to take licensure examinations, during the senior cadet period, the using agency—home or other civilian or governmental hospital or health service—paid the cadet a minimum of $30 a month and maintenance. The student participant agreed to remain in essential civilian or military nursing service for the duration of the war, a pledge later determined not legally binding. For their senior experience, cadets served not only in their home hospitals but also in hospitals of the army, navy, Veterans Administration, Public Health Service, and Indian Affairs, plus other civilian hospitals and public health agencies. "Some 22 Negro cadets had served in six Army hospitals by the end of 1945" (Maxwell, 1976) (Fig. 3–3).

It was deemed expedient and economical to strengthen the instructional staff and facilities of existing civilian schools of nursing. Although the establishment of the Cadet Nurse Corps was a defense measure, a precedent had been established—schools of nursing were given recognition as essential agencies in the protection of the nation's health (Shields, 1981). During the 1940s the corps recruited 169,000 of the nation's 179,000 nursing students (Kalisch, 1988) and of the 1,300 schools of nursing, 1,125 participated (U.S. Public Health Service, 1950).

Figure 3–2   First meeting of the National Nursing Council for War Service Committee on Recruitment of Student Nurses. Seated, left to right, are Mrs. E. B. Wickenden, Mildred Reese, Edith H. Smith (Chairperson), Dr. Donald Smelzer (Vice-chairperson), Lucile Petry Leone, Mrs. Eben J. Carey. Standing, left to right, are Leah Blaisdell, Lucille Reynolds, Dr. Walter C. Ellis, Florence Meyers, Mary Elizabeth Lancaster Carnegie, Sr. Charles Marie, Katherine Faville, Mary Anita Perez, Mildred Tuttle, M. Cordella Cowan, Jean Henderson. (Courtesy, National Library of Medicine)

In cooperation with the Cadet Nurse Corps, the NNCWS selected nurses with collegiate backgrounds to visit about 600 junior and senior colleges. Two black nurses, Orieanna Collins Syphax (Fig. 3–4) and Pauline Battle Butler "visited 82 [black] campuses and talked with thousands of black women students about the leadership positions awaiting the college-prepared nurse and about the free education offered through membership in the Cadet Nurse Corps" (Kalisch & Kalisch, 1978, p. 561).

The Cadet Nurse Corps proved beneficial to many black students, who otherwise might not have had a nursing education. By September 1944,

> there were some 2,000 black nursing cadets representing all but 500 to 600 of the total number of black students enrolled in all nursing schools. By the end of the Cadet Nurse Corps program in 1945,

Figure 3–3   Senior cadets from Tuskegee University en route to Boston City Hospital to gain senior experiences, March, 1945.

Figure 3–4   Orieanna Collins Syphax, recruiter for Cadet Nurse Corps.

2,600 black students had been enrolled. Of the nursing schools accepting black students, 20 were all-black schools enrolling 1,600 to 2,000 students, while the remaining 400 black students were distributed among 22 integrated schools. [Staupers, 1951, p. 223]

When the war started in 1941, only 14 white schools had ever admitted blacks (Staupers, 1961).

The Cadet Nurse Corps, composed of student trainees, was not a branch of the armed forces or the civilian personnel force of the U.S. government. The training and experience of its nurses did not constitute federal service, and, therefore, no veterans benefits accrued. The corps pledge was a statement of good intentions, rather than a legal contract. However, in 1984, Beth Bohannon, a former cadet, started a major campaign to initiate national legislation that would credit time spent in the Cadet Nurse Corps during World War II toward civil service retirement (Larson, 1987).

On June 4, 1985, Congressman Jim Slattery of Kansas introduced a bill (H.R. 2663) in the House of Representatives. This bill, as originally written, mandated civil service status for all cadet nurses who served at least two years in the corps. The House Bill met with much resistance from the Office of Personnel Management, the Budget Office, and members of the Reagan Administration who were concerned about the budgetary impact of the bill. Reluctantly, the bill was amended so that it applied only to registered nurses who were employed by the federal government on the date of enactment and who had at least two years of cadet service. The bill (P.L. 99-638) as amended was passed by the House and Senate and signed by President Reagan on November 10, 1986 ". . . to credit time spent in the Cadet Nurse Corps during World War II as creditable service for civil service retirement. . ." (CIS Annual Legislative History of U.S. Public Laws, 1986, p. 725).

BREAKTHROUGH

The National Student Nurses' Association (NSNA) is the only national organization for students in nursing. Its purpose is to aid in the development of the individual student and to urge students of nursing, as future health professionals, to be aware of and to contribute to improving the health care of all people.

In 1963, NSNA became actively involved in recruiting members of minority groups for schools of nursing. Recruitment of minorities continues to be a priority for the association. "Breakthrough to Nursing" was first developed on the local level; it is now a project of national scope. From 1965 to 1970, the project was maintained solely by nursing students who volunteered their time. Funding came from local philanthropy and NSNA.

In June 1971, the first contract of $100,000 from the Division of Nursing, DHEW, enabled NSNA to employ a program director (Fig. 3–5) and staff to assist students to organize Breakthrough volunteer recruitment programs through local and state constituent student nurses associations, to establish five selected target areas for intensive effort as test project sites, and to develop program plans to identify strategies to recruit students from minority groups to enroll in nursing programs.

Although the money stabilized Breakthrough activities in the five selected target areas—Los Angeles, California; Phoenix, Arizona; Denver, Colorado; Columbus, Ohio; and Charlotte, North Carolina—it was not sufficient to mount a nationwide program. By the end of the contract period, over 600 potential candidates for nursing had been reached through Breakthrough efforts, and there had been enough statistical data collected to justify expansion of the project.

In June 1974, NSNA obtained a three-year grant from the DHEW Division of Nursing to initiate and maintain programs in 40 local target areas where career opportunities for minority group students were available. During the first year of the grant, approximately 500 NSNA members of various racial backgrounds worked on the Breakthrough project as recruiters in the target areas. This was an average of about 20 percent

Figure 3–5   Alberta "Kit" Barnes, Project Director, NSNA Breakthrough Project, 1974–1977.

more than had worked at Breakthrough target areas the preceding year. Thirty-six students from various minority groups were recruited and accepted into schools of nursing by the end of the first year.

During the 1975–76 year of the grant, approximately 1,000 NSNA members were involved in recruiting in the 40 target areas. By June 1976, 86 more candidates had been recruited and were admitted to nursing programs, and 286 prospective applicants were targeted for the year 1976–77.

The basic approach to the Breakthrough project has been the establishment of one-to-one relationships with prospective candidates. When a candidate expresses interest in pursuing the study of nursing, the person is invited to meet with the local Breakthrough Committee. The committee, composed of faculty associates and students, determines the type of assistance needed by the candidate and helps in finding ways of providing it. Some students need encouragement only, while others may need assistance in filling out admission applications, in making financial plans, or in determining high school course requirements (Fig. 3–6).

Through the persistent efforts of the student volunteers and faculty associates, the Breakthrough project has achieved the following:

1. Encouraged schools of nursing to be more responsive to needs of minority-group students

2. Kept national nursing organizations aware of their responsibilities to minority-group people in and out of nursing, and established good working relationships with these organizations

3. Established, through local campaigns and the mass media, good working relations with secondary schools, guidance counselors, and schools of nursing

4. Developed recruitment materials geared specifically to minority-group recruitment

5. Developed leadership ability and skill in intergroup relations among minority- and nonminority-group student nurses

6. Obtained national and local scholarship funds for minority-group students.

More than 50,000 pieces of literature about Breakthrough have been distributed in junior and senior high schools, community centers, churches, and neighborhood organizations. The effect of the literature distribution is not known; however, the NSNA office receives thousands of inquiries from prospective candidates who do not reside in the target areas. In one week, over 3,000 inquiries were received at the NSNA office from persons in the New York metropolitan area following an NBC Television Network broadcast in which Dr. Frank Field, science editor, filmed a

Figure 3–6   Frances Knight, Chairperson, NSNA Breakthrough Project.

recruitment session in the Manhattan/Bronx area and interviewed two
Breakthrough student recruiters.

NSNA believes acceptance of and respect for minorities have increased
markedly over the last few years. Three of eight members of the NSNA
Board of Directors elected in 1976 were black. It is reasonable to assume
that without Breakthrough this would not have happened. As McGee
said, "The Breakthrough to Nursing Project . . . is foregoing a leadership
position in changing the image of the registered nurse as a 'white female
in a starched white uniform' as student nurses expand and increase their
local projects recruiting in minority communities all over the country"
(Breakthrough, 1972, p. 11).

Breakthrough has had an impact on schools, students, and the nursing
profession as the volunteer student recruiters have impressed admin-

istrative heads of nursing programs with the seriousness of purpose and support of the project's goals. Hundreds of students, faculty, and practicing nurses are now more aware of the need to bring more people from minority groups into the mainstream of American nursing. Students who are involved in Breakthrough realize that recruitment alone is insufficient, and that efforts must also be directed toward helping students complete the program so that they will become licensed practitioners. Efforts to reduce attrition rates through a planned tutoring-advocacy-counseling program are also part of the project.

In 1988, Breakthrough celebrated its 25th anniversary and "has proved to be one of the major avenues by which all nursing students can work in a unified way to ultimately improve the quality of nursing care given to diverse cultural groups, thus making nursing a more visible and attractive profession" (Carnegie, 1988, p. 59).

SEALANTIC

Since the early part of this century, the Rockefeller Foundation has acted on the fundamental belief that trained intelligence can and does promote human welfare, and has been for many years deeply engaged in working with a number of outstanding universities and colleges in the United States to create new opportunities for students from deprived backgrounds (Schickel, 1965). In keeping with the Rockefeller Foundation's long-standing interest in helping the disadvantaged in the United States and other countries and its interest in helping to meet the health needs of the people, the Sealantic Fund (one of the Rockefeller Brothers' Funds) was organized in 1935 by John D. Rockefeller, Jr., specifically to provide aid to nursing. Sealantic had funded several programs in nursing: the pilot project for the establishment of associate degree programs, the National League for Nursing Career Program to recruit more students, and conferences for faculties of associate degree programs. In 1965, the fund began sponsoring a program in nursing education for the disadvantaged.

The purposes of the Sealantic Project for the Disadvantaged in Nursing were (1) to assist selected schools of nursing to reach out for black and other disadvantaged youth and engage in educational and social action needed to prepare them for entering and completing programs in nursing and (2) to experiment with different ways of increasing the number of blacks and disadvantaged youth who enter nursing, with the expectation that many other schools, with or without financial assistance, would be stimulated to focus attention on this significant source of nurse power and on the expansion of educational opportunities for these youth.

In 1966, ten nursing programs participated in the Sealantic Project: Opening the Doors Wider in Nursing (ODWIN), Roxbury, Massachusetts; Cornell University-New York Hospital, New York; Goshen College, Indiana; Hunter College, New York; Loyola University, Chicago; Spalding College, Louisville, Kentucky; University of Arizona, Tucson; University of Cincinnati, Ohio; University of Portland, Oregon; and Wagner College, Staten Island, New York. ODWIN, an outgrowth of a project sponsored and conducted by the Alumnae Association of Boston University School of Nursing to assist persons from minority and low-income groups to enter and complete a program in nursing, became independently incorporated.

The initial grants awarded for all projects were for two years. While all projects had the same goal of helping disadvantaged young people prepare for careers in nursing, each project identified different strategies for the attainment of the goal. Common elements in all programs included recruitment, academic remediation, counseling, cultural enrichment, and financial assistance.

An advisory committee, composed of nurse educators, representatives from the federal government, the National Urban League, national nursing organizations, and the Rockefeller Foundation formulated the criteria for participation in the Sealantic Project. The schools selected were required (1) to offer a baccalaureate program that was accredited by the National League for Nursing (NLN); (2) to admit freshmen directly from high school, or to admit students as sophomores or juniors; (3) to offer intensive counseling and special instruction, if needed, to students in the first or first two years of study in other colleges on the same campus; (4) to be desegregated and not admit a predominant number of Negroes; (5) to be located in a community where a considerable number of blacks or other minority candidates were available; and (6) to have a dean and instructional staff who were known to possess interest in the purpose of the program.

On the basis of these criteria and the geographic spread, 58 baccalaurate nursing programs were selected and invited by letter to submit proposals to Sealantic that would include an estimate of funds needed. The schools were also informed of the availability of consultation services by the advisory committee through site visits. (The consultants who made the site visits were Lucile Petry Leone, Mary Elizabeth Carnegie, and Lillian Bischoff.) Twenty-four of the schools contacted indicated an interest, and visits were made. Nine schools submitted proposals, of which seven were approved for funding in 1966, with three additional programs funded later, bringing the number of participating programs to ten.

Since there were no forms for preparing the proposals, there was no uniformity among the proposals. However, all of the schools requested funds for project directors, summer and Saturday school instructors, counselors, tutors, scholarships, and stipends for students. In all instances, universities contributed physical facilities, educational resources, and financial aid to enrolled Sealantic students. The budgets approved by Sealantic for individual schools ranged from $17,600 to $59,866. Four programs received $25,000, three received less than $25,000, and three received more than $25,000.

The project directors (Fig. 3–7), six of whom were nurses, were responsible for identifying potential candidates for nursing among the disadvantaged junior and senior high school students with identifiable potential and interest; preparing students for admission to nursing programs; maintaining the students' interest in nursing as a career; increasing the motivation of students to undertake and successfully complete the program; providing the students with an opportunity to pursue nursing as a career; working with high school counselors in providing information on nursing and in selecting promising students for nursing; expanding and maintaining enrollment of disadvantaged students; helping students to qualify for admission to nursing school; providing an opportunity for students to identify with nursing; raising the level of the intellectual and vocational aspiration of students; assisting students with financial aid; providing information about nursing to counselors; preparing students to function within the nursing career; and creating

Figure 3–7   Sealantic Project Directors meet in Washington, D. C., March 1967. In the front row, left to right, are Susan Dudas, Alice Cicerich, Orpah B. Mosemann, Lucile P. Leone, Anita Smith, Mary Malone, Doris B. Clement, Jean Scheinfeldt. In the second row, left to right, are Virginia Kettling, Vernia Jane Huffman, Mary Elizabeth Carnegie, Sr. Agnes Miriam, Fannie L. Gardner, Doris Schwartz, Katharine Faville, Daphne A. Rolfe, Rhodes Arnold.

an awareness within the school and the university of the needs of the disadvantaged (Kibrick, 1970).

In addition, the project directors visited the families of the students to help them understand nursing, the Sealantic Project, and opportunities available in nursing. They also worked with community groups such as the Urban League and conducted field trips to hospitals, clinics, and public health agencies to sustain the students' interest in nursing and raise the level of their educational and professional aspirations. The project directors were also responsible for arranging cultural and social enrichment experiences. To provide further guidance, seven projects also had advisory committees composed of people in the community representing high school faculty and public service agencies. Members of these advisory committees represented various racial and ethnic groups in the community.

Recruitment plans and procedures varied. Six schools recruited specifically for baccalaureate programs and four recruited for all types of nursing education programs. Most efforts, however, were aimed at high school students who had been identified by their counselors or teachers as having the interest in and potential for succeeding in nursing.

All projects conducted a pre-nursing program throughout the academic year, which included Saturday activities, and all but one had a summer program ranging from six to ten weeks. All the projects gave continued support to students, including financial aid and counseling, after admission to a nursing program. The summer programs included academic subjects and cultural enrichment activities, and several schools provided housing on campus. For those students who would ordinarily have to work, the Sealantic grants provided modest stipends. The amount varied from $30 to $40 per week.

The goal of the Sealantic Project was twofold: successful admission and completion of the program through graduation. After admission to a nursing school, the Sealantic students were given continuing counseling and guidance, academic assistance by volunteers who were often other students, and financial assistance by Sealantic in the form of scholarships for tuition and living expenses.

A study conducted in 1971 compared the Sealantic students who had had specialized counseling with a similar group of students in the NLN Career-Pattern Study, who had had no such help (Carnegie, 1974). Findings of the study revealed that the dropout rate of the Sealantic students, who had been provided with special assistance, was 28.1 percent in contrast to those in the Career-Pattern group, who had a dropout rate of 48.4 percent. This finding alone supported the conclusion that the Sealantic Project was well worth the effort and money contributed, and resulted in adding more baccalaureate graduates to the population of black nurses. Although the Sealantic Project ended in the 1960s, it is still used by universities as a model.

ANA MINORITY FELLOWSHIP PROGRAMS

Doctoral education in nursing is relatively young; the first doctor of nursing science program was established in 1960 at Boston University. For years, however, nurses had been (and still are) pursuing doctoral studies in other disciplines to prepare them not only for leadership roles in service and education but also to conduct research in order to improve the quality of patient care. The first known nurse to hold a doctorate was Edith Bryan, who earned a PhD in psychology in 1927 from Johns Hopkins University, Baltimore, Maryland.

One of the main objectives of the American Nurses' Foundation (ANF), the research arm of ANA, is the encouragement of nursing research. To help meet this objective, ANF compiled a directory of nurses with doctoral degrees and published the first listing in the September-October 1969 issue of *Nursing Research*, with supplements in 1970, 1971, and 1972.

In 1973, the foundation's directory, which included 1,019 nurses with doctorates in 19 countries, was presented in a separate publication entitled *International Directory of Nurses with Doctoral Degrees*. This directory included data such as educational preparation, country of residence, area of doctoral study, and subject of dissertation. A unique feature of the directory was the identification of minorities. Such identification was made with the permission of the persons involved. The data revealed that of the 964 nurse doctorates reporting in the United States, 41 (4.2 percent) were black, and three of these were men. Twenty-six (63 percent) of the 41 black nurses had acquired their basic nursing education at 13 historically black schools of nursing: Lincoln School for Nurses in New York and Freedmen's in Washington, D.C.—five each; Meharry in Nashville—three; Dillard University in New Orleans, Harlem Hospital in New York, and Florida A & M University in Tallahassee—two each; and Good Samaritan Hospital in North Carolina, Lincoln in Durham, Tuskegee in Alabama, St. Philip in Richmond, Mercy in Philadelphia, Hampton Institute in Virginia, and Kansas City General in Missouri— one each. Two of the 26 had earned doctorates in medicine.

In the 1973 directory, it is reported that the first black nurse to hold a doctorate was Elizabeth Lipford Kent. She earned her PhD in public health in 1955 at the University of Michigan, Ann Arbor. Kent had earned a bachelor's degree at Spelman College in Atlanta, Georgia, before entering the basic nursing program at St. Philip Hospital School of Nursing, Richmond, Virginia. At retirement, she was Director of Nursing and Psychiatric Nurse Executive, Lafayette Clinic, Detroit, Michigan, and Adjunct Assistant Professor, Wayne State University College of Nursing, Detroit.

In 1980, the ANA published a *Directory of Nurses with Doctoral Degrees*.

This publication was funded by a grant from the DHEW Division of Nursing. Of the 1,964 respondents to a mailed questionnaire, 57 were identifiable as black, although race was not reported. However, 22 of these had appeared in ANF's 1973 directory, which did include data concerning race. Although the 1980 directory does not give the name of the nurse's basic program, of the 35 new black entries, 16, or nearly half, were known to have received their basic education at historically black schools: Freedmen's in Washington, D.C.; Florida A & M University; Harlem; Dillard University; Lincoln in New York; Homer G. Phillips in St. Louis; North Carolina A & T State University; and Tuskegee University. The two directories (1973 and 1980) presented a total listing of 76 black nurses with doctoral degrees. Of the questionnaires mailed in 1983 by ANA to 4,500 nurses, 3,650 elicited responses, which appear in the 1984 directory. Again, race was not included; however, 77 (2.1 percent) of the nurses were identifiable as black, 24 of whom were new entries. Although ANA has not issued a directory since 1984, the *National Sample Survey of Registered Nurses* indicates that in 1988 there were 5,415 nurses with doctoral degrees who have maintained their license in nursing (*National Sample Survey*, 1988). Of this number, approximately 300, or five percent, are black.

Based on the data in ANF's directory, an editorial which appeared in the November-December 1973 issue of *Nursing Research*, entitled "ANF Directory Identifies Minorities with Doctorates," drew attention to the small number of minorities with earned doctorates (Carnegie, 1973). Two years earlier, in 1971, the Center for Minority Group Mental Health Programs, a major component of the National Institute of Mental Health (NIMH), DHEW, was established. According to Harper (1977), the idea of minority representation within NIMH began to ferment in the early 1960s but did not succeed through its three initial attempts until black psychiatrists met with the director, Dr. Bertram Brown, expressing the desire for an organized unit to basically serve four minority groups: American Indians, Asian-Americans, Spanish speaking/Spanish surnamed, and blacks.

Following four national conferences with each of the ethnic groups, priorities in the areas of manpower, research, education, and training were identified. Because of the lack of manpower, especially, it was decided to fund five fellowship programs: the American Psychological Association, the American Sociological Association, the American Nurses' Association, the American Psychiatric Association, and the Council on Social Work Education. These programs were designed to increase the number and quality of competent minority researchers, with the aim of enhancing the professional minority manpower and providing scientific data through research to improve mental health and nursing care to ethnic minority consumers. In essence, the programs would supply researchers who could direct research and identify priorities by indigenous groups. The center's support includes doctoral traineeships for careers through grants administered by the above professional organizations.

Because ANA was concerned about research in the area of ethnic minorities and the small number of doctorally prepared minorities to conduct such research, in 1974 it submitted a proposal to NIMH for a grant to help minority nurses earn doctorates. The grant of nearly $1 million was approved, and ANA received the funds in July of that year. This provided for a project director (Dr. Ruth Gordon [Fig. 3–8] was the first project director), secretarial services, and an advisory committee which included representatives of the racial minority categories and two white nurses. (The original advisory committee members were Hazle W. Blakeney, Mary Elizabeth Carnegie, Effie Poy Yew Chow, Signe Cooper, Herlinda Q. Jackson, Carmen D. Janosov, Myra E. Levine, Martha Primeaux, Gloria Smith, and Ethelrine Shaw-Nickerson.) The advisory committee was selected by the ANA Task Force on Affirmative Action and the ANA Board of Directors.

The purpose of the 1974 grant was to support candidates in behavioral and social science doctoral studies who had engaged in or who had demonstrated an interest in conducting research relating to the racial/cultural influences on mental health care delivery systems in ethnic minority communities. The objectives of this first ANA research grant were (1) to increase the quantity and quality of ethnic/racial minority nurse researchers and (2) to provide scientific data derived from research on ethnic/minority clientele as a basis for quality mental health and nursing

Figure 3–8   Dr. Ruth Gordon, first Project Director, ANA Minority Fellowship Program, 1974.

service delivery. Since the first fellowships were given, the Registered Nurse Fellowship Program has changed its focus to center on the behavioral sciences only, as a result of the policies of the Reagan administration, which dictated fewer research and training monies going to the social sciences.

The second grant to ANA was received in 1977 for the Clinical Fellowship Program (CFP) for Ethnic/Racial Minorities so that nurses could pursue doctoral studies in the area of psychiatric and mental health nursing. (Members of the CFP Advisory Committee were Bette Evans, chairperson; Rosalie Jackson; Don Matheson; Helen Nakagawa; Oliver Osborne; and Janie Wilson.) The CFP prepares nurses to provide, supervise, and consult in the delivery of psychiatric and mental health nursing, particularly to ethnic and racial minority groups. Also in 1977, the current director, Dr. Hattie Bessent (Fig. 3–9) joined the project, bringing with her a vast amount of experience in administration, teaching, research, and consultation.

The rationale for the need for these minority nurse fellowship programs can be better understood in light of the mission of the Center for Studies of Minority Group Mental Health of NIMH, which is the funding agency. The center's primary function is to improve the quality and quantity of research, manpower, and services to minority groups by funding supplemental technical assistance and developmental and enabling assistance. The center's goal is to affect the health care delivery system for ethnic/racial minority groups through its programs and col-

Figure 3–9   Dr. Hattie Bessent, current Director, ANA Minority Fellowship Programs.

laborative efforts with other federal, state, and local agency programs; regional and national consumer and professional programs; and private health and funding sources. Thus, although the two fellowship programs differ in the type of mental health disciplines being supported for doctoral study, both programs have a common objective—to improve the delivery of mental health care to ethnic/racial minority persons by increasing the pool of minority nurse researchers, educators, and administrators. According to the project director, Dr. Hattie Bessent, the fellows have been enrolled in 47 universities throughout the country since the first fellowships were awarded in 1975. As of December 31, 1990, a total of 202 fellows have been funded, and 110 have earned their doctorates.

As part of the minority fellowship program, a legislative internship (Fig. 3–10) was instituted in 1977 to provide the fellows with an opportunity to observe and participate in the legislative process at the national level, with particular emphasis on the enactment process of legislation dealing with the nursing profession, health care policy, and mental health

Figure 3–10   ANA Minority Legislative Interns, past and present (1989) with Dr. Mary Elizabeth Carnegie (far right).

and illness issues. The rationale for this was that the fellows would benefit from having this kind of experience in public policy formation, and an internship would provide them with firsthand knowledge of the steps involved in having a bill introduced and its evolution into law. This political expertise helps the fellows, as leaders in the health care profession, make an impact in the legislative arena. As of 1990, 37 percent of the fellows have interned in the offices of congressional lawmakers and committees, federal health regulatory agencies, and centers for research and development and policy studies. Placement of fellows as interns in congressional offices and in federal health regulatory agencies is a means of monitoring and influencing federal legislative and administrative policies and their implementation as they affect the characteristics and numbers of nurses and the scope of their practice and accountability.

In addition to administering the project for ethnic/racial minorities funded by NIMH, the staff has been responsible for administering the Clara Lockwood Fund, the ANA Baccalaureate Scholarship Fund, the Allstate Foundation Fund, and the W.K. Kellogg Foundation project on leadership training. The Clara Lockwood Fund was originally established to assist in the education of American Indian nurses. However, in December 1983, the ANA Board of Directors approved the use of interest from the fund to help finance graduate education for all ethnic minority nurses.

The ANA House of Delegates at successive conventions passed two resolutions sponsored by the Commission on Human Rights. The 1978 resolution called for ANA to create a scholarship fund to support baccalaureate education for registered nurses, with the criteria for reflecting "national priorities for increasing access to nursing care" in medically underserved areas. The 1980 resolution proposed specific actions to increase informational, legislative, and financial support for minority students in basic and graduate nursing education programs, in response to the proposed changes in educational requirements for entry into practice. At their December 1983 meeting, the ANA Board of Directors committed $50,000, to be paid over a period of five years, toward the establishment of this fund, which was geared toward ethnic minorities, but not limited to them. In the five years that the program was in existence, 40 nurses complete bachelor's degrees.

From 1985 to 1989 the Allstate Foundation had financed education for American Indian/Alaska Native descent nurses through the Indian Nurses Association. When this association dissolved in 1985 because of financial difficulties, the ANA Minority Fellowship Program (MFP) assumed the administrative responsibility for the scholarship fund. Before the funds were depleted, 22 Indian nurses received assistance and completed the bachelor's or associate degree in nursing.

Also in 1983, with the strong conviction that a postdoctoral leadership training program was needed for the ANA fellows, discussions toward this end were held between the MFP staff and officials of the W.K. Kellogg Foundation for possible funding. The preliminary proposal was submitted which would involve alumnae from all five minority fellowship programs—psychology, psychiatry, sociology, social work, and nursing. In 1986, a three-year grant was secured from the Kellogg Foundation to provide postdoctoral leadership and management training in mental health and to improve the fellows' "contributions to the clients they serve. The thrust of the program recognized that our society . . . is in the process of change in terms of its perspectives in leadership roles and opportunities for women. The challenge was to design a program of excellence that would assist ethnic minority women in maintaining themselves in this environment of social change and in coping with those extra burdens placed on them because of the long history of society-imposed limitations" (Bessent, 1989). A second three-year grant was made in 1989, which will terminate in 1991.

The Kellogg program trained participants in a series of workshops that covered a wide range of administrative and communication skills. Faculty were selected from such prestigious sources as the Harvard School of Business and included America's leading women administrators. In the six years of the Kellogg program's existence, a total of 120 women of color participated (Fig. 3–11). They included directors of university

Figure 3–11   Dr. Hattie Bessent (center front) with Kellogg Fellows, Los Angeles, California, 1989.

counseling centers, administrators, social and behavioral practitioners, and university faculty members. Most were interested in moving toward leadership roles in their academic, medical, and social service institutions where they could improve the status of their race and sex (Bessent, 1989).

SUMMARY

During World War II, the federal government financed basic nursing education through the Cadet Nurse Corps in an effort to procure more nurses to help meet military and civilian needs. Nearly 3,000 black students benefited from this program and received a nursing education.

To increase the number of blacks entering and successfully completing a basic program in nursing, special projects were established in the 1960s and 1970s, two of which have been reported in this chapter: Breakthrough to Nursing and the Sealantic Project.

To increase the number of doctorally prepared minority nurses, including blacks, the Fellowship Program of the American Nurses' Association was developed. This project, which began in 1974, has been responsible for 110 minority nurses earning the highest academic credential—the doctorate.

REFERENCES

Bessent, H. (1989). Postdoctoral leadership training for women of color. *Journal of Professional Nursing, 5*, 279–282.

Breakthrough to Nursing. (1972). *Imprint, 4*, 11.

Carnegie, M.E. (1964). Are Negro schools of nursing needed today? *Nursing Outlook. 12*, 52–56.

Carnegie, M.E. (1973). ANF directory identifies minorities with doctoral degrees (editorial). *Nursing Research. 22*, 483.

Carnegie, M.E. (1974). *Disadvantaged students in RN programs*. New York: National League for Nursing.

Carnegie, M.E. (1988). Breakthrough to nursing: Twenty-five years of involvement. *Image, 35*, 55–59.

CIS Annual Legislative History of U.S. Public Laws. (1986). Bethesda: Congressional Information Service.

Deloughery, G.L. (1977). *History and trends in professional nursing* (8th ed.). St. Louis: C.V. Mosby.

Directory of Nurses with Doctoral Degrees. (1980). Kansas City: American Nurses' Association.

Directory of Nurses with Doctoral Degrees. (1984). Kansas City: American Nurses' Association.

Goodnow, M. (1948). *Nursing history* (8th ed.). Philadelphia: Saunders.

Harper, M.S. (1977, Spring). The origin of the minority fellowship programs. *Fellowship*, 4.

International Directory of Nurses with Doctoral Degrees. (1973). New York: American Nurses' Foundation.

Kalisch, P.A. (1988). Why not launch a new cadet nurse corps? *American Journal of Nursing, 88*, 316–317.

Kalisch, P.A., & Kalisch, B. (1978). *The advance of American nursing*. Boston: Little, Brown & Co.

Kibrick, A. (1970). A report of the Sealantic Project Concerned with Recruiting the Disadvantaged in Schools of Nursing. New York: Sealantic Fund (unpublished).

Larson, D.V. (1987). Cadet nurses seek help from KNSA. *The Kansas Nurse, 5*, 14–15.

Maxwell, P.E. (1976). *History of the Army Nurse Corps 1775–1948*. Washington, D.C.: U.S. Army Center of Military History (unpublished), 92.

National Sample Survey of RNs. (1988). Bureau of Health Professions, Division of Nursing, Department of Health and Human Services.

Riddle (Osborne), E., & Nelson, J. (1945). The Negro nurse looks toward tomorrow. *American Journal of Nursing, 45*, 627–630.

Roberts, M.M. (1954). *American nursing: History and interpretation*. New York: Macmillan.

Schickel, R. (1965, Spring). *Equal opportunities for all*. New York: Rockefeller Foundation.

Shields, E.A. (1981). Highlights in the history of the Army Nurse Corps. Washington, D.C.: Government Printing Office.

Staupers, M.K. (1951). Story of the National Association of Colored Graduate Nurses. *American Journal of Nursing, 51*, 222–223.

Staupers, M.K. (1961). *No time for prejudice*. New York: Macmillan.

U.S. Public Health Service. (1950). The United States Cadet Nurse Corps and other federal nurse training programs, 1943–1948. Washington, D.C.: Government Printing Office.

Chapter 4

Struggle for Recognition

This chapter discusses the involvement of black nurses in those national and regional organizations that have been significant in their history. It begins with the National League for Nursing because its forerunner, the American Society of Superintendents of Training Schools for Nurses in the United States and Canada, established in 1893, was the first nursing organization that was national in scope. This is followed by 17 other national organizations and two regional ones. Reference is also made to four specialty organizations that have or have had black nurses in top leadership positions—elected or appointed.

THE NATIONAL LEAGUE FOR NURSING

At the Congress of Hospitals and Dispensaries at the World's Fair in Chicago in 1893, held to celebrate the 400th anniversary of the "discovery" of America, the nursing section provided occasion for the first meeting of nurses on the North American continent. By that time, many schools of nursing had been established in the United States and Canada to train nurses. Concerned about the lack of educational standards for these existing schools, the directors, or superintendents of nurses who were attending the fair, created the American Society of Superintendents of Training Schools for Nurses in the United States and Canada for the purpose of exchanging ideas and establishing high educational standards. The work of the society concentrated on (1) higher minimum entrance requirements to attract top students into nursing,

(2) improvement of living and working conditions (for students), and (3) increased opportunities for postgraduate and specialized training. The society was also concerned about the need for laws to protect the public from poorly trained nurses (Flanagan, 1976). Although there were a few trained black nurses in the country when the society was formed, there was no indication of black involvement at the initial meeting.

In 1912 the Canadian nurses discontinued their membership in favor of establishing their own national organization, and so the name of the society was changed to the National League of Nursing Education (NLNE), and membership was open on an individual basis to those nurses engaged in administration and education in schools of nursing.

As the result of an in-depth study of the structure of the major national nursing organizations, NLNE, along with the Association of Collegiate Schools of Nursing and the National Organization for Public Health Nursing, and several national committees merged in 1952, becoming the National League for Nursing.

The primary purpose of NLNE was to further the best interests of the nursing profession by establishing and maintaining a "universal" standard of training (*First Annual Report of the American Society*, 1897). NLN's primary function is to work with health care agencies (of which nursing services are a basic component), with educational institutions, and with communities to improve health care services and to provide nursing education programs needed by society through services in accreditation, consultation, testing, continuing education, research, and publications.

Black nurses had participated in the NLNE on all levels—national, state, and local—presenting scientific papers at conventions, and the like. As early as 1934, Estelle Massey Osborne read a paper at a general session of the 40th annual convention in Washington, D.C., entitled "The Negro Nurse Student." At its last convention in Atlantic City in 1952, Mary Elizabeth Carnegie participated in the symposium on curriculum. The papers by both these black nurses were published in the *American Journal of Nursing* (Massey, 1934; Carnegie, 1952).

When the structure was changed in 1912 from an organization of administrators, NLNE admitted to membership those who served in any teaching capacity in a school of nursing, directors in public health work, members of state boards of nurse examiners, and others actively concerned with education. For many years, however, black nurses in southern states were denied membership in NLNE because membership in their state nurses' association was a prerequisite. By virtue of their being denied membership in the state constituents of ANA, they were barred from NLNE membership.

In 1942, NLNE set a precedent for individual membership by a change in its bylaws. This change was particularly significant because it broke the barriers related to race. Black nurses were also represented on committees related to areas such as curriculum, vocational guidance, postwar planning, educational policies in wartime, and the National Committee on Nursing School Libraries.

From its inception in 1952, NLN had black representation on the board of directors, and it has continued to involve blacks on its boards, councils, committees, and professional staff. Willie Mae Johnson Jones (Diploma, Tuskegee University School of Nursing, Tuskegee, Alabama; BS, New York University), a black nurse on the staff of the Community Nursing Services of Montclair, New Jersey, was elected to the first NLN Board of Directors in 1952. She retired in 1974 as educational supervisor and died in 1982. While Lillian Harvey was on the board (1957 to 1961), she was a board-appointed advisor to the National Student Nurses' Association. Currently (1990), Dr. Beverly H. Bonaparte is on the board.

In 1954, Estelle M. Osborne joined NLN staff as associate general director for administration and served in this capacity until her retirement in 1966. Many other blacks have held executive positions at NLN among whom were Eleanor Lynch, Test Construction Unit; Claudia Durham, Consultant, Maternal-Child Health project; Dr. Edith Ramsey Johnson, Dr. Betty Martin Blount, and Sylvia Edge, Council of Associate Degree Programs; Dr. Alma Yearwood Dixon, Director of Consultation; and Julia Kelly Jackson, Director, Commonwealth-funded Fellowship Program. Under Jackson's direction, the fellowship program helped nurses with outstanding ability obtain advanced educational preparation. During its existence, from 1955 to 1963, 195 scholarships were given, 162 of which were for post-master's study. Currently serving as Director of Council Affairs, Council of Baccalaureate and Higher Degree Programs is Dr. Ruth W. Johnson (Fig. 4–1),

At each biennial convention, NLN presents awards to outstanding persons for various achievements. In 1975, Mabel K. Staupers, first executive director and last president, NACGN, received the Linda Richards Award. In 1975, Lillian Stokes (Fig. 4–2), Faculty of Indiana University School of Nursing, Indianapolis, was the recipient of the Lucile Petry Leone Award for innovative teaching methods. Stokes is currently pursuing a doctoral degree as a fellow of the ANA Minority Fellowship Program, and was profiled at the Indianapolis Children's Museum as one of the "Black Achievers in Science." In 1985, Vernice Ferguson received the Jean Mac Vicar Outstanding Nurse Executive Award. In 1987, the Marine Midland Bank/Margaret Heckler Award of $10,000 went to Carolyn Cuello, a black student at North Carolina A & T State University School of Nursing, Greensboro, for excellence in writing.

In 1953, NLN issued a statement on civil rights: "All activities of NLN shall include all groups regardless of race, color, religion, and sex." This statement was reviewed in 1964 by the executive committee of the board

Figure 4–2   Lillian Stokes, 1975 recipient, NLN Lucile Petry Leone Award for outstanding young teacher in nursing.

Figure 4–1   Dr. Ruth Johnson, Director of Council Affairs, National League for Nursing Department of Baccalaureate and Higher Degree Programs.

which expressed its conviction that the principles inherent in the statement had been practiced and that the statement should not be changed or amplified. The League vowed to continue its past policy of nondiscrimination in employment practices and all other activities.

In 1990, NLN produced a videotape, edited by Ellen Baer, entitled, *Nursing in America: A History of Social Reform*, which includes black nurse leaders. In addition, NLN published a 1991 historical calendar, compiled by M. Elizabeth Carnegie, saluting the 23 baccalaureate and higher degree nursing programs at historically black colleges and universities (see Chapter 2 for a listing of these schools).

THE AMERICAN NURSES' ASSOCIATION

As schools of nursing developed, graduates of these schools formed alumnae associations not only for social and professional purposes but also for promoting their own schools (Flanagan, 1976). The graduates of Bellevue Hospital Training School were first to organize, in 1889, followed by the Illinois Training School in 1891, Massachusetts General and Johns Hopkins in 1892, and St. Louis Protestant Hospital in 1895 (Seymer, 1933; Christ, 1957). In addition to social and professional purposes, many of these organizations had the more serious intention of providing both moral support and financial assistance to their members in time of need. The service feature of the St. Louis Protestant Hospital Alumnae, for example, provided for "pecuniary assistance in time of illness, or death among its members" (Christ, 1957, p. 103). Such a provision was a common function of American secret societies originating during the 18th and 19th centuries, many of which, even today, offer their members mutual assistance in the form of burial insurance, life insurance, endowment plans, and so forth (Gist, 1940).

In 1896, with the support of the American Society of Superintendents of Training Schools for Nurses in the United States and Canada, representatives of nurse alumnae societies formed a national association to embrace the general betterment of the profession. The name chosen for the new organization was the Nurses' Associated Alumnae of the United States and Canada. For legal reasons that involved matters of incorporation, the Canadian members in 1911 withdrew from the association. In 1911, the name was changed to the American Nurses' Association.

Today, the ANA is the national professional organization of registered nurses, comprising 53 constituent state and territorial associations in the 50 states, the District of Columbia, the Virgin Islands, Guam, and over 900 district associations. The association establishes the standards of nursing practice, education, and service, and promotes the professional and educational advancement of nurses, and the general welfare of nurses, to the end that all people may have better nursing care. These purposes are unrestricted by consideration of nationality, race, creed, color, or sex (This Is ANA, 1975).

From its founding in 1896, the ANA had offered membership to all qualified professional nurses regardless of race, color, creed, or national origin, and until 1916, all nurses joined ANA through their alumnae associations. The 1916 reorganization set up the state association as the basic unit of membership. Because of segregation laws at that time, black nurses in 16 southern states and the District of Columbia were denied membership on the state level, thereby precluding their membership in ANA. Black nurse membership in ANA was one problem upon which the NACGN, which had been established in 1908, spent most of its time and efforts. The first major step taken by the ANA House of Delegates in 1942 toward this end was the authorization of the Committee on Constitution and Bylaws to consider some type of membership for those black nurses who were barred from membership in a state association because of race. With ANA's encouragement, a few southern states that year dropped their color bars and admitted black nurses—Delaware was first, followed by Florida and Maryland (Staupers, 1951). It was a simple procedure to admit blacks to membership in Florida: the word "white" was merely deleted from the bylaws. Simple, yes, but not the total solution. It took years before the black nurse was permitted to participate fully in the Florida Nurses' Association.

The 1942 action was followed in 1946 by the adoption of a plank in the ANA 1946–48 platform, which read: "Removal, as rapidly as possible, of barriers that prevent the full employment and professional development of nurses belonging to minority racial groups." At the 1946 convention, there was vigorous debate on this issue—pro and con—with some nurses from the southern states voicing their strong objections to black membership. Georgia delegates were particularly vocal and almost vehement in their protests, with one referring to black nurses as "our darkies." The house immediately voted that this be stricken from the record. The house was reminded by the president, Katharine Densford Dreves, that the barring of professionally qualified black nurses from membership in a state or district association was clearly against the non-discriminatory policies of the ANA. After the convention, Tennessee dropped its color bar. In 1947, a subcommittee of a joint committee of ANA and NACGN, chaired by Anna Heisler of the U.S. Public Health Service, was set up to study and plan ways in which ANA could absorb the functions of NACGN should the latter vote to dissolve. In a letter to Rita Miller dated July 1, 1949, Linnie Laird, Secretary, ANA, wrote, "You have been appointed by the President and Board of Directors of ANA as a member of the Special Committee to study the functions of the NACGN as they relate to comparable areas within the ANA program."

In 1948, the ANA House of Delegates inaugurated the Individual Membership Program, which offered direct membership and benefits in ANA to those qualified nurses who were not accepted by a state or district association. To implement the program, Elizabeth Ann Edwards was appointed assistant executive secretary. She was the first black to hold position as an executive on the staff of ANA. Edwards, a Harlem Hospital School of Nursing in New York graduate with a master's degree from Teachers College, Columbia University, New York, had served as secretary of Health and Housing, Urban League of Greater New York. She had also been an instructor in psychiatric nursing at Bellevue Hospital, New York, and director of student personnel and guidance at Harlem Hospital School of Nursing.

Also in 1948, the first black nurse, Estelle M. Osborne (Fig. 4–3), was elected to the ANA Board of Directors for a four-year term, having been

Figure 4–3   Estelle M. Osborne (sixth from left, top row) was first black to be elected to the ANA Board of Directors, 1948. (Courtesy, American Journal of Nursing Co.)

nominated by the state of Oregon. Osborne brought with her to the board not only professional knowledge and experience but also experience as former president of NACGN. In 1949, the board selected her to represent ANA as one of its delegates to the International Congress of Nurses in Stockholm, Sweden.

At NACGN's final convention in 1949 in Louisville, Kentucky, the report of the ANA Special Committee to Study the Functions of NACGN as they Related to Comparable Areas Within the ANA Program was unanimously approved. In essence, ANA had agreed to absorb the functions of NACGN should the membership vote to dissolve. Votes to accept the report of the ANA committee and to dissolve NACGN were taken in Louisville, and the wheels were set in motion immediately for legal dissolution, which would take a couple of years to accomplish.

At the final NACGN convention (1949), a panel of presidents of State Associations of Colored Graduate Nurses in those southern states that had accepted black nurse membership to the formerly all-white associations described the different problems. A common problem was finding meeting places that would accommodate both races. In 1947, the board of the Florida State Nurses' Association (FSNA) first gave courtesy membership without voice or vote to Grace Higgs, president of the Florida State Association of Colored Graduate Nurses, followed by Mary Elizabeth Carnegie. However, at the 1949 meeting of FSNA, the president of the Florida State Association of Colored Graduate Nurses, Mary Elizabeth Carnegie (Fig. 4–4), was placed on the ballot and elected to the board of FSNA for a one-year term and reelected the following year for

Figure 4–4   Dr. Mary Elizabeth Carnegie (sixth from left, top row) was first black to be elected to the board of directors of a nurses association (Florida), 1949.

a three-year term. Florida was the first state to elect a black to its state nursing association board of directors.

At the 1950 convention of ANA, a Code for Professional Nurses, embracing 17 principles, was adopted. The preface states:

> Service to mankind is the primary function of nurses and the reason for the existence of the nursing profession. Need for nursing service is universal. Professional nursing service is therefore unrestricted by consideration of nationality, race, creed, or color.

The code had been prepared by a committee after receiving suggestions from some 5,000 persons, chiefly nurses, representing a cross section of the profession (Roberts, 1954). Adoption of such a code had a significance in that a democratic philosophy was expressed.

The platform adopted by the ANA House of Delegates in 1950 carried a clear statement of the association's policy in Plank 14, which emphasized "full participation of minority groups in association activities," and the elimination of "discrimination in job opportunities, salaries, and other working conditions." As a follow-up of this unprecedented action, the house of delegates further approved a resolution urging that biracial committees be set up in district and state associations to implement programs of education and interpretation in their respective areas to promote sound development of intergroup relations, a program that had been inaugurated by ANA in 1950. The ANA's Intergroup Relations Committee was charged with the responsibility of seeing that these policies were carried out (Staupers, 1951). Serving on the committee was Rita Miller Dargan, Chairperson, Division of Nursing, Dillard University. In her letter of appointment to the committee dated October 15, 1952, Agnes Ohlson, secretary of ANA, referred to its function as "To consider problems in relation to the promotion of participation by nurses of the minority groups in the affairs of the professional nursing organization. Currently, the major problem of the committee is to effect the absorption of the functions of the NACGN into the ANA program."

In 1951, Elouise Collier Duncan (Fig. 4–5), the first black nurse to graduate from Yale University School of Nursing in New Haven, Connecticut, was appointed to ANA's executive staff to work across the board, that is, her responsibilities in the area of Constitution and Bylaws were not race related. She remained in this position until 1953, when she resigned to marry the Honorable Henry B. Duncan, secretary of Public Works and Utilities, Liberia, West Africa. She has since represented nursing in numerous capacities: president of the Liberian Nurses Association, member of the Board of Directors of the International Council of Nurses, and advisor to the Liberian delegation to the 19th General Assembly of the United Nations.

In 1951, NACGN dissolved its organization, largely through the patient and persistent effort of its leaders who worked for many years for the integration of black nurses into the profession. Mabel K. Staupers

Figure 4–5 Elouise Collier Duncan, first black nurse appointed to ANA staff to work "across the board."

was president of the NACGN at the time of its dissolution. Upon acceptance of the statement of the formal dissolution of NACGN, Elizabeth K. Porter, president of ANA, pledged the assumption by ANA of NACGN functions. NACGN then began to make preparations for its final hours. At NACGN's testimonial dinner, January 26, 1951, certificates of honor were distributed to organizations and individuals who had been involved in its mission. ANA's certificate read:

> For the recognition of the problems . . . [of] Negro nurses and the resulting action of the House of Delegates in 1946, in voting to make membership available to all American nurses, regardless of color, and the substantial interest in encouraging the removal of all restrictive barriers on the district and state levels.

From 1936 to 1951, NACGN presented the Mary Mahoney Award to persons for their contributions to the profession in the area of intergroup relations. At the convention in 1952, ANA awarded its first Mary Mahoney Medal to Marguerette Creth Jackson, public health nurse and long-time nurse leader in Harlem, who led the fight for the integration of the Henry Street Visiting Nurse Service. The Mary Mahoney Award is still given by ANA (Fig. 4–6). It is awarded to a person (or group of persons), regardless of race, who, in addition to making a significant contribution to nursing generally, has been instrumental in achieving

Figure 4–6   Mary Mahoney Medal recipients attending the 1990 ANA Convention in Boston. From left to right are Dr. Ethelrine Shaw-Nickerson, 1990; Dr. Hattie Bessent, 1988; Verdelle Bellamy, 1984; Dr. Mary Elizabeth Carnegie, 1980; Vernice Ferguson, 1970; Mary Mills, 1972. (Courtesy, American Nurses' Association)

the opening and advancement of opportunities in nursing on the same basis to members of all races, creeds, colors, and national origins.

Because of the concerted efforts of nurses, and aided by ANA, the state associations gradually accepted the nondiscriminatory principles. By 1953, all states but one (Georgia) admitted all professionally qualified nurses to membership. At the 1960 biennial convention of ANA in Miami Beach, the house of delegates considered the question of whether Georgia, which had not complied with the ANA nondiscriminatory principle of membership, should continue to be accepted as a constituent. After much discussion, the house accepted a resolution stating that "The state association be further encouraged in its efforts to provide membership for all qualified professional nurses, so that by at least the time of the next biennium, all states will accept all professional nurses as members." Georgia finally dropped its color bar in 1961, but one district in Louisiana (New Orleans) held out until 1964.

Although the ANA bylaws for many years had included a nondiscriminatory principle as one of the association's functions, in 1962 this principle was more appropriately placed within the statement of purposes of the organization. The statement (Section 2 of ANA Bylaws) now reads as follows:

> The purpose of the American Nurses' Association shall be to foster high standards of nursing practice, promote the professional and educational advancement of nurses, and promote the welfare of nurses to the end that all people may have better nursing care. The purposes shall be unrestricted by consideration of nationality, race, creed, or color.

The platform of ANA states that the association will "encourage all members, unrestricted by consideration of nationality, race, creed, or color, to participate fully in association activities and to work for full access to employment and education opportunities for nurses."

In 1964, through one of the membership memos, members were encouraged to recruit nurses from minority groups and to involve them in the work of the state and district associations. In addition, that year, the Economic Security Unit reviewed the Minimum Employment Standards of state nurses association sections. Wherever the standards did not include provisions against discrimination in employment, omission was called to the attention of the state nurses association.

For nearly 20 years, from 1952, the year that Estelle M. Osborne, the first black elected to the ANA Board, completed her four-year term, until 1970, when Fay Wilson (Fig. 4–7), was elected to the board, there was no black representation on the board. This lack of representation on the policymaking level concerned the black membership. It was pointed out to the house of delegates at the 1972 convention that the only func-

Figure 4–7   Fay Wilson, second black to be elected to ANA Board of Directors, 1970.

tion of NACGN that ANA had assumed responsibility for was the awarding of the Mary Mahoney Medal.

Despite the perceived inaction on behalf of state and local constituents, the ANA House of Delegates at the 1972 convention did pass an affirmative action resolution calling for a task force to develop and implement a program to correct inequities. The resolution had been drafted by the Commission on Nursing Research, of which two black nurses were members: Dr. Lauranne Sams and Dr. Mary Harper. It was resolved that the ANA honor its commitment by taking immediate steps to establish an affirmative action program at the national level, which would include the appointment of a task force to develop and implement such a program; to appoint a qualified black nurse to the ANA staff to work with the task force in developing and implementing the program; and to actively seek greater numbers of minority-group members in elected, appointed, and staff positions within ANA and urge states and districts to do likewise. It was also resolved that ANA encourage and promote affirmative action programs on the state and local levels and that an ombudsman be appointed to the ANA staff (*ANA Proceedings*, 1972). At the same convention, the house of delegates adopted a comprehensive resolution on the Universal Declaration of Human Rights. This placed the organization on record in support of specific issues on human rights and race relations; for example, employment opportunities, education, and implementation of the 1964 Civil Rights Act.

An Affirmative Action Task Force was established in 1972 and was chaired by Ethelrine Shaw-Nickerson (Fig. 4–8), a black nurse who had

Figure 4–8   Dr. Ethelrine
Shaw-Nickerson, First Chair,
ANA Affirmative Action Task
Force, 1972.

just been elected to the office of third vice president. Other members
of the task force were Teresa Bello (California), Gean Mathwig (New
York), Janice E. Ruffin (Connecticut), Lauranne Sams (Alabama), Betty
Williams (California), and Rosemary Wood (Oklahoma). Irene Minor
was appointed staff coordinator.

This action marked the beginning of a new commitment by the ma-
jority-group nurses to the minority membership. The house of delegates
also provided for the position of ombudsman to evaluate involvement
of minorities in leadership roles within the organization and to resolve
complaints received from applicants or members that they had been
discriminated against in participating in ANA because of nationality,
race, creed, life-style, color, age, or sex.

Through the establishment of the affirmative action program, ANA
joined a widespread movement that had grown dramatically during the
1960s. Affirmative action programs exist today within industry; government agencies; educational institutions; hospitals; and trade, professional, and community organizations (Minor & Shaw, 1973). During
1975, the ANA Affirmative Action Task Force held two regional conferences that focused on improving nursing care and health care delivery

for ethnic/minority consumers and on promoting affirmative action programs in nursing (Flanagan, 1976).

In 1974, Barbara Nichols, a black nurse who had been president of the Wisconsin Nurses' Association, was elected to the ANA board and served until 1978, when she became president. The year 1974 is significant because that was when ANA received a million dollar grant from the National Institute of Mental Health, designed to increase the quality and quantity of ethnic/racial minority nurse researchers with doctorates (see Chapter 3).

As a result of the house of delegates action establishing the ANA Task Force on Affirmative Action, the need to establish a broader permanent unit focusing on human rights became evident, and a Commission on Human Rights was established in 1976. It was chaired for two terms by Ethelrine Shaw-Nickerson, prime mover in the development of ANA's affirmative action program. The first item in Article 8 of the 1976 Bylaws states: the Commission (retitled Cabinet) on Human Rights "shall establish the scope of the Association's responsibility for addressing and responding to the equal opportunity and human rights concerns of nurses and health care recipients, with the major focus on ethnic people of color."

Looking at the cabinet in terms of its scope and long-range goals, Shaw-Nickerson pointed out that although the focus was on ethnic people of color at that time, she expected that eventually programming will be broadened to encompass many significant human rights issues. Marian Whiteside (Fig. 4–9), chairperson from 1980 to 1982, added that "the Cabinet's primary focus is to protect the rights of nurses and patients, particularly those who are racial and ethnic minorities." Whiteside also viewed the cabinet as needing to be sensitive to the sociopolitical issues that affect the inalienable rights of people around the world. The

Figure 4–9   Marian Davis Whiteside, Chairperson, ANA Cabinet on Human Rights, 1980–1982.

cabinet has, since 1976, been influential in having the vast majority of the states change their bylaws to incorporate provisions for a formal mechanism for human rights.

In 1977, the Commission on Human Rights honored with a luncheon in New York the surviving leaders of NACGN. Present were Mabel K. Staupers, Estelle M. Osborne, Mabel Northcross, Marguerette Jackson, Alma John, Leota Brown, and Verdelle Bellamy. At the 1978 ANA convention, the Commission on Human Rights initiated an award to a constituent association or structural unit that had evidenced the most growth in programming and policies reflecting affirmative action efforts and human rights concerns.

Under the jurisdiction of the Cabinet on Human Rights is the Council on Intercultural Nursing, composed of interested members. The council's purpose is to improve the quality of nursing care by being responsive to cultural and ethnic variances among consumers. One function of the council is to promote the inclusion of cultural diversity in the curriculum of nursing programs throughout the country.

In 1984, the Council on Intercultural Nursing was renamed the Council on Cultural Diversity in Nursing Practice. Its new purpose—to improve nursing practice based on the inclusion of cultural conditions, values, beliefs, and attitudes of our society, health care consumers, and practitioners of nursing—takes into account the need to change with our society as the character of that society changes.

At the 1976 convention in Atlantic City, as part of the country's bicentennial celebration, ANA paid tribute to 15 pioneers in nursing and named them as the first members of ANA's Hall of Fame. These women, all deceased, were recognized for their crusades and reforms in health care through the significant contributions they had made in nursing practice, education, service, and research, at least 20 years before the time of selection. Three of the 15 nurses were black: Mary Eliza Mahoney, Martha M. Franklin, and Adah B. Thoms. Mahoney (1845–1926), America's first black professional nurse, was known for her outstanding personal career and her contributions to local and national professional organizations. Franklin (1870–1968) founded the NACGN in 1908 to promote the standards and welfare of black nurses and to break down racial discrimination in the profession. Thoms (1879–1943) worked for acceptance of black nurses as members of the American Red Cross and for equal rights in the U.S. Army Nurse Corps. She also wrote the first account of black nurses, *Pathfinders*, published in 1929. Thoms was president of NACGN for seven years and received the first Mary Mahoney Medal in 1936. Estelle M. Osborne (1901–1981), another black nurse, was one of the 13 new members inducted into the hall of fame at the 1984 ANA convention.

In 1978, for the first time in the history of the ANA, a black nurse, Barbara Nichols (Fig. 4–10), a member of the board of directors for four years, was on the ballot for president. Nichols ran against two white candidates, Marion Murphy and Laura Simms, and won the election. At the 1980 convention in Houston, Texas, Nichols was elected to a second two-year term. In balloting by the 773-member house of delegates, she received 452 votes; Jean Steel, a white nurse from Boston, who was nominated from the floor, received 282 votes.

During her four years in office as president of ANA (1978–1982), Nichols spent much of her time traveling to represent ANA, addressing hundreds of meetings of state nurses associations; meeting with officials of other health organizations and government officials; traveling to Nairobi, Kenya, and Geneva, Switzerland, for conferences of the International Council of Nurses; and walking the picket line with nurses in Ashtabula, Ohio. In answer to the question by the *American Nurse*, "What do you consider to be your greatest achievements as president," Nichols said,

> I consider the following to be developments that I have helped to influence: movement toward baccalaureate education as the basis of

Figure 4–10   Barbara Nichols (left), first black president of ANA, and Anne Zimmerman.

the professional nursing practice; legitimizing the professional association's right to represent registered nurses for collective bargaining; and strengthening the interaction with the American Hospital Association, the Joint Commission on Accreditation of Hospitals, the American Medical Association, the National Council of State Boards of Nursing, and the Federation of Specialty Nursing Organizations. [ANA Presidency, 1982]

At the convention in 1986, Nichols was the recipient of the ANA Honorary Recognition Award.

At the 1982 ANA convention, presided over by Nichols, Lillian Harvey (Diploma, Lincoln School for Nurses, New York; EdD, Teachers College, Columbia University, New York) (Fig. 4–11), Dean Emerita, Tuskegee University School of Nursing in Alabama, was the 29th recipient of the Mary Mahoney Award. Because her experiences were typical of many of the Mahoney Awardees, presented here is the full text of Harvey's citation:

Her life is a profile of dynamic leadership, an example of service dedicated to advancing opportunities for thousands of black young people to enter nursing and to become successful practitioners. Dr. Harvey arrived in Tuskegee, Alabama, as a young woman in 1944, becoming the first dean of the School of Nursing at Tuskegee Institute. Upon her arrival at Tuskegee, Lillian met 75 students who were enrolled in a three-year diploma program. While engaging in activities to assure their successful completion of the program in which they were enrolled, she also embarked upon activities necessary for the establishment of the first baccalaureate program in the state of Alabama, which began in 1948.

Figure 4–11   Dr. Lillian Harvey, 1982 recipient, ANA Mary Mahoney Award.

Lillian was instrumental in advancing opportunities for black nurses to enter the Army Nurse Corps during World War II. She maintained a program at Tuskegee Institute that prepared black nurses for military service.

Our Mary Mahoney Award recipient has been an active participant in community and nursing activities at all levels: local, state, and national.

She used her talents to work through established organizations for the purpose of contributing to and advancing causes of the nursing profession. She is a former member of the Nursing Advisory Committee of the American National Red Cross and the Kellogg Foundation, and was a member of the Board of Directors of the National League for Nursing. She is a former member of the Board of Directors of the American Journal of Nursing Company and a former secretary of the Educational Administrators, Consultants, and Teachers Section of the American Nurses' Association and of the Alabama Nurses' Association. She has held committee membership in the Alabama State Nurses' Association and in the Alabama League for Nursing.

While it was necessary to work within the segregated system that was mandated by law in the Deep South, Lillian worked endlessly toward breaking these barriers and promoting an open social system. Some of her efforts may seem diminished because of the passing of time, and changes that have occurred over time. The impact of some of her actions, however, cannot be measured by time. For example, during the early years of her career, she singularly undertook the task of desegregating the Alabama Nurses' Association by attending its meetings. This required an 80-mile round trip drive from Tuskegee to Montgomery. Although she had to sit in a separate section of the room, she spoke for the needs of black nurses and to nursing students without hesitation. It took courage to bear humiliation. Moreover, going into white communities in southern cities was an actual physical threat that most black people chose not to chance.

That the baccalaureate program, which Lillian started in 1948, remains an active, viable, accredited offering that admits students without regard to race, sex, or national origin, is the strongest statement necessary for demonstrating the current and perpetual nature of her work.

Dr. Lillian Harvey is an example of a truly authentic nursing leader who knew how to face and tackle problems no matter how difficult, always maintaining belief in the ability to attain that which countless others would have viewed as unattainable.

Dr. Lillian Harvey is an example for us all. As Phillips Brooks said, if every person were such as you and every life like yours, this earth would be God's paradise. [*Summary of Proceedings*, 1982, p. 16–17]

Another event that had significance for black nurses at the 1982 ANA convention was the address by the president of the International Council of Nurses, Eunice Muringo Kiereini (Fig. 4–12), a black nurse from Kenya, East Africa, who had been elected at the 17th quadrennial International Congress of Nursing—the first black to hold that office.

Figure 4–12 Eunice Muringo Kiereini of Kenya, President, International Council of Nurses. (Courtesy, American Nurses' Association)

When elected to the presidency of the ANA, Barbara Nichols (Diploma, Massachusetts General Hospital School of Nursing, Boston; MS, University of Wisconsin-Madison) was director of inservice education for all employees at St. Mary's Hospital, Madison, Wisconsin. Among her many honors, Nichols has had three honorary doctoral degrees bestowed upon her: one from the University of Wisconsin at Milwaukee; one from Rhode Island College, Providence; and one from Lowell University, Massachusetts. She was one of eight women to receive the 1984 Outstanding Women of Color Award, sponsored by the National Institute for Women of Color. Established in 1981, the purpose of the award is "to enhance the strength of diversity and to promote educational and economic equity for women of color." Nichols joins a celebrated group of recipients: Coretta Scott King, civil rights activist; Connie Chung, television news reporter; and Patricia Roberts Harris, former secretary, U.S. Department of Health and Human Services.

On July 29, 1984, at its convention in Montreal, Quebec, Canada, the National Medical Association, an organization of black physicians in the United States, presented to Nichols a Scroll of Merit,

... in recognition of her distinguished leadership and service as secretary of the Department of Regulation and Licensure for the

State of Wisconsin, and her unique contribution as teacher, nurse, and scholar in the field of health care and human services.

In June 1985, Nichols was elected International Council of Nurses (ICN) North America Area Member of the Board. She had been member-at-large of the ICN Board since 1981.

In working toward the objectives set forth in ANA's platform, which placed greater emphasis on legislative activities, in 1951 the association opened the Division of Governmental Affairs office in Washington, D.C. Staff are responsible for the review of congressional and state bills affecting nurses, nursing, and health care; preparation and distribution of informative materials on legislation, legislative problems, and the government relations program of ANA; and preparation of congressional testimony reflecting nurses' interests and concerns (Flanagan, 1976). From 1984 to 1986, Retired Brigadier General Hazel Johnson-Brown served as director of the Washington office.

In 1983, a black nurse, Donna Rae Richardson (Fig. 4–13),who also holds a law degree, was added to the staff of the Washington office as senior staff specialist/lobbyist. She now holds the title, "Director of Congressional and Agency Relations."

Richardson (Diploma, Akron City Hospital School of Nursing, Akron, Ohio; JD, Howard University, Washington, D.C.) represents the ANA's position and policy statements on nursing and health issues to federal agencies, Congress, the executive branch, and constituent forums. She assists in the development and implementation of legislative strategy,

Figure 4–13   Donna Rae Richardson, nurse and lawyer, Senior Staff Specialist/Lobbyist, ANA Washington Office.

prepares ANA testimony and witnesses for public presentations, and acts as liaison with state nurses' associations and regional congressional delegates. Eunice Turner, senior staff specialist for governmental affairs in the Kansas City office, is the liaison with ANA's Washington office.

In a memorandum to the executive director, dated July 12, 1990, Richardson referred to specific initiatives and activities undertaken by the Governmental Affairs Division on issues related to ethics and human rights. Among these activities were lobbying for the Civil Rights Act Reauthorization (passed in 1989) and Civil Rights Restoration Act (1990); pushing for examination of federal pay classification systems to determine whether wage discrimination is based on sex or race; and lobbying for the Minority Health Professionals bill which is intended to increase the numbers of minority health professionals as well as access to care for minorities. In addition, ANA participates in a number of coalition activities which support human rights and ethics positions.

Because so many national nursing organizations had developed since the major ones were restructured in 1952, the ANA deemed it timely to reexamine organizational arrangements. To that end, in 1982, ANA appointed the Commission on Organizational Assessment and Renewal (COAR). The goal of COAR was to strengthen ANA on behalf of its members, the nursing profession, and the American people through study of its structure, function, membership base, and interorganizational relationships.

The commission proposed a number of recommendations, which were voted on by the 1989 ANA House of Delegates. Recommendations, which resulted in the disbanding of the ANA cabinets, including the Cabinet on Human Rights, called for the strands of ethics, human rights, nursing education, and nursing research to be recognized as part of the work of all ANA units.

The house further directed that the board appoint an ad hoc committee to determine what mechanism should be developed to address human rights and ethics issues. The committee, chaired by Dr. Beverly Malone, proposed that a Center for Ethics and Human Rights be established. The proposal was adopted by the board in December of 1989, and a program director was appointed in 1990—charged with the responsibility for ensuring that ethics and human rights are considered in all activities of ANA, including its strategic plan, labor relations, and governmental and practice programs. The new center will make ANA's efforts and resources more available to nurses across the country.

The 1982 ANA bylaws revision created the Nursing Organization Liaison Forum (NOLF) in an attempt to permit ANA to collaborate with representatives from the growing number of other national nursing organizations—general and specialty. According to the operating guidelines adopted by the ANA Board of Directors in 1984, NOLF has two purposes: (1) to provide within the formal structure of ANA a forum for discussion between national nursing organizations and ANA regarding questions of professional policy and national health policy issues of mutual concern; and (2) to promote concerted action by national nursing organizations on professional policy and national health policy issues, as participating organizations deem appropriate (*Evolution of Nursing Professional Organizations*, 1987). In 1987, NOLF listed 41 participating organizations, two of which were black: Chi Eta Phi Sorority and the National Black Nurses' Association. When the Association of Black Nursing Faculty in Higher Education was organized, it, too, became a member of NOLF. The forum now includes 47 national nursing organizations and 12 ANA councils.

As has been pointed out, blacks have had representation on the board and staff of ANA since 1948, but not consecutively. From 1978 to 1982, there was an elected black president, and today, 1990, there are elected and appointed black officials and a few on the professional staff—one is deputy executive director.

THE NATIONAL ASSOCIATION OF
COLORED GRADUATE NURSES

Until the structure of the ANA changed in 1916, setting up the state association as the basic unit of membership, black nurses who were members of their nursing school alumni associations could join ANA, and many of them did. However, little was done to encourage their participation, nor was any concern shown for their special problems of segregation and discrimination (Staupers, 1961).

Scattered throughout the country, black nurses had little or no medium through which they might keep abreast of developments in nursing in general and little opportunity for useful action to advance the standards of nursing among black nurses. There was, however, a unity of desire on the part of black nurses to organize. As a result, local groups began to form as early as 1900 in cities such as Norfolk, Washington, New York, and Chicago. It was not until 1908 that the first group of black graduate nurses came together for the purpose of considering plans for organizing a permanent national association to help improve their conditions. The title selected was the National Association of Colored Graduate Nurses. (See Appendix B for a list of the NACGN charter members.)

The guiding light in the movement toward a national organization was Martha M. Franklin (1870–1968) (Fig. 4–14) of Connecticut, a grad-

Figure 4–14　　　Martha M. Franklin, Founder, National Association
of Colored Graduate Nurses, 1908.

uate of Women's Hospital in Philadelphia in 1897, the only black in her class. Because of her concern for the welfare of black nurses, she zealously studied the status of the colored graduate nurse in America by writing hundreds of letters in her own hand to Negro nurses, superintendents of nursing schools, and nursing organizations. The survey took two years to complete. Finally, in 1908, she mailed 1,500 letters at her own expense to all the black nurses with whom she had been in contact, polling them on the advisability of a national gathering. Franklin, one of the first to campaign actively for racial equality in nursing, was the catalyst for collective action by black nurses. She not only recognized that black nurses needed help to improve their professional status, but that they would have to initiate it themselves.

At the invitation of the Alumnae Association of Lincoln School for Nurses in New York City, under the leadership of Adah B. Thoms, 52 nurses attended the organizing three-day meeting, which began on August 23, 1908, at St. Marks Methodist Church. They heard a statesmanlike report from Franklin, in which she outlined the manifold need for a national organization of their own. After much discussion, the group adopted the following purposes for the new organization: (1) to achieve higher professional standards; (2) to break down the discriminatory practices facing Negroes in schools of nursing, in jobs, and in nursing organizations; and (3) to develop leadership among Negro nurses. By organizing, these women proclaimed to the entire profession that they had created an instrument through which they could oppose discrimination in the nursing field on all fronts. Franklin, the founder of the NACGN, was elected president and served two terms.

Lavinia Dock, nursing's premier historian, and Lillian Wald, founder of the Henry Street Settlement House—both social activists—supported the formation of NACGN and hosted a reception at Henry Street for this new organization (Staupers, 1961). Dock went on record with her support, saying, "Negro nurses are held among the most valuable members, not only for good nursing, but for intelligent altruism" (Dock, 1912, p. 198).

Franklin seldom missed a national meeting of NACGN. Her last attendance was at the convention in Washington, D.C., in 1921. Those attending were received at the White House by President Warren G. Harding. The membership presented the president and his wife with a large basket of American Beauty roses and requested that NACGN be placed on record as an organization of 2,000 trained nurses ready for world service when needed.

In the early days of NACGN's existence, the work of the organization, which served as an instrument for the advancement of the black nurse, was done by volunteer members. Among the projects of these volunteers was a central registry, begun in 1918 and operating out of New York, to serve black nurses in every area of work and in every section of the country. This was an important program because at that time private and official registries, which had sprung up all over the United States, seldom accepted black registrants.

Along with the registry program, a campaign was instituted to focus attention on better opportunities for black nurses in leadership positions in hospitals, schools of nursing, and public health agencies. NACGN was not only concerned with the plight of the black nurse, but with the general improvement of conditions of all Negroes. To this end, NACGN worked with other civic organizations, including those that focused on civil rights.

Because of her experience in a number of professional and community organizations and knowledge of the many facets of nursing, Mabel C. Northcross (Fig. 4–15) of St. Louis, Missouri, was elected president of the NACGN in 1930 and served four years. During her administration, she was responsible for several innovations, the most important of which was the conduct of educational programs, called institutes, held during the national conventions as a form of postgraduate education to help increase the level of skills, knowledge, and job potential of members. The first institute was held during the national convention in 1932. Northcross was ahead of her time in terms of continuing education, a vital part of most conventions and meetings today.

To meet the continuing education needs of black nurses, beginning in 1934 under the presidency of Estelle Massey Riddle Osborne and with

Figure 4–15   Mabel C. North-cross, President, NACGN, 1930–1934.

the support of a grant from the General Education Board of the Rocke-feller Foundation, NACGN instituted regional conferences as a vehicle through which black nurses could keep abreast of developments in the nursing profession. Participants in the first regional conference, held in New York City, included the executive secretaries of the three major national nursing organizations—the ANA, the National League of Nurs-ing Education, and the National Organization for Public Health Nursing; officials of the Rosenwald Fund, the National Medical Association, and the National Health Circle for Colored People; directors of schools of nursing for Negro students; and the black press. At the time of this conference, America was feeling the effects of the Great Depression. There was great need for a program that would bring into clear focus the fact that black nurses not only needed jobs, but that these needs were aggravated by racial bias (Staupers, 1951).

The many projects, educational programs, consultation services, and day-to-day business of operating a national organization made it man-datory that NACGN establish a headquarters with a paid staff. In 1934, through the generosity of the National Health Circle for Colored People, office space was shared, and Mabel K. Staupers was employed as exec-utive secretary, the position she held for 12 years. With grants from the GEB and the Rosenwald Fund, NACGN acquired its own permanent office, located in the same building with the three major national nursing organizations. As executive secretary, Staupers was responsible for col-lecting facts; advising the black nurse and translating her to the com-munity; holding conferences; organizing state and local nursing associations, as well as strengthening those already in existence; and working closely with the national advisory council, biracial in composition, which was organized in 1938 as a means of developing greater interest in and support for the programs of NACGN. In short, she had the tremendous responsibility for developing greater unity in order to combat the policies and practices that were hampering the growth of black nurses. Staupers was truly the ombudsman for the black nurse.

The year 1936 was the year that NACGN established the annual Mary Mahoney Award in recognition of individual achievement in nursing, presenting it to Adah B. Thoms (Fig. 4–16), past president of NACGN and author of the first account of black nurses, *Pathfinders*. (See Appendix C for a list of Mary Mahoney Award recipients.) Thoms was also recognized for her active single-handed campaign during 1917 and 1918 in opposing discrimination in the military against black nurses.

NACGN also worked to promote progressive health legislation, making its voice heard and its influence felt regarding health and nursing legislation, as well as other progressive legislation which would benefit all Americans. A major feat was NACGN's joining with other organizations to support the amendment to the Bolton Bill of 1943 for the creation of the Cadet Nurse Corps during World War II. This amendment ensured for students in black schools the privilege of joining the corps. By the end of the war, over 2,000 black students had participated in the Cadet Nurse Corps.

Figure 4–16   Adah B. Thoms, first recipient of the Mary Mahoney Award, 1936.

At the time of the attack on Pearl Harbor, NACGN was in the midst of leading a vigorous campaign to break down racial barriers in the army and navy. In 1941, the army established a quota of 56 black nurses and the navy flatly refused to admit any. Through the efforts of NACGN, the army quota was abolished before the end of the war, and the navy dropped its color bar in January 1945. By the end of the war, over 500 black nurses had served in the army and four in the navy. NACGN's campaign, led by Staupers, stimulated wide public interest and support because discrimination was costing the lives of American fighting men (Staupers, 1951).

In 1946, for health reasons, Staupers (1890–1989) resigned as executive secretary of NACGN, and Alma Vessells John (Fig. 4–17) was appointed to fill this position, which she held until NACGN dissolved in 1951. John, a graduate of Harlem Hospital School of Nursing in New York with a bachelor's degree from New York University, had, since 1943, served on the staff of the National Nursing Council for War Service as assistant consultant. She brought to her position with NACGN first-hand knowledge of the problems of the black nurse in this country. She had worked closely with NNCWS consultant, Estelle Massey Riddle Osborne, to help integrate blacks into schools of nursing, as well as into the military nursing services. John died in New York in 1986.

Of all battles waged by NACGN, whose quest was to place the black nurse into the mainstream of professional nursing in America, the longest and hardest was with the ANA, the professional organization which nurses joined through their states. When the barriers were finally re-

Figure 4–17   Alma Vessells John, Executive Director, National Association of Colored Graduate Nurses, 1946–1951.

moved, the NACGN, at convention in Louisville, Kentucky, in 1949, under the presidency of Alida Dailey (Fig. 4–18), voted itself out of existence. By that time, provisions had been made for black nurses to bypass those southern states that denied them membership and join the ANA directly as individual members.

At the 1949 convention, Staupers (Fig. 4–19), who had been executive secretary from 1934 to 1946, agreed to serve as president of NACGN until the organization legally dissolved in 1951. The forward steps that had been made during NACGN's lifetime are not as important in themselves as in the development of capable leadership, broadened understanding on both sides, and determination to accept nothing less than full and equal opportunity for all nurses—developments made possible by the existence of NACGN (Staupers, 1951).

On January 26, 1951, approximately 1,000 persons, including members of the boards of the three major national nursing organizations, representatives from government and private agencies, and many distinguished citizens, assembled at the Essex House in New York for the formal dissolution of NACGN, which had purposefully and successfully worked itself out of existence. This occasion was also used to present

Figure 4–18   Alida Dailey, President, NACGN, in 1949 when a vote was taken to dissolve the organization.

Figure 4–19   Mabel K. Staupers, first executive director and last president of NACGN.

certificates of honor to 11 individuals and 21 organizations who had worked with and for Negro nurses.

As keynote speaker at the dinner, the Honorable Judge William H. Hastie, former Governor of the Virgin Islands and Judge of the First District Federal Court, said:

> The passing of an organization can be only somewhat less sad than the death of a human being, but in this case I rejoice, as I believe all of the guests here tonight do, that a splendid organization has accomplished its mission and then deliberately determined to release its membership to continue work under more comprehensive auspices. It is a grand thing that there is no longer need for a separate organization of Negro nurses.... To me the meaning of this far transcends the nursing profession, its organization, and its internal policies. It points up something of great consequences which is happening to American life as well as the reaction of the Negro to the change.... I can think of no incident which symbolizes the dynamics of constructive social evolution at its best more effectively or more dramatically than this gathering and its occasion.

Writing in a column in the Chicago *Defender* after attending the testimonial dinner, Walter White, then executive secretary of the National Association for the Advancement of Colored People (NAACP), said:

> For the first time in my life I have enjoyed a funeral, instead of being lugubrious the obituaries were gay and congratulatory. The quite lively corpse handed out thank you scrolls to individuals and organizations which had helped and cooperated with the late departed. Stripping off its sable shroud, the corpse promptly marched into a new life of greater usefulness . . . [through amalgamation with the ANA]

While happy about the progress NACGN had made from 1908 to 1951, the nurse leaders in the movement for integration reflected seriously on the challenges still to be faced. They recognized that although Negro nurses had taken a giant step forward in the fight for equality, there was still much that remained to be done. In presenting certificates of honor at the testimonial dinner, NACGN's past president Estelle M. Osborne, had this to say:

> There are still the problems of segregated and inadequately supported nursing schools for Negroes, salary differentials on a racial basis, inequalities in job opportunity and advancement, racial inequalities in preliminary education, and frequently there is merely token or no representation of Negro nurses in the policy-making areas at the higher levels of participation. These and other problems constitute a considerable amount of the unfinished business of democracy, as well as the unfinished business of NACGN. These problems [with dissolution of NACGN] automatically become a part of the unfinished business of the entire nursing profession.

So, 1951 marked the end of one era in the fight for equality for all nurses and the beginning of another. That is, to the public, it was the formal recognition of a giant step taken by the nursing profession to prove that its democratic principles are real and workable.

Because of her devotion to the nursing profession and to the advancement of black nurses, Mabel Staupers received many honors, none more deserved than the Mary Mahoney Award presented to her in 1947. She has also received the Spingarn Medal, black America's highest honor, from the NAACP for leadership in the movement to integrate black nurses as equals in the national professional nursing organization in 1951 (Fig. 4–20). (The Spingarn Medal was established in 1914 by Joel E. Spingarn, then Chair, NAACP Board of Directors, to call attention to distinguished merit and achievement by Americans of African descent, and thus stimulate black youth to similar aspiration.) Other awards presented to Staupers have been; the Sojourner Truth Award; the National Urban League Team Work Award; the John V. Lindsay Citation, presented by the mayor of New York City to an immigrant (Staupers was born in Barbados, British West Indies) who has become an outstanding American citizen and leader; the Medgar Evers Human Rights Award; Howard University Alumni Award for distinguished achievement in the fields of nursing and community service; Caribbean American Intercultural Organization Award for outstanding contributions to the field of nursing and civil rights; and the Linda Richards Award for unique and pioneering contributions to nursing, given by the National League for Nursing.

In 1972, Staupers was invited to the ANA convention in Detroit to attend a reception given by ANA for Mary Mahoney Medal awardees. She declined the invitation because, as she explained, "The ANA has not completely acted upon the Resolution accepted from the NACGN in 1951 and therefore, I cannot in good conscience accept recognition from the ANA. The Board of Directors has not given full attention to the problem of minority nurses, but rather has shown mere tokenism" (Bourne, 1989, p. 37).

THE AMERICAN RED CROSS NURSING SERVICE

Aware of Florence Nightingale's work in the Crimea, Henri Dunant, a native of Switzerland, used his influence to establish national societies that would render aid to all combatants in time of war. Beginning in 1864, National Red Cross societies were organized, but it was not until 1882 that one appeared in the United States (Jamieson & Sewall, 1944).

Figure 4–20   Mabel K. Staupers (left) presented NAACP Spingarn Medal by
Lillian Smith.

Upon her return from service with the Red Cross Society in Germany in the Franco-Prussian War of 1870, Clara Barton was determined to win her country's approval of this new type of neutral society. In 1882, the American Red Cross Society was founded, and Barton became its first president, serving in this capacity until 1905 (Jamieson & Sewall, 1944).

Public health nursing was first proposed as a Red Cross program by Lillian Wald as early as 1908, and the American Red Cross Nursing Service was established in 1909, created by Jane Delano. The public health nursing component was financed mainly by Jacob H. Schiff, an officer of the New York branch of the Red Cross. Because the number of nurses employed was inadequate to meet the needs of the country, in 1912 the Red Cross organized its rural nursing service, known as the American Red Cross Town and Country Nursing Service. This was the first plan of a nationwide scope to supply trained nurses to rural districts. By 1913, the service was extended to towns having populations as large as 25,000. After 1918, the service was known as the American Red Cross Public Health Nursing Service.

Frances Reed Elliott Davis (Fig. 4–21), a graduate of Freedmen's Hospital School of Nursing in Washington, D.C., was the first black nurse to be accepted in the American Red Cross Nursing Service in 1918. Her pin read "1-A"—"A" designating "Negro." Before being accepted by the Red Cross, Elliott was required to take a year's course at Teachers College, Columbia University, New York. She was the first black nurse to take the course, which included conferences each week with Adelaide

Figure 4–21   Frances Reed Elliott Davis, first black nurse accepted by the American Red Cross Nursing Service, 1918.

Nutting, the head of the Nursing Department. Davis's practice work was performed at the Henry Street Visiting Nurse Service and the New York Board of Charities. Upon completing the course, she was assigned to work in Jackson, Tennessee, which had requested a black Red Cross nurse.

Sixty-four years after Davis received her Red Cross pin, Irmatrude Grant (Fig. 4–22), a black nurse who had become Chairperson of Recruitment and Enrollment, Nursing and Health Services, American Red Cross in greater New York, received the Ann Magnussen Award, the highest recognition given for outstanding volunteer nursing leadership in the American Red Cross. The award was made at the 1982 National Convention of the Red Cross in St. Louis, Missouri, and presented by Dr. Jerome Holland, a black man and former U.S. ambassador to Sweden, who was national chairman of the Red Cross.

THE NATIONAL ORGANIZATION FOR PUBLIC HEALTH NURSING

By the turn of the century, public health nursing had been identified as a separate field, and the nurses in this specialty felt the need to form an organization that would meet their needs. As a result, in 1911, a joint committee was appointed by the ANA and the American Society of Superintendents of Training Schools for Nurses for the purpose of standardizing nurses' services outside the hospital. Lillian Wald, the founder of public health nursing was appointed chairperson. In June 1912, at the meeting of the two established nursing organizations in

Figure 4–22   Irmatrude Grant, recipient of the American Red Cross Ann Magnussen Award.

Chicago, with invited representatives from 800 public health agencies, the National Organization for Public Health Nursing (NOPHN) was voted into existence with Wald as president.

Wald was also one of the moving spirits in the establishment of the NAACP, which was formed to press for full citizenship rights for blacks and public understanding of their contribution to America's stability and progress. She was one of the "60 persons of distinction" who in 1909 signed the call to hold a conference on the 100th anniversary of Abraham Lincoln's birthday that became the driving force in the establishment of the NAACP several months later. On the eve of the conference, Wald hosted a reception for the group at her Henry Street Settlement House (Hughes, 1962, p. 22).

As an association of nurses, lay persons, and education and service agencies, NOPHN grew out of a pressing need for a mechanism through which standards could be developed for public health nursing services operating under voluntary auspices with direction of lay boards (Fitzpatrick, 1975). During its lifetime of 40 years (it became part of NLN in 1952), black nurses were involved. Unlike the ANA, NOPHN was not confronted with any significant difficulties regarding membership of blacks. Members joined NOPHN directly, while members joined ANA through their state associations. NOPHN accepted black members if they met the usual eligibility requirements. Its purposes were to stimulate the general public and the visiting nurse associations to extend and support public health nursing service, to facilitate harmonious cooperation among the workers and supporters, to develop a standard of ethics and teaching, and also to act as a clearing house for information for those interested in such work.

After the Gage and Haupt survey of black schools in the South, made under the auspices of NOPHN in 1932 (see Chapter 2), NOPHN became concerned about the poor quality of education for blacks in these southern schools, many of which made no provisions for public health nursing theory or practice in the curriculum, thus prohibiting their graduates' acceptance as nurse members of the organization. To help remedy this situation, NOPHN awarded public health nursing scholarships to black nurses. In addition, NOPHN members participated in conferences held to discuss the health of blacks, making the services of its Education Committee available for advice and consultation to black schools of nursing. After the Gage and Haupt tour, Estelle Massey Riddle Osborne and Mabel K. Staupers were invited to join two important NOPHN committees. Osborne represented NACGN on the Education Committee and Staupers represented NACGN on the Committee on Organization and Administration.

Along with ANA and NLNE in 1940, NOPHN was represented on a special joint committee to work with the NACGN. An additional mechanism to work with black nurses was NOPHN's establishment of a Council on Negro Nursing to study the education and development of the black public health nurse. The council's objective was to foster and enhance the complete integration of Negro nurses in all phases of public health nursing so that they would receive all benefits and emoluments based on the effort and programs achieved in their work (*Report of NOPHN Council on Negro Nursing*, 1942).

The problems faced by black nurses continued to be of vital interest and concern to NOPHN, and it, probably more than any other nursing organization, took action to support and help NACGN.

THE AMERICAN PUBLIC HEALTH ASSOCIATION

The American Public Health Association (APHA) is the largest organization of public health professionals in the world, representing more than 32,000 members from 77 occupations of public health. The association and its members have been influencing policies and setting priorities in public health since 1872. APHA brings together researchers, health service providers, administrators, teachers, and other health workers in a unique, multidisciplinary environment of professional exchange, study, and action.

APHA is concerned with a broad set of issues affecting personal and environmental health. In recent years this has included topics such as state and federal funding for health programs, movement toward a national health program, air pollution control, promotion of water fluoridation, health care in jails and prisons, full funding for the World Health Organization, public health programs and policies related to AIDS, a smoke-free society by the year 2000, and professional education in public health.

The association's programs are based on scientific study of health problems and service issues, utilizing the expertise and diverse resources of its members. Whether APHA is proposing solutions based on research, helping to set public health practice standards, or working closely with national and international health agencies to improve health worldwide, it continually strives to improve public health.

In 1988, Iris R. Shannon, PhD, RN, FAAN, Associate Professor, Community Health Nursing, Rush University, Chicago, Illinois, was elected president of APHA and presided at the 117th annual meeting in Chicago in 1989 with 8,700 people in attendance (Fig. 4–23).

Figure 4–23   Dr. Iris R. Shannon,
elected president of APHA in 1988.

SIGMA THETA TAU INTERNATIONAL

Sigma Theta Tau International, Honor Society of Nursing, which was founded by six nursing students in 1922 at Indiana University, Indianapolis, is now the second largest nursing organization in the United States. It boasts of approximately 150,000 members and 301 chapters at colleges and universities with accredited baccalaureate and higher degree programs in nursing. Chapters exist in all 50 states, Canada, Korea, and Taiwan/Republic of China. The organization's mission encompasses recognizing superior achievement in nursing, facilitating leadership development, fostering high nursing standards, stimulating creative work, and strengthening the commitment to ideals of the profession.

Vernice D. Ferguson, a black nurse serving as Deputy Assistant Chief Medical Director for Nursing Programs, Department of Veterans Affairs, became the society's 16th president in 1985. She served for two years (Fig. 4–24). In 1987, Mary Elizabeth Carnegie was nominated to receive the Founders Award for Excellence in Leadership, one of Sigma Theta Tau's most prestigious awards recognizing nursing excellence and scholarship.

In 1989, Sigma Theta Tau International dedicated its new International Center for Nursing Scholarship and Virginia Henderson Inter-

Figure 4–24   Vernice Ferguson, President, Sigma Theta Tau International, 1985–1987.

national Nursing Library on the Indiana University/Purdue University-Indianapolis campus. The 32,000-square foot facility serves as an international focal point for nursing research, continuing education, and other professional activities. It also houses Sigma Theta Tau's international headquarters. The state-of-the-art electronic library offers quick, easy, on-line computer access to a unique information data base featuring 'fugitive," or unpublished, nursing literature, and additional information valuable to nurse clinicians, educators, researchers, and entrepreneurs, as well as other health care professionals. More than 16,000 nurses, 100 nursing groups, 75 foundations and corporations, 270 Sigma Theta Tau chapters, and friends of nursing contributed approximately $5 million to the center and library. Many black nurses who participate in Sigma Theta Tau's national activities and hold chapter offices throughout the country strongly supported the fund raising effort. The successful campaign for the Center for Nursing Scholarship was the first national capital funds campaign ever conducted by a nursing organization.

Sigma Theta Tau's strong commitment to research is exemplified by its numerous scholarly publications, including *IMAGE: Journal of Nursing Scholarship*; the *Directory of Nurse Researchers*, which lists and classifies the work of more than 3,600 nurse researchers; and periodic research monographs. The society underwrote the first known nursing research grant in 1936, and has since that time funded an impressive body of work through a series of small grants to nearly 200 highly qualified nurse researchers. In 1989, it presented the first Baxter Foundation Episteme

Award for breakthrough nursing research, which includes a $10,000 honorarium and original onyx sculpture. Local, national, and international theory, research, and writers' conferences and congresses are frequently sponsored by Sigma Theta Tau. Hundreds of thousands of nurses around the world have benefited from these events and the society's other scholarly activities.

CHI ETA PHI

Chi Eta Phi is a national sorority of registered professional nurses, founded at Freedmen's Hospital, Washington, D.C., in 1932 by Aliene Carrington Ewell (Fig. 4–25) and 11 other women—all Freedmen's nurses. (See Appendix D for a list of the charter members.) The organization was incorporated in 1934 under the laws of the District of Columbia.

Chi Eta Phi has 83 chapters—65 graduate and 18 active undergraduate—in 23 states, the District of Columbia, Monrovia, Liberia, West Africa, and the U.S. Virgin Islands. Its goals are to elevate the high standards of the nursing profession; to encourage continuing education among its members; to maintain a recruitment program for students interested in a nursing career; to stimulate a close, friendly relationship among members; to develop working relationships with other professional groups for the delivery of health services; and to provide contin-

Figure 4–25   Aliene Carrington Ewell, Founder, Chi Eta Phi Sorority, 1932.

uous identification of nursing leaders within the membership who will function as agents of change on all levels.

Among the 55 honorary members of Chi Eta Phi was the late Lillian Carter ("Miss Lillian"), a nurse and the mother of Jimmy Carter, the 39th president of the United States (see Appendix E). Its official publication, the *Glowing Lamp*, published annually, presents scientific articles as well as chapter news. The organization also supports civic and charitable efforts.

Except for the NACGN, there was little opportunity for black nurses to develop leadership skills in professional nursing organizations when Chi Eta Phi was organized in 1932. In the South, including the District of Columbia, black nurses were barred from membership in their state nurses' associations. In the North, even with open membership, there was little evidence of black nurses at that time having held office in the state and district constituents of the ANA, let alone on the national level.

For 20 years, between 1951 when NACGN was dissolved and 1971 when the National Black Nurses' Association came into existence, Chi Eta Phi was the only organization in which black nurses were given the opportunity to develop organizational leadership skills. Many of the black nurses who have occupied and are now occupying leadership roles in ANA and other organizations on all levels—national, regional, state, and local—rose through the ranks of Chi Eta Phi, where they had held key offices. When Fay Wilson, for example, was elected to the ANA Board of Directors in 1970, she not only brought with her a history of experience in nursing service, education, administration, and consultation, but valuable experience from having served three terms as national president of Chi Eta Phi. She has also served on the California Board of Nursing.

Others with leadership experience in Chi Eta Phi include Marguerette Creth Jackson, who had been first vice president of the joint boards of the six national nursing organizations (ANA, NLNE, NOPHN, Association of Collegiate Schools of Nursing, American Association of Industrial Nurses, NACGN) to study the structure of these national organizations to avoid duplication; Fostine Riddick Roach, member of the Virginia State Board of Health and alumni representative on the Board of Trustees of Tuskegee University; Verdelle Bellamy, president of the Georgia State Board of Nursing; Helen Miller, who had been vice president of NLN and member of the North Carolina Board of Nursing; and Mary Long, president of the Georgia Nurses' Association and ANA board.

Beginning as an organization of black female nurses, Chi Eta Phi has become interracial and also accepts men as members. With chapters in Africa and the Caribbean, this organization can also be classified as international in scope. In keeping with its goals of encouraging continuing education among its members and scholastic achievements, all chapters of Chi Eta Phi conduct continuing education workshops and award generous scholarships to worthy students in their communities to study nursing.

THE AMERICAN JOURNAL OF NURSING COMPANY

Upon the suggestion in 1895 of the American Society of Superintendents of Training Schools for Nurses that nurses needed a journal "managed, edited, and owned by the women of the profession," the Nurses' Associated Alumnae (forerunner of ANA) appointed a Committee on Periodicals, led by Mary E. P. Davis. The committee formed a joint stock company and sold shares to nurses only at $100 each. With this capital, plus 550 subscriptions pledged at $2 each, the nursing profession in 1900 launched its own magazine titled the *American Journal of Nursing* (Fondiller, 1990).

The company conducts its business under the direction of a board of directors, but since ANA is the sole stockholder of the company, the journal company board members are elected by the ANA Board of Directors. Since 1951, black nurses have been represented on the *American Journal of Nursing* Board of Directors, with Estelle M. Osborne being the first. Dr. Ora Strickland became chairperson of the board in 1984. Currently serving on the board (1990) is Barbara Nichols.

Until 1952, the *American Journal of Nursing* was the company's only publication, serving as the official organ of ANA and NLNE. Although there had been a few other magazines for nurses (e.g., *The Nightingale* and *Trained Nurse and Hospital Review*), the *Journal* was the first official professional nursing journal established in the United States.

In 1952, at the request of the Association of Collegiate Schools of Nursing (ACSN), the journal company began publishing its second magazine, *Nursing Research*, devoted exclusively to research reporting in nursing. From 1953 to 1980, when NLN started publishing its own journal, *Nursing and Health Care*, *Nursing Outlook* had been published by the company as the official organ of NLN. In 1966, the company began publishing the *International Nursing Index; MCN, the Journal of Maternal Child Nursing* in 1975; *Geriatric Nursing* in 1980, and the *AJN Guide*. The company also produces multimedia materials (books, other printed matter, audiocassettes, filmstrips, videocassettes, and films) through its Educational Services Division. In addition, the company manages seminars, holds national professional conferences, and conducts other communications activities.

In July 1953, Mary Elizabeth Carnegie was the first black nurse to join the American Journal of Nursing Company as assistant editor of the *American Journal of Nursing*. She moved to *Nursing Outlook* in 1956 as associate editor. In 1970, she became senior editor of *Nursing Outlook*, and in 1973, equipped with a doctoral degree, she was made chief editor of *Nursing Research* (Fig. 4–26), the position she held until her retirement from the American Journal of Nursing Company in 1978. At that time, the board, in the form of a resolution, commended her "for her illustrious record and meritorius service in the editing of its publications," and expressed "its gratitude . . . for her quarter of a century of contributions and accomplishments."

THE NATIONAL STUDENT NURSES' ASSOCIATION

When the National Student Nurses' Association organized in 1953, it was under the aegis of the ANA and NLN. Today NSNA is an auton-

Figure 4–26   Dr. Mary Elizabeth Carnegie, Editor, *Nursing Research*.

omous, student-financed and student-run organization. According to its bylaws, its purpose is "to aid in the development of the individual student and to urge all students of nursing, as future health professionals, to be aware of and to contribute to improving the health of all people."

The functions of NSNA are related to its purpose and demonstrate the scope of its work: promoting community participation directed toward improved health care and related social issues; speaking for nursing students when and where this is indicated; influencing the development of recruitment of minorities into schools of nursing; and promoting collaborative relationships with ANA, NLN, ICN, and other nursing and related health organizations (*National Student Nurses' Association Bylaws*, 1972).

At the 1976 convention of NSNA, a black student, Cleo Doster (Fig. 4–27) from California, was elected president. After serving one term, he was made one of the 12 honorary members of NSNA. Doster organized and chaired the Student Assembly at the ICN in Tokyo in 1977. He died November 25, 1985, at the age of 44.

In 1988, Ronaldo Futtrell, a lecturer in the Department of Nursing at New York City Technical College and a major in the Army Nurse Corps, U.S. Army Reserves, joined the staff of NSNA as director of programs. In this post, she coordinated activities in the areas of education, community health, legislation, and student recruitment. NSNA's major and most successful project is its Breakthrough to Nursing (see Chapter 3).

NURSES' EDUCATIONAL FUNDS

Nurses' Educational Funds (NEF) was incorporated in 1954 as an extension of the Isabel Hampton Robb Memorial Fund, established in 1910, and the Isabel McIsaac Loan Fund, established in 1914. An independent, nonprofit organization, it grants and administers scholarships to registered nurses for master's and doctoral study. The corporation, with a chief executive officer, is governed by an interracial board consisting of members selected from nursing and business leaders. Membership includes Dr. Mary Elizabeth Carnegie, Dr. Beverly Bonaparte, and Dr. Hattie Bessent. NEF is supported by contributions from the business community, foundations, nurses, and individuals interested in the advancement of nursing.

In addition to providing scholarships from interest on the endowment funds, NEF administers named grants. Although black nurses may win any of the awards, two of the named scholarships are designated for black nurses: The Mary Elizabeth Carnegie Scholarship for doctoral

Figure 4–27   Cleo Doster, elected President, National Student Nurses' Association, 1976.

study and the Estelle M. Osborne Memorial Scholarship for master's study. (Major annual donors to the Osborne Scholarship are Chi Eta Phi Sorority and Freedmen's Hospital School of Nursing Alumni Association.) The first recipient of the Carnegie Scholarship in 1982 was Bobbie Jean Primus Heath, an alumnus of Florida A & M University, Tallahassee, who has subsequently completed her doctorate at Virginia Polytechnical Institute and State University, Blacksburg. The 1989 recipient, Marcia Wells, a doctoral student at Harvard University is also Chairperson, Editorial Board, *Harvard Educational Review*. The first recipient of the Osborne Scholarship in 1983, Vicki Hines-Martin, a faculty member of Indiana University, earned her master's degree at the University of Cincinnati.

In the spirit of helping future awardees, Sadie Smalls, a 1983 Carnegie Scholarship recipient, along with Charles Hargett and Barbara Holder, initiated an annual fund-raising activity for the Carnegie Scholarship Fund (Fig. 4–28).

THE AMERICAN NURSES' FOUNDATION

The American Nurses' Foundation (ANF) was established by the ANA in 1955 pursuant to action of the 1954 house of delegates calling for a mechanism through which tax-exempt funds could flow in support of nursing programs, particularly those in nursing research. ANF grants

Figure 4–28   At NEF fund-raising reception, New York, 1983. Left to right are Charles Hargett, Dr. Barbara Holder, Dr. Mary Elizabeth Carnegie, and Sadie Smalls.

funds for research to universities, colleges, research centers, institutes, and individuals. Its competitive extramural grants program supports nursing research directed by registered nurses. It was created chiefly for beginning nurse researchers, but consideration is also given to experienced nurse researchers who are entering new fields of investigation.

Several black nurses have received grants from ANF to support their research: Dr. Juanita Fleming's project in 1970–71 was "Understanding Hospitalized Children Through Drawings"; Dr. Willa Doswell's research in 1979 was entitled "Physiology and Behavior: An Investigation of the Relation Between Race, Repression-Sensitization and Systolic Blood Pressure Response in Female Registered Nurses."

In 1976, Dr. Evelyn K. Tomes, professor and chairperson of the Department of Nursing Education at Meharry Medical College in Nashville, Tennessee, received one of six grants from ANF to investigate the contributions of black nurses to health services and health education. Says Tomes,

> Black nurses are interested in being recognized for their contributions to the progress of nursing in this country. Throughout the development of the profession, there have been black women so concerned about the improvement of health services, and the involvement of black nurses in the profession that they have overcome many insurmountable odds to accomplish these goals. It is such con-

tributions that need to be researched, highlighted, and incorporated into nursing history. Bringing these events into focus should provide a long overdue redress to this group of nurse pioneers, and also influence the future direction of professional nursing. [*Nursing Research Report*, 1976, p. 7]

The 29 grants awarded by ANF in 1990 marked the largest number of nurse researchers funded since its beginning in 1955. Funded recipients are titled scholars of the sponsoring corporation, organization, or individual. In 1987, Dr. Gloria Smith became the fourth recipient of the ANF Distinguished Scholar Award, and conducted a study titled, "Influencing Public Policy: Rethinking Public Health Nursing Practice Dilemmas."

ANF is directed by a nine-member board of trustees—all registered nurses. In 1985, Dr. Ethelrine Shaw-Nickerson became president—the first black—and served until 1989: Beverly Malone, PhD, was elected to the board in 1990; other black board members are Dr. Juanita Fleming and Mary Long.

THE AMERICAN ASSOCIATION OF COLLEGES OF NURSING

Beginning in 1966, a group of deans and directors, concerned about making baccalaureate preparation for beginning professional nursing practice a reality, and who were also members of the NLN Department of Baccalaureate and Higher Degree Programs, held a series of meetings with NLN staff to explore the kind of organizational arrangement that could focus on significant issues and take the necessary actions (Fondiller, 1989).

In 1969, the deliberations of these early sessions culminated in the formation of an independent conference of deans of college and university schools of nursing. By 1972, the name of the group had become the American Association of Colleges of Nursing (AACN), which became incorporated in the District of Columbia in 1973. From the original 80-member institutions in 1969, AACN today represents 415 schools of nursing at public and private universities and four-year colleges nationwide.

The mission of AACN, with offices in Washington, D.C., focuses on three main areas: to advance the quality of baccalaureate and graduate nursing education, promote nursing research, and provide for the development of academic leaders. AACN administers programs in education, research, government relations, publications, public affairs, and data base operations (Fondiller, 1989). In 1985, AACN began publishing its official organ, *The Journal of Professional Nursing*—a bimonthly.

From its inception, black deans have played an active role—holding office, serving on task forces, and so forth. In 1988, Geraldene Felton, EdD, RN, FAAN, Dean, University of Iowa College of Nursing, was elected president and served until 1990 (Fig. 4–29). The historically black schools that hold membership as of 1990 are: Tuskegee University, Alabama; University of Arkansas at Pine Bluff; Howard University, Washington, D.C.; Florida A & M University, Tallahassee; Bowie State University, Bowie, Maryland; Coppin State College, Baltimore, Maryland; Alcorn State University, Natchez, Mississippi; North Carolina A & T State University, Greensboro; Winston-Salem State University, North Carolina; Tennessee State University, Nashville; Prairie View A & M University, Texas; Grambling State University, Grambling, Louisiana; Hampton University, Hampton, Virginia; Norfolk State University, Norfolk, Virginia; North Carolina Central University, Durham; and Southern University and A & M College, Baton Rouge, Louisiana. The predominantly black member schools are: Chicago State University, Chicago, Illinois; Medgar Evers College of the City University of New York, Brooklyn, New York; and the University of the District of Columbia, Washington, D.C.

Figure 4–29   Dr. Geraldene Felton, President, AACN, 1988–1990. (Courtesy AACN)

THE NATIONAL BLACK NURSES' ASSOCIATION

In 1970, ANA's national convention was held in Miami, Florida, with approximately 200 black nurses in attendance. To learn more about those present, one black nurse from Indiana, Dr. Lauranne Sams (Fig. 4–30), called for a caucus to which over 150 black nurses responded. This was an initial attempt to develop a channel of communications among concerned black nurses. It was determined at the caucus that black nurses were concerned about and accountable to black people in a special way. The caucus also felt there was a need to articulate the health needs of the black community, as well as provide equal access to and mobility within the health care system.

Later, a small group of black nurses was called by Sams and met in Dr. Mary Harper's home in Cleveland, Ohio. The primary purpose was to organize a black nurses association that would be an independent group. They also met to plan for a caucus at the next ANA convention. Those present noted what many other black nurses had voiced: concern over the absence of black nurses in leadership positions in ANA (at that time, there had never been a black president or vice president); limited opportunities for blacks to share in shaping ANA policies and priorities; persistent tokenism; limited recognition of the black nurse's contribution to nursing; no significant increase in the number of black registered nurses; no recognition of achievement in terms of awards, other than the Mary Mahoney Award honoring the first black trained nurse; limited appointments to committees and commissions, presentation of papers, and so forth.

Figure 4–30   Dr. Lauranne Sams, first President, National Black Nurses' Association.

In December 1971, the National Black Nurses' Association (NBNA) was formed with Sams as its president. In 1972, NBNA was incorporated, with membership open to all registered nurses, licensed practical nurses, licensed vocational nurses, and student nurses. (See Appendix F for a list of the charter members.)

The purpose and objectives of the NBNA are as follows:

1. Define and determine nursing care for black consumers for optimum quality of care by acting as their advocates

2. Act as change agent in restructuring existing institutions and/ or helping to establish institutions to suit [black nurses'] needs

3. Serve as the national body to influence legislation and policies that affect black people and work cooperatively and collaboratively with other health care workers to this end

4. Conduct, analyze, and publish research to increase the body of knowledge about health needs of blacks

5. Compile and maintain a national directory of black nurses to assist with the dissemination of information regarding black nurses and nursing on a national level by the use of all media

6. Set standards and guidelines for quality education of black nurses on all levels by providing consultation to nursing faculties and by monitoring for proper utilization and placement of black nurses

7. Recruit, counsel, and assist black persons into the field

8. Be the vehicle for unification of black nurses of varied age groups, educational levels, and geographic locations to insure continuity and flow of our common heritage

9. Collaborate with other black groups to compile archives relevant to the historical, current, and future activities of black nurses

10. Provide the impetus and means for black nurses to write and publish on an individual or collaborative basis. [Smith, 1975]

In addition to regular organization business, NBNA sponsors annual national institutes. The first one, held in Cleveland in 1973 with the theme, "Emerging Roles for Black Nurses," focused national attention on the relationship between the health needs of the black consumer and the current practice of nursing. The purpose of this institute was to design and implement a program which would provide an opportunity for black nurses and other health-related workers to begin systematically to explore the health needs of the black consumer.

NBNA, with headquarters in Washington, D.C., has several thousand members in more than 51 chapters working to provide quality health care. With a special focus on minorities, the association recruits for nursing, serves as a job bank, functions as an information resource for federal agencies concerned with health care, and monitors federal legislation. It is an active member of the Black Congress on Health and Law. NBNA's refereed journal, *Journal of the NBNA*, is edited by Dr. Hilda Richards,

Provost and Vice President for Academic Affairs, Indiana University of Pennsylvania (Fig. 4–31).

Beginning in 1986, at each ANA biennial convention, the ANA Minority Fellowship Program and the ANA Cabinet on Human Rights present awards to women of color who have made a contribution to public service. In 1990, Alicia Georges (Fig. 4–32), president of NBNA, and Hilda Richards were among those so honored.

THE AMERICAN ASSOCIATION FOR THE HISTORY OF NURSING

Spearheaded by Teresa Christy, nurse historiographer, the International History of Nursing Society was founded in the Midwest in 1978. Because of problems with making the organization international in scope, in 1980 the name was changed to the American Association for the History of Nursing. From 1982 to 1984, Mary Elizabeth Carnegie served as corresponding secretary.

Annual conferences, cosponsored by the association and a university upon invitation, have been held since 1984. The conferences are designed to provide a forum for members to share their historical research.

Figure 4–31   Dr. Hilda Richards, Editor, *Journal of the National Black Nurses' Association*.

Figure 4–32   Alicia Georges (center), President, National Black Nurses' Association.

Among the many presentations have been a few that focused on black nurses and their contributions; for example, Dr. Althea Davis's paper, based on her dissertation, paid tribute to three early "architects" of integration: Adah B. Thoms, Martha Franklin, and Mary Eliza Mahoney. A paper by Janice Barnes Young described black nurses' experiences in the Cadet Nurse Corps. A paper by Pegge L. Bell was on the "Influence of the Tuskegee School of Nurse Midwifery for Colored Nurses on the Health Status of Southern Blacks in the 1940's." Still another paper, by Dr. Arlene Lowenstein, described "Racial Segregation in Nursing Education: The Lamar Experience."

At the 1990 conference, held at the University of Texas—Galveston, Darlene Clark Hine (Fig. 4–33), John Hannah Professor of History at Michigan State University, who has written five books and 11 journal articles on the history of blacks, was the recipient of the Lavinia Dock Award (Dock was America's first nurse historian). Hine's latest book is *Black Women in White: Racial Conflict and Cooperation in the Nursing Profession, 1890–1950,* published by Indiana University Press in 1989. According to the *Women's Review of Books,* "the book is full of poignant and sympathetic portraits of black nurses in their dedication and idealism, in their pain and anger . . . and in their deep concern for their community's health needs. . . ."

Figure 4–33   Dr. Darlene Clark Hine (right), recipient of Lavinia Dock Award, 1990. (Courtesy, University of Texas Medical Branch of Galveston)

Since 1988, The American Association for the History of Nursing has been cooperating with the Museum of Nursing History in Philadelphia and the Center for the Study of the History of Nursing at the University of Pennsylvania in holding an annual invitational Nursing History Conference at the historic Pennsylvania Hospital. The conference not only addresses important issues in the history of nursing, such as the ethics of historical research, but also serves as a forum for the critique of historical research.

THE SOCIETY FOR NURSING HISTORY

Spearheaded by Dr. Nancy Noel, who called a group of nurses she thought would be interested in forming a national organization for the history of nursing, the first meeting of the Society for Nursing History was held in October 1979 at Teachers College, Columbia University, New York. This group, who for the most part had been doctoral students at Teachers College, voted to organize and were considered charter members. Noel was elected president.

The following objectives were formulated: (1) to stimulate interest in historical research in nursing; (2) to share information about nursing history and historical research with society members; (3) to provide a channel for the exchange of information with other nursing history and interdisciplinary groups; (4) to contribute ideas and support for the development and maintenance of nursing archives; and (5) to facilitate the incorporation of the history of nursing into the curriculum.

Purposes agreed upon at the first meeting were: (1) to create further interest in historical research in nursing; (2) to share information and expertise among its membership as well as with interested others; and (3) to contribute ideas and lend support in the development and maintenance of the nursing archives at Teachers College and elsewhere.

From its inception, black nurses have been involved as members, beginning with Mary Elizabeth Carnegie, a charter member, and have also held elected offices. The first black president was Dr. Pamella E. Ho Sang, who served from 1986 to 1988 (Fig. 4–34).

THE ASSOCIATION OF BLACK NURSING FACULTY IN HIGHER EDUCATION

In 1986, at the invitation of Dr. Sallie Tucker-Allen, a group of black nursing faculty from several universities in Illinois met to share expe-

Figure 4–34   Dr. Pamella E. Ho Sang, President, Society for Nursing History, 1986–1988.

riences on how to best meet their professional needs and to determine how to best serve their constituencies. The result was the founding of the Association of Black Nursing Faculty in Higher Education, Inc. (ABNF), with Tucker-Allen as president (Fig. 4–35). Her full-time position is Chairperson, Professional Nursing Program, University of Wisconsin— Green Bay.

Membership in ABNF consists of black registered nurses with an earned graduate degree in nursing who are teaching at an institution of higher education offering a baccalaureate program in nursing. The functions of the ABNF are to provide a center for communication among members; develop strategies for promulgating group concerns to other individuals, institutions, and communities; assist members in professional development; develop, initiate, and sponsor continuing education activities; encourage and support research efforts among members; support black consumer advocacy issues; act and speak on health-related issues of legislation, government programs, and community activities; and serve as a forum for the exchange of new ideas and research findings.

ABNF's first annual meeting was held in 1988 in Washington, D.C. At this conference, awards of recognition were presented to two outstanding nurses—Dr. Hattie Bessent and Dr. Helen Grace. Honorary membership was bestowed upon Dr. Mary Elizabeth Carnegie. At its second annual meeting in August 1989, in the Bahamas, Mary Elizabeth Carnegie received the ABNF Lifetime Achievement Award in Education and Research.

Figure 4–35   Dr. Sallie Tucker-Allen, Founder and President, ABNF.

Like other professional nursing organizations, ABNF has an official journal which is refereed. ABNF is also a member of the ANA Nursing Organizational Liaison Forum.

THE AMERICAN ACADEMY OF NURSING

Within most professions is a body referred to as an academy, composed of a cadre of scholars who deal with issues that concern the profession and take positions in the name of the academy. Nursing, a young profession, has such an academy under the aegis of the professional association. The academy was established by the ANA Board of Directors in 1973. The board, acting on the criteria that had been established to recognize substantial achievement and contributions to nursing, designated 36 charter fellows, among whom were two blacks: Rhetaugh Dumas and Geraldene Felton. The charter fellows were chosen from more than 100 nominees and symbolize the high degree of commitment of nursing to providing high-quality care. Those selected for charter membership were highly expert clinical practitioners, academicians, administrators, and researchers.

The American Academy of Nursing is constituted to provide visionary leadership to the nursing profession and the public in shaping health policy and practice that optimize the well-being of the American people. The academy identifies emerging nursing and health care issues, promotes their scholarly exploration, challenges the status quo, and proposes creative solutions.

The mission of the academy is framed within nursing's historic commitment to an ethos of caring and the responsible generation and application of science. The academy facilitates the synthesis of scientific and philosophic knowledge as the basis for effective health care policy and practice. The academy pursues its mission by facilitating scholarly debate on issues that are identified as significant to nursing and health care; evaluating and interpreting scientific and philosophic knowledge as a basis for proposing new directions in health care policy and practice; initiating studies to generate new knowledge relevant to health care; disseminating proposals for health policy and practice through publications, conferences, and other professional activities; and forming interactive linkages with other groups to recommend health care policy and practice to meet emerging health care needs (*American Academy of Nursing Mission Statement*, 1990).

More than 700 nurses have been admitted to the academy, 38 of whom have been black—36 regular and two honorary. The academy also has had three black elected presidents: Mary Elizabeth Carnegie, 1978–1979

(Fig. 4–36); Vernice Ferguson, 1981–1983; and Rhetaugh Dumas, 1987–1989. Listed below are the black fellows, regular and honorary, with biographical sketches of each by year of induction into the academy.

Regular Fellows

1973   **Rhetaugh Dumas** (BS, Dillard University Division of Nursing, New Orleans, Louisiana; PhD, Union Graduate School, Yellow Springs, Ohio, [Fig. 4–37]) was Chief, Psychiatric Nursing Education Branch, Division of Manpower and Training Programs, NIMH, when she was

Figure 4–36   Dr. Mary Elizabeth Carnegie (right), outgoing president, American Academy of Nursing, hands over gavel to Dr. Linda Aiken, incoming president, 1979.

Figure 4–37　　Dr. Rhetaugh Dumas, Charter Fellow, American Academy of Nursing.

selected by the ANA board for membership in the American Academy of Nursing as a charter fellow. She became deputy director of that division in 1977. In 1979, she was promoted to Deputy Director, NIMH, Alcohol, Drug Abuse, and Mental Health Administration, Public Health Service, U.S. Department of Health and Human Services. Since 1981, Dumas has been Dean, University of Michigan School of Nursing, Ann Arbor.

Prior to Dumas's appointment to federal posts beginning in 1972, her career had spanned teaching, clinical practice, administration, consultation, and research. She had served as chairperson of the Psychiatric Nursing Program at Yale University and Director of Nursing Service at the Connecticut Mental Health Center at Yale-New Haven Medical Center. In the area of research, she is credited with being the first nurse to conduct clinical experiments to evaluate nursing practices. In this connection, she was principal investigator of federally funded research projects. Robert C. Leonard, PhD, was her collaborator. Results of their studies on "The Effect of Nursing Care on Postoperative Vomiting" (1961) have been widely published and have stimulated many similar studies over the years. Dumas is the author of numerous publications.

Dumas is in constant demand, in this country and abroad, as a consultant to organizations and as a speaker at conventions and scientific meetings. In the spring of 1982, she was invited by the U.S. Department of Health and Human Services to travel with a team of nurses to Nigeria,

West Africa, to consult with the Federal Ministry of Health on nursing and nursing education. In July 1983, she participated in a Working Conference for the Examination of Group Behavior Within an Institution, sponsored by the Washington-Baltimore Center of the A.K. Rice Institute and the University of Maryland European Division for the 7th Medical Command, United States Army, Walldorf, Germany.

Four honorary doctorates have been bestowed on Dumas: Doctor of Public Service by the University of Cincinnati; Doctor of Public Service by Simmons College, Boston; and Doctor of Humane Letters by both Yale University and her alma mater, Dillard University. Her numerous awards include Distinguished Alumnae Award from Yale University, which reads, "No catalogue of her personal and professional accomplishments does justice to the power of her person, the scope of her service, or the depths of the ways she has touched the lives of others." In 1985, she received the University of Michigan's First Annual Academic Women's Career Award. In 1986 and 1987, she served on the Advisory Committee to the Director of the National Institutes of Health (NIH).

Geraldene Felton (Diploma, Mercy Hospital School of Nursing, Philadelphia; EdD, New York University [Fig. 4–38]) was on loan from the Department of the Army in the position of Associate Professor, University of Hawaii School of Nursing, when she was named a charter fellow of the American Academy of Nursing by the ANA Board of Directors. At the time, she was also principal investigator on a Health, Education, and Welfare research project: "Rhythmic Correlates of Shift

Figure 4–38   Dr. Geraldene Felton, Charter Fellow, American Academy of Nursing.

Work." Later she was a research nurse and Deputy Director, Walter Reed Army Institute of Research, Division of Nursing, Washington, D.C.

After 20 years of service with the U.S. Army Nurse Corps, and as professor and researcher, Felton retired and became professor and dean of nursing at Oakland University in Rochester, Michigan. In 1981, she assumed the position of Professor and Dean, College of Nursing, University of Iowa, Iowa City.

Felton has published widely in professional and refereed journals; has delivered innumerable papers at scientific meetings; is a member of Sigma Xi, Scientific Research Society of North America; has held office in major nursing organizations; and has served on the boards of the American Journal of Nursing Company and St. Joseph Mercy Hospital, Pontiac, Michigan. With her administrative responsibilities, she continues to be actively engaged in teaching, consultation, research, and scholarly publication. In 1984, she became the assistant editor for research for the *Journal of Professional Nursing*, the official publication of the AACN. She was Chair, Iowa Academy of Science Nursing Section, 1984–1985; President Elect, AACN, 1986–1988; President, AACN, 1988–1990; Chair, Nursing Research Study Section, National Science Institutes of Health (NIH) Division of Research Grants, 1987–1991; and Member, Special Advisory Group, Department of Veterans Affairs, 1988–1992.

1974 **Juanita Fleming** (BS, Hampton University School of Nursing, Hampton, Virginia; PhD, The Catholic University of America, Washington, D.C. [Fig. 4–39]) was Professor and Associate Dean and Director of Graduate Education, University of Kentucky College of Nursing, Lexington, and professor with a joint appointment in the College of Education when she was inducted into the academy. In August 1984, she was promoted to associate vice chancellor for academic affairs at the

Figure 4–39   Dr. Juanita Fleming.

Medical Center, University of Kentucky. Currently, she is special assistant to the president of the university for Academic Affairs. She also served on the governing council of the academy from 1982 to 1984.

From the beginning, Fleming's nursing career has been characterized by outstanding achievements. While a senior nursing student at Hampton University, she suggested the possibility of students having public health experience in Washington, D.C. With the director's approval, she made initial contact and all the arrangements for the experience. Later, while on the staff of Freedmen's Hospital School of Nursing in Washington, D.C., she initiated clinical experiences for the students at Children's Hospital in Washington and Howard University. She also gave the first Lillian B. William Lecture at Children's Hospital.

In 1963, Fleming won the Mary M. Roberts Journalism Fellowship with a paper she wrote entitled "Black Tract." This fellowship, awarded by the American Journal of Nursing Company, permitted her to study journalism and human development at the University of Maryland. A paper she wrote in 1966 was later used as a guide in caring for children at Children's Hospital in Washington, D.C. Another paper, written in 1985, titled "Maternal-Child Nursing in the Decade Ahead," was cited by several leaders, including Surgeon General C. Everett Koop, as a guide for future directions in maternal-child care. This pattern of excellence has continued with numerous honors and recognition awards, including induction into the Hall of Fame at Hampton University.

One of Fleming's most notable areas of achievement is nursing research. She was active in the ANA Conference on Research when attendance was by invitation only; has participated in ANA's Council of Nurse Researchers, presenting her own research for criticism; and has been a member of the council's executive committee. She also served as a member of the ANA Commission on Nursing Research. She has done considerable research on the nursing needs of children and has served as consultant in this area. Her excellence as a teacher is irrefutable, and she has received the University of Kentucky Alumni Association's Great Teacher Award. She is highly respected by students and peers alike for her pursuit of excellence, scholarly presentations, and wealth of knowledge. In the community at large, she has received several gubernatorial appointments to statewide advisory boards. Her publications include two books, *Care and Management of Exceptional Children* and *Issues in Nursing Research*, coauthored with Florence Downs.

Fleming has served on research review panels including the Maternal Child Health Research Review Panel in the Division of Maternal Child Health, Public Health Service, NIH Behavioral Medicine Study section. She also serves as a reviewer for *Nursing Research*, *Advances in Nursing Science*, *Applied Nursing Research*, *Scholarly Inquiry for Nursing Practice: An International Journal*, and *Nursing Outlook*.

In 1985, Fleming was elected to the ANA Board of Directors and was reelected in 1987, serving as secretary. She is currently on the ANF Board of Directors and is a member of the NIH Behavioral Medicine Study Section.

Myrtis J. Snowden (Diploma, Homer G. Phillips Hospital School of Nursing, St. Louis, Missouri; Dr PH, Tulane University, New Orleans, Louisiana, [Fig. 4–40]) is Professor, Graduate Program, Louisiana State University School of Nursing, New Orleans.

Snowden's field of concentration has been community health nursing, beginning with her experience while living at the Henry Street Settlement House in New York. Her greatest contribution to the field of public health was probably made in Louisiana, where she organized a demonstration school health program for the New Orleans Health Department and instituted school-wide educational programs. Her teaching career in community health nursing began at Dillard University in New Orleans, where she organized and implemented a field education center for baccalaureate students in community health nursing. Subsequent to that, she held teaching positions at Northwestern State University, Natchitoches, Louisiana, and the University of Southern Mississippi, Hattiesburg, before joining the faculty of Louisiana State University School of Nursing.

Snowden's many professional responsibilities include supervising the writing of master's theses, writing grants, and conducting workshops. She has been deeply involved in many funded research projects as director and co-director and has had her work published in professional books and journals. Her honors have been many, including Zeta Phi

Figure 4–40
Dr. Myrtis J. Snowden.

Beta and Milbank Memorial scholarships and honorary membership in Chi Eta Phi Sorority.

1975   **Lucille Davis** (BSN, University of Illinois at the Medical Center, Chicago, Illinois; PhD, Northwestern University, Evanston, Illinois [Fig. 4–41]) was associate dean of the graduate program at Rush College of Nursing, Chicago, when she was admitted to the academy. Before going to Rush, she was Director of Nursing Education, Chicago State University. Until 1990 she was Director of the Center for Nursing, Northwestern University. She then returned to the University of Illinois at Chicago as a research associate in the College of Nursing. Since 1987, Davis has been serving as a consultant to a W.K. Kellogg Foundation Project in Zimbabwe.

According to her peers:

> Dr. Davis has combined a sensitivity as a nurse practitioner with a broad background in sociology and has retained her initial devotion to nursing itself. She is a creative and innovative teacher, stimulating intellectual growth in her students by a demonstration of a mind that is always seeking new avenues of understanding . . . Her current interest is in gerontology and she has a clinical appointment at Northwestern Hospital where she works with aged patients. While she is an articulate spokesman for black nurses, she has also had a global view of the academic problems of nursing and has introduced innovative and humanistic concerns into the graduate program (personal communication, Myra Levine, 1975).

Figure 4–41   Dr. Lucille Davis.

Vernice Ferguson (Diploma, Bellevue Hospital School of Nursing, New York; MA, Teachers College, Columbia University, New York [Fig. 4–42]) was Chief, Nursing Service, Clinical Center, NIH, Bethesda, Maryland, when she was admitted to the academy. She is now Deputy Assistant Chief Medical Director for Nursing Programs and Director of Nursing Service, Department of Veterans Affairs, Washington, D.C.

In recognition of her many achievements in the field of nursing, Ferguson has been the recipient of numerous awards, including honorary doctorates from Marymount College of Virginia; Adelphi University, New York (Doctor of Science); LaSalle College in Philadelphia (Doctor of Science); Villa Maria College in Erie, Pennsylvania (Doctor of Laws); Villanova University (Doctor of Social Science); and Northeastern University (Doctor of Public Science). She has received numerous honors including the Distinguished Service Award, U.S. Public Health Service; the ANA Mary Mahoney Award; Distinguished Nurse Award, Clinical Center Nursing Department, NIH; The R. Louise McManus Award for Distinguished Service to Nursing, Teachers College, Columbia University, Department of Nursing Education Alumni, New York; and the U.S. Public Health Service Surgeon General's Recognition Award given to outstanding leaders in the health field.

In 1984, Ferguson was one of four nurses who received the Royal College of Nursing Fellowship in London, England. The fellowship, awarded to non-British nationals only in rare instances, is granted in recognition of outstanding contributions to the advancement of the science and art of nursing. In announcing her honorary fellowship, the Council of the Royal College said that this selection of a non-British

Figure 4–42   Vernice Ferguson.

national was merited because of her "outstanding example of innovative leadership, not only within the nursing profession in the United States, but in other countries as well, which has set a standard for others to follow." This citation was recorded in the October 2, 1984, issue of the *Congressional Record.* In the international arena, she served as first vice president of the International Society of Nurses in Cancer Care and has lectured in Norway, Italy, Korea, Scotland, England, and Australia.

Ferguson's professional experience is wide and varied, having been a clinician, consultant, academician, and chief nurse at Veterans Administration (VA) medical centers in Madison, Wisconsin, and Chicago West Side, Illinois. In addition to her position at the VA, she is an administrative faculty associate at the University of Maryland School of Nursing, Baltimore, and adjunct professor at Georgetown University School of Nursing, Washington, D.C.

From 1981 to 1983, Ferguson served as the elected president of the American Academy of Nursing. In 1983, she was elected president-elect of Sigma Theta Tau and served as president of that society from 1985 to 1987. Ferguson served on the National Commission on Nursing, the Secretary's Commission on Nursing of the Department of Health and Human Services (DHHS) in 1988. She is also on numerous boards, including the Board of Trustees of the Washington Hospital Center—the first nurse appointed.

1976 **Mary Elizabeth Carnegie** (Diploma, Lincoln School of Nurses, New York; DPA, New York University [Fig. 4–43]) was editor of *Nursing*

Figure 4–43
Dr. Mary Elizabeth Carnegie.

Research when she was inducted into the academy, becoming treasurer of the academy in 1977 and president in 1978.

Before joining the editorial staff of the American Journal of Nursing Company, where she began as an assistant editor, *American Journal of Nursing*, then Associate Editor and Senior Editor, *Nursing Outlook*, Carnegie had initiated the baccalaureate program at Hampton University in Virginia and had been the first Dean and Professor, Florida A & M University School of Nursing in Tallahassee.

For her contributions in elevating the status of all minority nurses and black nurses in particular, Carnegie has been the recipient of many honors, among which have been the Mabel K. Staupers Award by Chi Eta Phi; the ANA Mary Mahoney Award; Recognition Award, District 13, New York State Nurses' Association; Recognition Award, University of Pennsylvania; and recognition by Nurses House; *Dollars and Sense* magazine; Mugar Library; Association of Black Nursing Faculty in Higher Education; and Virginia Nurses' Association (for history).

Carnegie holds honorary memberships in Sigma Theta Tau; Chi Eta Phi; Teachers College, Columbia University Alumni; Freedmen's Hospital School of Nursing Alumni; and the Association of Black Nursing Faculty in Higher Education. Since 1974, she has been on the Advisory Committee of the ANA Minority Fellowship Program, an ANA Board of Directors appointee serving as chairperson since 1980, and on the NEF Board of Directors. Carnegie has received an Honorary Doctor of Laws from Hunter College, City University of New York, and an Honorary Doctor of Science from the State University of New York, Health Science Center, Brooklyn.

Since retiring from the editorship of *Nursing Research* in 1978, Carnegie has been Distinguished Visiting Professor, Hampton University School of Nursing in Virginia; Visiting Distinguished Professor, University of North Carolina, Greensboro; Visiting Professor, Pennsylvania State University; Visiting Scholar, University of Michigan, Ann Arbor; Visiting Scholar, Oakland University, Rochester, Michigan; and Distinguished Visiting Professor, Indiana University, Indianapolis. She has held two endowed chairs: The Vera E. Bender Chair, Adelphi University, Garden City, New York, and the Loewenberg Chair of Excellence in Nursing, Memphis State University, Memphis, Tennessee.

Carnegie is also an independent consultant on scientific writing, having published widely in professional journals. In addition to having contributed chapters to books, two of her own are *Disadvantaged Students in RN Programs*, published by NLN and *Historical Perspectives of Nursing Research*, published by Mugar Library, Boston University.

Virginia Ford (Diploma, Kansas City General No. 2 Hospital School of Nursing Kansas City, Missouri; PhD, The Catholic University of America, Washington, D.C. [Fig. 4–44]) was Dean, Chicago State Uni-

Figure 4–44   Dr. Virginia Ford.

versity College of Nursing, when she became a member of the academy. Before then, she was Associate Professor, DePaul University Department of Nursing, Chicago. She is now Dean and Professor Emerita, Chicago State University.

Ford has been instrumental in the development of public health programs in the United States and abroad, having served on an international team of health specialists in Liberia, India, Taiwan, and in recreational programs of the American Red Cross in Korea and Japan. She holds the permanent rank of captain in the U.S. Public Health Service. Recognized for her expertise as a nurse anthropologist, she is a national speaker and author in the fields of anthropology and nursing. She is also a fellow of the American Anthropological Association, the American Association for the Advancement of Science, and the Society for Applied Anthropology. Among her many publications is *Acceptance of Modern Medical Theory and Practice Among the Teton Dakota*.

Ford has served as a member of the board of directors of the Comprehensive Health Planning, Inc., of Metropolitan Chicago and is a former member of the executive committee of the Illinois Nurses' Association's Council for Nursing Research. She also served as a member of the Research in Nursing in Patient Care Review Committee of NIH.

1977   **Fostine G. Riddick Roach** (Diploma, Tuskegee University School of Nursing, Tuskegee, Alabama; MA, New York University [Fig. 4–45]), at the time of her induction into the academy, was Dean and Professor, Hampton University School of Nursing, Hampton, Virginia. While there,

Figure 4–45
Dr. Fostine G. Riddick Roach

she developed and implemented the first master's degree program in nursing at an historically black institution. As dean emerita, she does consultant work in the areas of education and administration.

Roach is credited with changing the public image of Norfolk Community Hospital while she was director of nursing there from 1957 to 1963. During this time, she created an environment for her multiracial staff that stimulated professional interest and growth. Under her leadership, most of her staff began pursuing advanced education, began taking an active interest in their professional organizations, and showed more inclination toward acceptance of inservice education.

From 1968 to 1981, Roach served as an accreditation visitor for the NLN Department of Baccalaureate and Higher Degree Programs and as a member of the Nurse Training Act Review Committee; Division of Nursing; Department of Health, Education, and Welfare; National Institutes of Health. Her publications, many of which were based on her speeches, have appeared in *Nursing Outlook*, the *Glowing Lamp*, *Nursing in Virginia*, and *Virginia Nurse Quarterly*.

Roach has received numerous honors, among which was the 1974 ANA Mary Mahoney Award. She served as a governor's appointee to the Virginia State Board of Health for eight years and as an alumni representative on the board of trustees of Tuskegee University. She is also past national president of Chi Eta Phi Sorority.

In 1986, Roach returned to Hampton University as Director of Alumni Affairs for a period of two and a half years. As a former dean, in March 1990 she was awarded emeritus status by the AACN.

Iris Shannon (Diploma, Meharry Medical College School of Nursing, Nashville, Tennessee; PhD, University of Illinois, Chicago [Fig. 4–46]) is Associate Professor, Community Health Nursing and Health Systems Management, Rush University, Chicago. At Rush, she has served as codirector of the pediatric, medical, and obstetrical-gynecological nurse associate continuing education programs and also of the graduate program for the preparation of community nurse practitioners.

Shannon has demonstrated excellence in both the teaching and practice of community health nursing. Her work in the Head Start program in the Chicago public schools and in the Mile Square Health Center during the 1960s showed innovative approaches to organizing and delivering health services to inner-city populations. She combined her knowledge of the health needs of poor communities with the potentials of nursing to institute a model program to meet those health care needs. Building on her experience and her appreciation for the underutilized potentials of nursing, she instituted one of the earliest programs for pediatric and medical nurse associates. These programs have served as models for similar programs throughout the country.

Continuing her involvement in practice and education, Shannon developed and implemented community health nursing programs for Rush

Figure 4–46   Dr. Iris Shannon.

Medical Center, which include discharge planning, ambulatory care, hospital-based home health service, and nurse-managed populations.

Shannon's memberships in professional organizations reflect her broad commitment. She is active in the ANA, the American School Health Association, the Institute of Medicine of Chicago, and the Institute of Medicine of the National Academy of Science. In addition, she is a fellow of the American Public Health Association (APHA) and serves on numerous committees on local, state, and national levels. In 1989, she served as president of the APHA, which represents over 50,000 public health workers. During the same year, she was elected as an honorary fellow in England's Royal Society of Health. Throughout her career, Shannon has shared her experiences with innovative services and educational patterns through her publications. Her literary contributions can be found in the *Journal of Practical Nursing, Inquiry, Nursing Outlook, The American Journal of Public Health*, and *Pediatric Digest*. She has presented papers to numerous professional and other groups. In 1988, Shannon led a delegation of public health workers on a technical exchange visit to the People's Republic of China.

Gloria Smith (BS, Wayne State University College of Nursing, Detroit, Michigan; PhD, Union Graduate School, Cincinnati, Ohio [Fig. 4–47]) was Dean and Professor, College of Nursing, University of Oklahoma, Oklahoma City, when inducted into the academy. In 1983, she was appointed by Governor Jim Blanchard as director of the Michigan Department of Public Health—the first nurse ever to be appointed to head a state agency in Michigan. One of the state's largest agencies, the Department of Public Health oversees the development and regulation of

Figure 4–47   Dr. Gloria Smith.

health care facilities, agencies, and providers; protects against environmental health hazards; and promotes improved health status of individuals, groups, and communities. In 1988, Smith was appointed dean of her alma mater, Wayne State University College of Nursing, Detroit, Michigan.

Throughout Smith's nursing career, her work has been characterized by the development of strategies to assist the disadvantaged and the culturally different to take advantage of available opportunities and/or to create new opportunity for gaining entry into both the health care delivery system and the health care industry. Beginning practice in the 1950s in an urban center, Smith worked with immigrants, southern Appalachian mountaineers, and southern blacks. She has influenced both education and service with her humanistic approach to nursing education. Her consultant work has been international as well as nationwide. In 1982, she was appointed as a member of a nursing consultant team to Nigeria, through a bilateral agreement between Nigeria and the United States. Currently, she serves as a consultant to W.K. Kellogg's international programs in Africa, India, China, South America, and the Netherlands.

A former member of the ANA Commission (now Cabinet) on Nursing Education, Smith has published widely in prestigious journals and provides leadership to minority nursing organizations. She serves on the governing council of the American Academy of Nursing; the Special Projects Review Committee, Department of Health and Human Services; and the Geriatric Curriculum Grants Review Committee. She holds membership in the NLN, the AACN, the NBNA, and the Midwest Alliance in Nursing.

1978 **Mary S. Harper** (Diploma, Tuskegee University School of Nursing, Tuskegee, Alabama; PhD, St. Louis University [Fig. 4–48]) was Deputy Chief, Center for the Study of Mental Health of Minority Groups, National Institute of Mental Health, Department of Health and Human Services, when she was inducted into the academy. Shortly thereafter, in 1979, she was on detail for two years as Director, Office of Policy Development and Research, White House Conference on Aging. In 1982, she returned to NIMH to become Coordinator, Long-Term Care Programs, Center for the Study of the Mental Health of the Aging.

Known nationally and internationally for the leadership she has exercised at NIMH and in her 30 years with the Veterans Administration, Harper's professional experience ranges from ten years as a staff nurse in Alabama; to 11 years as associate chief, Nursing Service for Education, at VA Hospitals in Alabama, Michigan, and California; to seven years as the chief of clinical research at a VA hospital in New York. While in New York, she assisted in establishing a plan for a $500,000 research laboratory for the study of immunology of schizophrenia.

Figure 4–48   Dr. Mary S. Harper.

In her current position as Director, Office of Policy Development and Research, Harper shares responsibility for the administration of a comprehensive nationwide program concerning the mental health of minority groups. She also provides technical assistance to researchers in developing and revising grant applications. Harper developed and initiated the National Research and Development Mental Health Center for Asian-Americans, American Indians, blacks, and Hispanics and was the principal staffer for the development of the first national fellowships in mental health for minorities in the disciplines of psychology, social work, psychiatry, nursing, and sociology. The ANA is one of the five national associations participating in this program.

Harper has presented papers at national meetings of the American Psychological Association, National Education Association, American Sociological Association, National Council on Aging, and the American Indian Physician's Association that were based on the activity and research generated at the Center for the Study of Mental Health and Minority Groups.

Honors awarded to Harper have been numerous, the most unique being the declaration of a "Mary Starke Harper Day" by Mayor Pete Wilson of San Diego in May 1975, recognizing her as an innovative administrator and nationally recognized educator and researcher. She received the Federal Nursing Award for Outstanding Service and Accomplishments in Professional Nursing, the Tuskegee University Alumni Meritorious Award in 1970, and the ANA Mary Mahoney Medal in 1978.

In 1983, Harper received special recognition for outstanding contributions in the area of health care by the University of Pennsylvania School of Nursing. Internationally, she is an approved World Health Organization (WHO) consultant and has provided consultation in Africa, Belgium, Thailand, United Kingdom, China, India, and Austria. Harper has been on the faculty of the University of Minnesota, University of California at Los Angeles, Tuskegee University, and Mount St. Mary's College in New York.

Barbara Martin McArthur (Diploma, Provident Hospital School of Nursing, Chicago, Illinois; PhD, University of Washington, Seattle [Fig. 4–49]) is Professor, College of Nursing, Wayne State University, Detroit, and was director of the nurse-epidemiologist program, the only program of its kind in the United States, which she conceived and developed. Until recently, in her position at Wayne State, 50 percent of her time was spent in laboratory research on hospital infections cause by a gram-negative organism and 50 percent of her time was spent developing, administering, and teaching in the nurse-epidemiologist program. She holds certificates from the Centers for Disease Control, Atlanta, in Surveillance, Prevention, and Control of Nosocomial Infections; from Regional Science Center, Oak Ridge Institute of Nuclear Studies in Radioisotope Techniques; and from the University of North Carolina at Greensboro Summer Institute in Molecular Biology.

A pioneer in research in epidemiology and clinical microbiology, McArthur was accorded a singular honor in 1976 when she delivered

Figure 4–49
Dr. Barbara Martin McArthur.

papers at the Fifth International Symposium on Acute Care held in Rio de Janeiro and Sao Paulo. The symposium was jointly sponsored by the Brazilian College of Surgeons, the Brazilian Medical Association, and the International College of Surgeons. McArthur has also addressed the annual meeting of the American Society of Microbiology and has delivered a paper in London on AIDS research.

In addition to her research activities and the direction of institutional epidemiology study, McArthur has maintained her long-time interest in working with minority students, providing tutorial services, serving on community health committees, and giving her time to a high school student summer program. She has numerous publications, including the editorship of a volume of *Nursing Clinics of North America*.

McArthur is a member of the Association for Practitioners of Infection Control, the American College of Epidemiology, the Michigan branch of the American Society for Microbiology, the Nightingale Society, and the American Association of University Professors. In addition, she was a member of the first Certification Board of Infection Control (CBIC) and chairperson of the CBIC Task Analysis Committee, which developed the first survey tool for a job analysis of infection control practitioners.

Oliver Osborne (Diploma, Central Islip State Hospital School of Nursing, New York; PhD, Michigan State University [Fig. 4–50]) is Professor, Department of Psychosocial Nursing, University of Washington, Seattle.

In the Pacific Northwest, Osborne has pioneered in the development of cross-cultural perspectives in the delivery of health care services through research, publications, and training programs. On the international level, he has been consultant to the King and Ogboni Elders, Yorubaland,

Figure 4–50   Dr. Oliver Osborne.

Nigeria, where he was elected chief (Adila of Ibara) for his services to Ibara people during a period of civil strife. He has also served as associate fellow at the University of Botswana and has been research consultant to governments and universities in Nigeria and Ghana.

Active in the ANA, Osborne has served in various capacities since 1972: as member of the Executive Committee, Division of Psychiatric and Mental Health Nursing Practice, and as a member of the Advisory Committee, Minority Fellowship Program. Many of his research publications focus on African health care, social structure, mental health nursing, ethnicity, and cross-cultural aspects of nursing.

Osborne pioneered in the expansion of nursing roles through development of a System-Oriented Community Mental Health program. This program prepares nurses for research, planning, program implementation, and evaluation in a variety of health care settings and has contributed to the creation of numerous innovative mental health agency programs in the Pacific Northwest. For a number of years, he has focused upon the development of state hospital nursing through university-public hospital collaborations.

In 1983, Osborne took a year's leave of absence and went to Spain to serve as a consultant to a psychiatric hospital. During that year, he traveled extensively to other parts of Europe, studying the relationships between value systems, public policy, and the organization of mental-health care systems. He also observed alternatives to traditional health care.

Ora Strickland (BS, North Carolina A & T State University School of Nursing, Greensboro; PhD, University of North Carolina at Greensboro [Fig. 4–51]) was Assistant Professor, University of North Carolina at Greensboro School of Nursing when she was admitted to the American Academy of Nursing. She now holds the position of Independence Foundation Research Chair and Professor, Nell Hodgson Woodruff School of Nursing, Emory University, Atlanta, Georgia.

Selected as one of the recipients of the first fellowships awarded through the ANA Registered Nurse Fellowship Program for Ethnic Minorities, Strickland was one of the first two fellows to complete the doctoral degree. A nationally known specialist in nursing research, measurement, evaluation, maternal and child health and parenting, Strickland is frequently called upon as a consultant nationally and internationally and has presented more than 150 lectures, speeches, and workshops. Exemplifying her commitment to nursing research, she has gained national recognition for her research on expectant fathers and responses of men to pregnancy. Results of her research have appeared in over 80 newspapers, and she has discussed her research on six television programs and over 1,200 radio stations internationally. She is also known for a videocassette production, *Giving Emotional Support to Parents of the High-*

Figure 4–51   Dr. Ora Strickland.

Risk Newborn. In addition to regularly contributing to professional journals, she has written or contributed to 14 books. Two of her books have won four *American Journal of Nursing* Book of the Year Awards. Strickland's newspaper column titled "Nurse Station," which appeared regularly in the health magazine section of the *Morning* and *Evening Baltimore Sun*, won two health journalism awards in 1988.

Beyond her research and educational activities, Strickland is active in the health care policy area. Following her selection as an ANA legislative intern, which led to her spending the summer of 1977 formulating policy relating to health care legislation through the offices of U.S. Congressman Ralph Metcalfe (Democrat, Illinois), she was invited to become a member of the Congressional Black Caucus Health Brain Trust. In this capacity, she served as a member of the advisory group on health issues to the U.S. Congressional Black Caucus.

Strickland is a member of the National Council on Family Relations, Society for Research in Child Development, Sigma Theta Tau International Honor Society in Nursing, ANA Council of Nurse Researchers, and ANA. She serves on the editorial boards or review panels of *Advances in Nursing Science, Research in Nursing and Health, Health Care for Women International, Journal of Professional Nursing, Scholarly Inquiry for Nursing Practice: An International Journal* and *Western Journal of Nursing Research.* Strickland also serves as chairperson of the Advisory Committee of *Nursing Outlook* and co-chairperson of the National Nursing Research Agenda

Steering Committee of the National Center for Nursing Research, NIH. In 1989, she was appointed to a four-year term on the National Advisory Committee of the National Center for Nursing Research, NIH, by the U.S. secretary of Health and Human Services.

In 1984, Strickland was chosen by the W.K. Kellogg Foundation's National Fellowship Program as one of 43 outstanding American professionals. The program is intended to help the nation expand its bank of capable leaders.

1979 **Elnora Daniel** (BS, North Carolina A & T State University School of Nursing, Greensboro; EdD, Teachers College, Columbia University, New York [Fig. 4–52]) was professor and coordinator of the master's program at Hampton University School of Nursing, Hampton, Virginia, when she was admitted to the academy. She is now dean of the School of Nursing at Hampton University.

Under Daniel's leadership, the master's program has expanded and now includes three new specialty areas and two graduate nurse-practitioner programs. The initiation of a self-paced auto-tutorial system in the nursing program at Hampton was another of her creative roles. The curriculum substance of this system was developed in line with the results of her research, which she has shared through publications, conferences, and workshops at other institutions. She is also responsible for the creation of the first nursing center with a mobile van to accommodate faculty practice, research, and student clinical learning experiences. The Nursing Center with its "Health Mobile" provides primary and acute care

Figure 4–52   Dr. Elnora Daniel.

services to unserved and underserved population groups, including the homeless, throughout southeastern Virginia.

Daniel's distinguished appointments in nursing include Chairperson and Member, NLN Board of Review; Consultant, Faculty Development in Nursing Education Project, Southern Regional Education Board; Member, Curriculum Project Liaison Committee for Demonstration Projects in Graduate Education, Southern Regional Education Board; Lieutenant Colonel, U.S. Army Reserve Nurse Corps; Accreditation Visitor, NLN; President, Virginia State Board of Nursing; Secretary, AACN; Peer Reviewer, NIMH, Psychiatric Nursing, Division of Nursing for Special Projects Grants and Advanced Nursing Training Grants; and consultant for the W.K. Kellogg Foundation to four African Countries: Lesotho, Botswana, Zimbabwe, and Swaziland.

Laurie Gunter (Diploma, Meharry Medical College School of Nursing, Nashville, Tennessee; PhD, University of Chicago [Fig. 4–53]) is Professor Emerita, Nursing and Human Development, Pennsylvania State University College of Nursing, University Park. She has had a long and distinguished career as an educator, having been professor at the University of Washington, Indiana University, and the University of California, and Dean, Meharry Medical College School of Nursing. She has also held visiting distinguished professorships at the University of California at Los Angeles, the University of Tulsa in Oklahoma, and the University of Delaware.

Figure 4–53   Dr. Laurie Gunter.

For many years, Gunter has been involved in the development of geriatric and gerontological nursing as an educator, researcher, and clinician and is considered an expert in these fields. She has been a nursing pioneer in efforts to integrate geriatric nursing content into the undergraduate curriculum and to develop graduate programs that prepare clinical nursing specialists in geriatric care.

At Pennsylvania State University, Gunter planned and implemented an innovative, creative curriculum to prepare nurses for health care roles. Using a growth and development model, this curriculum approaches health care in terms of new roles and functions. Inherent in the new curriculum was the incorporation of innovative independent-learning experiences.

Gunter's involvement in ANA has included participation on the executive committee and interim certification board of the Division on Gerontological Nursing Practice and Council on Research. Internationally, Gunter has served as a faculty member at the first Japanese Nursing Research Conference at Women's Tokyo Medical College. She has also written extensively. Among her published works are articles and books on the attitudes and interests of Negro nurses, the role of professional nurses in nursing homes, stress of mothers of premature infants, theoretical frameworks for nursing research, and a host of writings on the aging. In 1978, she was elected to membership in the Institute of Medicine of the National Academy of Science.

Faye Gary Harris (BS, Florida A & M University School of Nursing, Tallahassee; EdD, University of Florida, Gainesville, [Fig. 4–54]) is professor at the University of Florida in psychiatric and mental health nursing. She holds a joint appointment in the Department of Psychiatry,

Figure 4–54
Dr. Faye Gary Harris.

College of Medicine, and is vice chairperson of the Council of Advanced Nurse Specialists in Psychiatric and Mental Health Nursing.

Harris is nationally recognized as one of the outstanding leaders in psychiatric nursing. Her excellence in scholarship and research was recognized at the 1978 ANA convention in Hawaii through a special award from the Council of Advanced Psychiatric Nursing Specialists. She has done outstanding work in the prevention, treatment, and rehabilitation of children and adults with mental health problems. Her clinical and research activities have been focused on the mental health needs of underserved areas and populations. Her publications reveal significant contributions to the development of an appropriate methodology for a study of nursing problems. One paper, which focuses on the definition of psychiatric nursing, raises issues for the field and proposes a paradigm for organizing curricula for the preparation of psychiatric nurses.

Harris has written numerous articles and chapters in books that focus on psychopathology and intervention methods. Currently, she is program director of an NIMH-awarded grant to train master's students to care for the severely disturbed and chronic mentally ill. Through her approach to the training of psychiatric nurses and her collaboration with an interdisciplinary team of clinicians, she is contributing to better quality care for the poor, minority, and neglected groups. During the academic year, 1983–84, Harris served as an administrative intern assigned to the president's office at Georgetown University in Washington, D.C. She had been selected from a nationwide competition as a fellow of the Academic Administrative Fellows Program, an internship program sponsored by the American Council on Education.

Additional appointments for Harris include: Chairperson, Cabinet on Human Rights, ANA; co-editor of the Textbook, *Psychiatric Nursing*, Philadelphia, Lippincott; Member, Advocacy Committee for Disabled Persons, State of Florida; Vice President, Board of Directors, Arnette House (a shelter for runaway youths), Ocala, Florida; Editorial Board Member, *Archives of Psychiatric Nursing* and *Nursing Outlook*; W.K. Kellogg Fellow; Consultant, W.K. Kellogg Foundation's Southern African Project.

1980 **Betty Smith Williams** (MN, Frances Payne Bolton School of Nursing, Case Western Reserve University, Cleveland, Ohio; Dr PH, School of Public Health, University of California, Los Angeles [Fig. 4–55]) was Dean and Professor, School of Nursing, University of Colorado Health Science Center, Denver, when she was admitted to the academy. She is now Professor, Department of Nursing, California State University, Long Beach.

Prior to her Colorado deanship, Williams held appointments as Assistant Dean, Student Affairs, and Assistant Dean, Academic Affairs, at the School of Nursing, University of California at Los Angeles. Her

Figure 4–55
Dr. Betty Smith Williams.

earlier academic positions included tenured assistant professor of Public Health Nursing at Mount Saint Mary College, Los Angeles, where she was hired in 1956, becoming the first black nurse to teach in a higher degree program in California.

Williams is committed to facilitating excellence in nursing practice. This commitment has been manifested in her choice of professional positions, in her research and publications, and in her active participation in professional and community organizations. Through her research, Williams has contributed to the body of nursing knowledge about quality care. Specifically, she has found that public health nursing interventions that raise the patient's level of self-esteem will reduce anxiety, decrease evasive behavior, and increase movement toward solution of the health problem. Her publications are in both clinical nursing and on problems associated with the recruitment and retention of ethnic students in nursing.

Acutely aware of the underrepresentation of ethnic persons in nursing, Williams founded the Council of Black Nurses, Inc., in 1968, in Los Angeles. She served as president for five years and on the executive board for ten more years. She is a founding member of the NBNA and has provided dynamic leadership substantive to its growth and development since its inception. She currently serves as national parliamentarian, chairperson of Bylaws Committee, member of the board of directors, and associate editor of the *Journal of National Black Nurses' Association*.

Williams is recognized as a nurse educator, leader, and as a person with concern for contemporary issues. She was on the original ANA

National Affirmative Action Task Force and was an original member of the ANA Commission on Human Rights. She is a member of the board of directors of Blue Cross of California. She was president and member of the board of directors of Operation Womanpower, Inc. She is a former national treasurer of Delta Sigma Theta Sorority, Inc., and president of its Telecommunications, Inc.

Honorary membership in Chi Eta Phi was bestowed upon Williams in 1985. Recipient of many awards and honors, she was recognized by the School of Public Health, University of California at Los Angeles, by the establishment in 1989 of the Betty Smith Williams Scholarship for graduate education of African-American students.

1981   **Ethelrine Shaw-Nickerson** (BS, Ohio State University School of Nursing, Columbus; PhD, Union Graduate School for Experimental Colleges & Universities, Cincinnati, Ohio [Fig. 4–56]) is Associate Professor Emerita, Ohio State University School of Nursing. She has also served as Distinguished Scholar, Virginia Commonwealth University Medical College of Virginia College of Nursing and as Visiting Professor, University of Delaware.

Shaw-Nickerson has made outstanding contributions to nursing in many areas. In addition to her work in nursing education and nursing practice, she has worked with state and national nursing organizations, on governmental regulations and federal support programs, and in the area of minority affairs. As a member of the review panel and as consultant to the Division of Nursing, Department of Health, Education, and Welfare, she added to the quality of nursing-degree programs throughout the country. In other work with DHEW, she helped professional schools develop greater sensitivity to the needs and contributions

Figure 4–56
Dr. Ethelrine Shaw-Nickerson.

of women, particularly black women. Her paper, "Professional Schools and Their Impact on Black Women," comes out of her work on the Women's Research Program and was published by the National Institute of Education.

Shaw-Nickerson was instrumental in the development and implementation of the National Student Nurses Association Breakthrough to Nursing project to improve opportunities for minorities to enter the nursing field. Her work on the ANA Task Force on Affirmative Action, which grew into the Commission on Human Rights, which she chaired, contributed to the progress made by ANA in this direction. Shaw-Nickerson was the president of the American Nurses' Foundation from 1985 to 1989. She also serves on the Advisory Committee of the ANA Minority Fellowship Programs.

Shaw-Nickerson was an active participant in the founding of the National Black Nurses' Association and in the formation of the American Indian Nurses' Association. In the state of Ohio, she pioneered the Human Rights Committee of the Ohio Nurses Association and has provided leadership to the nursing program at the university. She has developed several films, which are widely used to teach concepts of maternal-child health nursing.

Irene D. Lewis (Diploma, Mt. Zion Hospital School of Nursing, San Francisco, California; DNSc, University of California, San Francisco [Fig. 4–57]) was associate professor, graduate faculty, and associate dean for research at Rutgers—the State University of New Jersey, Newark when she was admitted to the academy. She is now Professor, San Jose State

Figure 4–57   Dr. Irene D. Lewis.

University, California, and Director of "Special People, Inc.," San Mateo, California.

Many of Lewis's contributions to nursing have come through her research. She has done several studies on hypertension, especially among aging blacks. More recently, she completed an 18-month study titled, "Self-Help and Advocacy for the Underserved Elderly," for which she received a $112,000 Administration on Aging grant. Numerous articles and presentations have resulted from these studies. Lewis has helped conduct several workshops, including "Hypertension Management in the Black Family" at the National Health Educational Center, Oakland, California, and "Hypertension: An Update in San Francisco" for the Bay Nurses' Association. She has also given a number of speeches across the country, including "Regimen Management in Hypertension: Issues in Field Research" in Washington, D.C., before the Clinical Medicine Section of the National Gerontological Society, and "Role of the Patient in Hypertension Compliance," before the United Community Center, San Francisco. For *Health and the Black Aged*, 1977, she served as co-editor and wrote a chapter entitled "The Study of Hypertension Compliance in a Group of Elderly Third World Patients." She coauthored a chapter entitled "Health Problems of the Minority Elderly: Special Needs and Services" in *Comprehension Service Delivery Systems for the Minority Aged*. In community nursing, Lewis developed a system for making safe home visits in "at-risk" communities. This system was detailed in "Making Safe Home Visits," which she coauthored with J. Hallburg for the July–August 1980 issue of *Urban Health*.

Among Lewis's honors are the John B. Harris Award, University of California, San Francisco, for outstanding contributions on human rights activities and teaching and a National Research Fellowship Award by the National Institute of Mental Health. She has also been appointed to the NIMH Task Force on Nursing.

Barbara Logan (AA, Bronx Community College Department of Nursing; PhD, Northwestern University [Fig. 4–58]) is Associate Professor, University of Illinois, Chicago. Logan's contributions to nursing have come in varied areas. On two occasions, she discussed teenage pregnancy as a special consultant on ABC television programs, sponsored by the University of Illinois Consultation Series. A version of these programs was also aired on local radio stations. For three years, she served as chairperson to the Community Mental Health Advisory Board of a Chicago Medical center, where she brought the nursing perspective to a multidisciplinary group of mental health care providers and community representatives.

Logan has made a number of presentations to various groups: "Socialization and Professional Isolation of Black Nurses" at the ANA convention in 1976; "The Black Family: A Social Unit of Survival" at the

Figure 4–58   Dr. Barbara Logan.

National Black Nurses' Association; "Politics, the Art of the Possible—Possible Areas for Nurse Input in the Legislative Process" at the ANA Fellow's Symposium in Washington, D.C.; and "Perspectives on the Black Culture: Implications for Health Care" at the Philippine Nurses' Association.

Logan coauthored an article with Barbara Dancy, entitled "Unwed Pregnant Adolescents: Their Mother's Dilemma," in *Dynamics of Role Making: Family Studies for Nursing*, edited by Kathleen Knafl and Helen K. Grace, 1978. Logan convened an Ethnicity and Health Research interest group at the Fifth Midwest Conference in 1981. Her sabbatical leave, January to July 1983, was spent as associate professor at the Fanon Research and Development Center, Charles R. Drew Postgraduate Medical School and at the Center for Afro-American Studies, University of California, Los Angeles. This sabbatical gave her an opportunity to continue her own research, which is designed to explore intra-ethnic differences of urban black American families in such areas as the availability and use of support systems, health benefits, and health behaviors.

Logan was the recipient of an ANA Minority Fellowship. While a doctoral student, she served as a legislative intern to Congressman Ralph Metcalfe during the summer of 1978. In 1988, she was a Martin Luther King/Rosa Parks Visiting Scholar, University of Michigan School of Nursing, Ann Arbor.

Patricia E. Sloan (BS, Ohio State University School of Nursing, Columbus; EdD, Teachers College, Columbia University, New York [Fig. 4–59]) was acting chairperson and professor in the graduate department

Figure 4–59   Dr. Patricia E. Sloan.

at the School of Nursing, Hampton University, Hampton, Virginia, when she was admitted to the academy. She is now Chairperson, department of Undergraduate Nursing Education at Hampton, and director of the M. Elizabeth Carnegie Nursing Archives.

In 1977, Sloan established the M. Elizabeth Carnegie Nursing Archives. She had collected historical information by and about black nurses and early black nursing schools and interviewed nurses about their education. She presented the rationale for the development of a separate collection to the college president and received final approval on April 9, 1977. These were the first archives designed to centralize historical data by and about black nurses and their educational institutions, categorized under oral histories, trends and correspondence, and photographs.

Among Sloan's publications are "Commitment to Equality: A View of Early Black Nursing schools," in *Historical Studies in Nursing* by M. Louise Fitzpatrick (ed.), New York, Teachers College Press, 1978; "The Real vs. Ideal Content in Master's Curricula," *Nursing Outlook*, November 1980; "Essential Content in Master's Degree Nursing Programs" in *Nursing Education Research in the South*; "Why Minority Group Members Should Pursue Higher Education" in *They came and They Conquered*, by Frank Hale (ed.), Ohio State University Press; and "Geneva Estelle Massey Osborne" in *American Nursing*, by Vern Bullough et al. (eds.).

Sloan's presentations of papers include "Early Black Nursing Schools: Predictors of our Professional Future," at the NBNA, 1977; "Early Black Nursing Schools: Impact on Health Promotion," University of Pennsyl-

Figure 4–60
Dr. Beverly Bonaparte.

vania, 1981; "Black Hospitals and Nurse Training Schools: The Formative Years, 1886–1906," at the Berkshire Conference of Women Historians, Vassar College, 1981; and "Black Nursing Education: A Selected Oral History," and "The Piedmont Sanatorium School of Nursing: 1918–1960," in 1990, both at the Missouri Valley History Conference, Omaha, Nebraska.

1982 **Beverly Bonaparte** (AAS, Queens College Department of Nursing, Flushing, NY; PhD, New York University [Fig. 4–60]) was Dean and Professor, Lienhard School of Nursing at Pace University, Pleasantville, New York, when she was inducted into the academy. From 1986 to 1989, she was Assistant Vice President, Corporate Nursing Services, New York City Health and Hospitals Corporation.

Before going to Pace University, Bonaparte had been assistant professor at Hunter College School of Nursing, New York, and associate professor at New York University. Her earlier administrative experience includes work as an interim director of the Public Health Outreach Program at Phebe Hospital, Liberia, West Africa; a clinical specialist in medical and surgical nursing at Long Island Jewish-Hillside Medical Canter; and an associate director of nursing service and assistant evening administrator at Whitestone Hospital.

Bonaparte has been particularly concerned about health care delivery to minority populations. This concern has been demonstrated not only in her work in the United States but at her Liberian post as well. She has published two articles on this subject: "Understanding Culture: Nursing in a Developing Country," *Imprint*, December 1978; and "Ego Defensiveness, Open-Closed Mindedness and Nurses' Attitudes Toward Culturally Different Patients," *Nursing Research*, May–June 1979. Her concern for minority affairs is evident in her work for the Association of Black Women in Higher Education, a support network devoted to the professional development of black women. Bonaparte's efforts in the association have recently earned her a place on its board.

Bonaparte has given numerous speeches in the United States and other countries: Trinidad and Tobago, Israel, and Spain. She is a member of the Editorial Review Panel and the Editorial Advisory Committee of *Nursing Research*, has been a member of the board of trustees of Iona College, New Rochelle, New York, and is on the board of directors of NEF and the board of trustees of St. Cabrini Nursing Home, Dobbs Ferry, New York.

At the 1989 NLN Convention in Seattle, Bonaparte was elected to the board of directors. In addition to having her own international consultant firm, The Gladstone Group, she is director of the Mid-Atlantic Regional Nursing Association.

1984   **Hazel W. Johnson-Brown** (Diploma, Harlem Hospital School of Nursing, New York; PhD, The Catholic University of America, Washington, D.C. [Fig. 4–61]), retired Chief, Army Nurse Corps, with the rank of brigadier general (the first black woman general in U.S. military history), is Professor and Director, Center for Health Policy, George Mason University School of Nursing, Fairfax, Virginia, and is the former director of the ANA Division of Governmental Affairs. In her ANA position, she helped to influence legislation and develop a more professional relationship between the ANA, Congress, the White House, and nursing.

Figure 4–61
Dr. Hazel Johnson-Brown.

Johnson-Brown's dissertation, "A Description of the Administrative Activities of the Director of Nursing Service in Selected General Hospitals, as described by the Director of Nursing Service, the Hospital Administrator, and the Medical Director," has been used by nurses nationally and internationally—it was recently requested by nurses from some South African states. Among Johnson-Brown's many honors are the Distinguished Service Award for "Total commitment to promulgating the highest standard of nursing practice to insure the quality of patient care," and her honorary doctorate and Alumni Achievement Award from the College of Nursing, Villanova University which states, "You have served nursing and your country and have exemplified the highest quality of professionalism." She also has been awarded the Alumni Award for Government Work from The Catholic University of America.

Carolyn McCraw Carter (Diploma, St. Francis Hospital School of Nursing, Pittsburgh, Pennsylvania; PhD, University of Pittsburgh [Fig. 4–62]) is a retired Associate Professor of Psychiatric Mental Health Nursing and Assistant Dean of Student Affairs and Special Projects, School of Medicine, University of Pittsburgh. In this joint faculty appointment of nursing and medicine, Carter not only taught and conducted research, but also provided consultation to faculty and students on ethnicity and health care and did interdisciplinary collaboration.

When Carter became the recipient of the ANA Mahoney Award in 1976, she was Assistant Professor, University of Cincinnati College of Nursing and Health Care—the first black—where, in addition to her faculty responsibilities, she designed and implemented a Minority Recruitment Project funded by the Center for Minority Group Affairs,

Figure 4–62
Dr. Carolyn McCraw Carter.

NIMH. In 1973, special recognition of her expertise found Carter serving as the only nurse consultant to the Special Action Office of Drug Abuse Prevention, Executive Office of the White House. She was a member of a seven-person team to evaluate drug use among adolescent dependents of American military and civilian employees at Clark Air Force Base, Republic of the Philippines.

Carter is proudest of the following accomplishments: increasing the number of black graduates at the University of Cincinnati College of Nursing and Health, at the University of Pittsburgh School of Nursing, and at the University of Pittsburgh School of Medicine.

1986 **Barbara Nichols** (Diploma, Massachusetts General Hospital School of Nursing, Boston; MS, University of Wisconsin, Madison [Fig. 4–63]) was Secretary, Wisconsin Department of Regulation and Licensing—a cabinet-level post—when she was inducted into the academy.

Nichols has held 23 offices in professional associations, including two terms (1978–1982) as president of the ANA and one term as president of the American Society of Health Care Education. She is the 1986 recipient of the ANA Honorary Recognition Award; Member, Board of Directors, International Council of Nurses; and serves on the board of the American Journal of Nursing Company. In addition, she is the recipient of four honorary doctoral degrees and numerous awards of achievement for her contributions to the nursing profession. Since 1989, Nichols has held the position of Executive Director, California Nurses' Association.

Figure 4–63   Barbara Nichols.

1987 **May Louise Wykle** (Diploma, Ruth Brant School of Nursing, Martins Ferry Hospital, Martins Ferry, Ohio; PhD, Case Western Reserve University, Cleveland, Ohio [Fig. 4–64]) is Florence Cellar Professor, Frances Payne Bolton School of Nursing, Case Western Reserve University. Within the university, she holds positions as Director, Center on Aging and Health; Chairperson, Gerontological Nursing; and Professor, Psychiatric Mental Health Nursing. She also serves as Chairperson, Administrative Association in Nursing, Hanna Pavilion, University Hospitals of Cleveland.

Wykle has recently been honored by receiving the John S. Diekhoff Award for Excellence in Graduate Teaching. In 1990, Wykle served as Chairperson, Nominating Committee, American Academy of Nursing; Member, Case Western Reserve University's Review Panel for the Brookdale National Fellowship Program; and Board Member, Western Reserve Area Agency on Aging in Cleveland, Ohio.

As a noted expert in the field of gerontological nursing, Wykle has made presentations at numerous seminars and workshops on issues affecting this growing population. She has also published extensively in professional journals in the area of gerontology and has chapters in several books. Wykle is coauthor of four books: *Counseling, Evaluation and Student Development in Nursing Education*, Philadelphia, Saunders; *Decision-Making in Long-term Care Factors in Planning*, New York, Springer; *Memory and Aging*, New York, Springer; and *Elderly Rehabilitation as Art and Science*, New York, Springer.

1988 **Beverly Malone** (BSN, University of Cincinnati, Ohio; PhD, University of Cincinnati [Fig. 4–65]) is Dean and Professor, North Car-

Figure 4–64   Dr. May Wykle.

Figure 4–65
Dr. Beverly Malone.

olina A&T State University School of Nursing, Greensboro. She is a
therapist in private practice and adjunct faculty at the Union for Experimenting Colleges and Universities.

Malone serves as president of the North Carolina Council of Deans
and Directors of Baccalaureate and Higher Degree Nursing Programs
in addition to holding membership in ANA (board member), the America Black Psychology Association, the American Association of Colleges
of Nursing, the Southern Council on Collegiate Education for Nursing
(board member), and the Association of Women Administrators. She
has published extensively in professional journals and has been a well-
received speaker at many conventions.

1990 **Clara L. Adams-Ender** (BS, North Carolina A & T State Uni-
versity School of Nursing, Greensboro; MMAS, Command and General
Staff College, Fort Leavenworth, Kansas [Fig. 4–66]) is Chief, Army
Nurse Corps, and Director, Personnel Directorate Office for the Surgeon
General. Prior to this appointment, she served as Chairperson, Depart-
ment of Nursing, Walter Reed Army Medical Center, Washington, D.C.

Brigadier General Adams-Ender serves as adjunct assistant professor
at the Oakland University School of Nursing, Rochester, Michigan, and
at Georgetown University School of Nursing in Washington, D.C. In
1989, she was honored by *Washingtonian Magazine* as one of the 100 Most
Powerful Women in Washington, D.C. Other honors bestowed upon her
include being the first army nurse officer to be graduated from the U.S.
Army War College and the first black female nurse to be awarded the

Figure 4–66   Brigadier General Clara Adams-Ender.

Military Art and Science Degree. She has published extensively in professional and lay journals and has held consultant positions to the Defense Advisory Committee on Women in the Services and the Frances Payne Bolton School of Nursing, Case Western Reserve University, Cleveland, Ohio.

M. Linda Burnes-Bolton (BSN, Arizona State University, Tempe, DrPH, UCLA School of Public Health, Los Angeles [Fig. 4–67]) is Director, Nursing Research and Development, Cedars-Sinai Medical Center, Los Angeles, California. She has conducted research in the area of adolescent pregnancy, recruitment and retention of disadvantaged students, and hospital staffing patterns and trends. Active as childbirth educator and basic life support educator, she has been involved in the development and implementation of a city-wide health educator project for senior citizens. She has also published widely.

Burnes-Bolton serves on the Advisory Board of California State University Los Angeles School of Nursing; California State Northridge University; Los Angeles Valley College; and the Office of Minority Health, U.S. Department of Health and Human Services. She is chair of the Recruitment for Action Committee of the Council for Black Nurses, National Black Nurses' Association, and is currently the second vice president of NBNA.

Juanita K. Hunter (Diploma, E. J. Meyer Memorial Hospital School of Nursing, Buffalo, New York; EdD, State University of New York at Buffalo [Fig. 4–68]) is Assistant Professor and Project Director, State

Figure 4–67   Figure 4–68   Dr. Juanita Hunter.
Dr. M. Linda Burnes-Bolton.

University of New York at Buffalo Nursing Department. She received an excellence award from the New York Statewide Joint Labor/Management Committee in recognition of her outstanding performance and service to the State University of New York at Buffalo and the State of New York and the Mabel K. Staupers Award by Omicron Chapter, Chi Eta Phi, for her outstanding contributions to the growth and development of nursing. Hunter has been selected by Sigma Theta Tau as a distinguished lecturer to address chapters on contemporary issues in nursing.

Hunter's commitment to the homeless and underserved has been demonstrated by her numerous research and investigatory projects, many of which were funded by the Department of Health and Human Services Division of Nursing. Hunter has coauthored *Continuity of Care for Individuals with Chronic Illness*, Lexington, Ginn, and a chapter in the book entitled *Nursing Issues and Nursing Strategies for the Eighties, New York, Springer*. She has published extensively in lay and professional journals and acts as peer reviewer of the *Journal of the National Black Nurses' Association*. As a renowned nursing leader, Hunter has been invited to address audiences nationwide and has provided insight on topics relative to nurses and the general public alike. In 1990, she acted as consultant to New York's Governor Mario M. Cuomo regarding the nursing shortage—the outcome public service announcement by Governor Cuomo, on recruitment into nursing, aired in March 1990. Hunter was co-chairperson of the ANA Leadership Development Task Force in 1989 and currently serves as chairperson of the Minority Focus Group on Entry into Practice.

Bernardine M. Lacey (Diploma, Mississippi Baptist Hospital School of Nursing, Jackson; MA, Howard University, Washington, D.C. [Fig. 4–69]) is the director of the Howard University College of Nursing Homeless Project, which is funded by the W. K. Kellogg Foundation. She is also an instructor in nursing administration at Howard University. In 1976, she was recognized for her work by the Maryland House of Representatives and named Outstanding Educator of America. Her media presentation on Howard University College of Nursing's Health Care for the Homeless Project produced by WHMM-TV is a culmination of the video, "Taking Nursing Education to the Streets," which she has presented to many audiences throughout the country.

Lacey is president-elect of the District of Columbia League for Nursing and serves as Commissioner, Mayor's Council on the Homeless.

Cora Newell-Withrow (BSN, Meharry Medical College School of Nursing, Nashville, Tennessee; DSN, University of Alabama [Fig. 4–70]) is Professor and Chairperson, Department of Nursing, Berea College, Berea, Kentucky. In her position at Berea College, Newell-Withrow has demonstrated her commitment to continuing education and retention of minority students. Her effectiveness is reflected in the school's overall NCLEX scores, evaluation from employers, and the abilities of the graduates to function well beyond the entry level in practice.

Newell-Withrow's academic and professional commitment to health care is reflected in her initiation of the Charles P. Drew Comprehensive Health Center in a low-income, African-American community in the

Figure 4–69   Bernardine M. Lacy.

Figure 4–70
Dr. Cora Newell-Withrow.

1960s, long before government mandates. For nearly three decades, Newell-Withrow has contributed to nursing practice, research, and publications on school health and community health nursing. She has published her work in the *Journal of Comprehensive Pediatrics, Adolescence, Journal of Pediatric Health Care,* and *Academic Leader.*

Jeannette O'Neal Poindexter (Diploma, Homer G. Phillips Hospital School of Nursing, St. Louis, Missouri; PhD, University of Michigan, Ann Arbor, [Fig. 4–71]) is Associate Dean of Academic Affairs and Associate Professor, Wayne State University College of Nursing, Detroit, Michigan. She served as Dean, Prairie View A & M University College of Nursing, Houston, Texas, from 1982 to 1984. Currently (1990), Poindexter is a consultant for the Nursing Education Program in Botswana, southern Africa, a project funded by the W. K. Kellogg Foundation.

Poindexter's involvement in the area of maternal-child health is reflected in her research and publications, which include such topics as teenage pregnancy, youth programs, homeless shelters, and child abuse prevention. She is currently co-principal investigator in research involving predicting teenage pregnancy. This research is funded by the Bureau of Maternal and Child Health and Resources Development. Poindexter's work has been published in the *American Journal of Nursing, Journal of Professional Nursing,* and *Journal of Health Education.*

Among Poindexter's many honors and awards is the recognition by the ANA Minority Fellowship Program as one of 1990's "Outstanding Women of Color."

Figure 4–71   Dr. Jeannette O'Neal Poindexter.

Dorothy E. Ramsey (Diploma, Jewish Hospital and Medical Center of Brooklyn School of Nursing, New York; EdD, Teachers College, Columbia University, New York [Fig.4–72]) is a tenured associate professor at Adelphi University School of Nursing, Garden City, New York.

Ramsey was awarded a $10,000 grant by the Zlinkoff and Dolen Fund for Medical Research and Education at Adelphi University in 1990 for research into early assessment of neonates for hearing deficits. She was

Figure 4–72
Dr. Dorothy E. Ramsey.

also the recipient of the New York State Nurses' Association Membership Award for outstanding contributions to the objectives and programs of the association and the profession and of the Mabel K. Staupers Award for "Outstanding Leadership in Nursing" by Chi Eta Phi Sorority, Inc., New York.

Ramsey's research has been published widely and her interest in community services led her to a position of mentor with the New York City Board of Education Monitoring Project at Andrew Jackson High School, working with a student, the student's family, and school officials, and assisting with personal and academic progress. She also serves as a consultant for high risk families at the Carter Community Health Center, Jamaica, New York. As a member of ANA, Ramsey has served on the nominating committee and as a delegate to the house of delegates.

Honorary Fellows

Estelle M. Osborne. In 1978, Estelle M. Osborne (Fig. 4–73) was the first black nurse to be inducted in the American Academy of Nursing as an honorary fellow, and in 1984, she was inducted into the ANA Hall of Fame. The following is the complete text of the statement read in 1982 at the memorial service for deceased fellows.

In Memoriam

Estelle Massey Riddle Osborne, honorary fellow of the American Academy of Nursing, died December 12, 1981, in California at the age of 80 following a long illness.

During her distinguished career in nursing, Mrs. Osborne made lasting contributions to nursing in the areas of teaching; public health; educational administration; nursing service administration; organizational administration, consultation, and research; publications; and public service in local and nationwide communities. Mrs. Osborne's teaching experience occurred on all levels—from elementary school in rural Texas prior to entering nursing, to high school in Kansas City, Missouri, to diploma programs at Lincoln and Harlem in New York, to New York University Division of Nurse Education as assistant professor. Her first experience after graduating from nursing school was with the St. Louis Municipal Visiting Nurses. Upon earning the master's degree in 1931 from Teachers College, she served as educational director at Freedmen's Hospital School of Nursing in Washington, D.C. At the invitation of the board of directors of the nursing program from which she was graduated, Mrs. Osborne became the first black director of nursing at Homer G. Phillips Hospital in St. Louis.

Realizing the odds against the black nurse in the areas of education, employment, and organized nursing, Mrs. Osborne joined forces with other members of the National Association of Colored Graduate Nurses (NACGN) to fight discrimination on all those fronts. Not

Figure 4–73   Estelle M. Osborne,
Honorary Fellow, 1978.

only did she provide leadership as president for five years, striking hard for principles and convictions, but she was instrumental in securing financial support for NACGN from such sources as the Rosenwald Fund, the Rockefeller Foundation, and personal affluent friends among whom was Frances Payne Bolton of Ohio. Having been the recipient of two Julius Rosenwald fellowships to complete her bachelor's and master's degrees, Mrs. Osborne was invited by Rosenwald to join a team of scholars, called social explorers, to the rural South to do a behavioristic study in health and welfare, thus giving her experience in research.

During the years of Word War II, Mrs. Osborne opened many doors of opportunity for black nurses while serving officially as consultant on the staff of the National Nursing Council for War Service—the organization responsible for laying the groundwork for the Cadet Nurse Corps. After the war, she ran for election for the board of directors of the American Nurse' Association, won and served four years, 1948–1952. In this capacity, she was ANA's delegate to the International Congress of Nurses in Stockholm, Sweden, in 1949. While on the ANA Board, she served on the Board of the American Journal of Nursing Company. Mrs. Osborne also served as a member of the Federal Citizens Committee to the United States on Education and as a member of the Advisory Committee to the Surgeon General, United States Public Health Service.

With such a rich background in education, nursing service, community health, research, and organizational affairs, it was logical that Mrs. Osborne would be invited shortly after the establishment of the National League for Nursing to join the staff (1954) in an administrative capacity. She retired 12 years later (1966) as Associate General Director and Director of Services to State Leagues.

Mrs. Osborne was a prolific writer with articles to her credit in the *American Journal of Nursing, Public Health Nursing, Journal of Negro Education, Harpers, Opportunity Magazine, Crisis,* and the *Trained Nurse and Hospital Review.* Her life story has been included in many books and periodicals. She did not confine her voluntary activities to the nursing community. She extended herself to the broader community serving such organizations as the National Council of Negro Women (1st Vice-President); the National Urban League; the Legal Defense Fund of the National Association for the Advancement of Colored People (board); Alpha Kappa Alpha Sorority; Women's Africa Committee; the United Mutual Life Insurance Company (board); and other civic associations.

In recognition of her contributions, Mrs. Osborne received numerous honors and awards; the Mary Mahoney Award (1946) for opening opportunities for the black nurse to move into the mainstream of professional nursing; the establishment of the Estelle Massey Scholarship at Fisk University, Nashville, in recognition of her contributions to community life; Nurse of the Year by the New York University Division of Nurse Education (1959); and Honorary Life Membership Award, Nursing Education Alumni Association, Teachers College, Columbia University (1976); and Honorary member, Omicron Chapter, Chi Eta Phi Sorority. These are in addition to the many testimonials in her lifetime, tapes, and documentary films.

Mrs. Osborne was a great lady and a pioneer in nursing who exemplified the ideal for all nurses regardless of race . . . a lady who carried out her personal and professional responsibilities with dignity, majesty, sincerity, and warmth. In appreciation of her many contributions, Academy Fellows enter this tribute in the records of the American Academy of Nursing. [Written and presented by Mary Elizabeth Carnegie at the 1982 Annual Meeting of the American Academy of Nursing, Portland, Oregon, September 1982.]

Marie Bourgeois (Diploma, Freedmen's Hospital School of Nursing, Washington, D.C.; PhD, The Catholic University of America, Washington, D.C. [Fig. 4–74]) was admitted to the American Academy of Nursing as an honorary fellow in 1982. At that time, she was assistant professor in the nursing administration major at Georgetown University in Washington, D.C. She performs consultant work in nursing education nationally and internationally for directors and administrators concerned with doctoral programs in nursing and for nurses at the baccalaureate and master's level who are preparing for a career in nursing research. She has been instrumental in assisting 276 graduate nurses complete their doctoral training, providing encouragement and consultation about career patterns, goals, and the scientific merit of the doctoral degree. Currently, Bourgeois is adjunct Associate Professor, Graduate Program, Howard University College of Nursing, Washington, D.C.

Bourgeois is one of the most recognized nurse researchers in the United States in predoctoral and postdoctoral training. As a former chief of the Research Training Section of the Nursing Research Branch, Di-

Figure 4–74   Dr. Marie Bourgeois,
Honorary Fellow, 1982.

vision of Nursing, Department of Health, Education, and Welfare, she founded and administered the National Research Service Awards Fellowship Program, which provided funding for nurses in predoctoral and postdoctoral studies throughout the nation. She was the organizer of the National Conference on Doctoral Education for Nurses in 1971, which resulted in a publication entitled *Future Directions of Doctoral Education for Nurses*. This conference had a significant impact on fostering doctoral study for nurses and the promotion of the development of doctoral programs in nursing. The conference focused the attention of the nursing community nationally on the goals and objectives of doctoral education for nurses.

In the field of doctoral education for nurses, Bourgeois has presented numerous papers before various assemblies and has published a number of reports and articles, including "The Special Nurse Research Fellow: Characteristics and Recent Trends," published in *Nursing Research* in 1975; "Research Training Beyond the Doctoral Degree," co-authored with Phillips and Wood, in *Glowing Lamp*, 1987; and *The Fifty Year Graduates of Freedmen's Hospital Tell Their Story, 1913–1935*, published in 1987.

Bourgeois has maintained her interest in anthropology, the field in which she did her doctoral studies. She has written several articles and has presented papers on the relationships between nursing and anthropology. She was on the board of directors of the Anthropological Society of Washington, D.C., from 1973 to 1976 and became president in 1979. She is also a fellow of the American Anthropological Association.

Bourgeois organized a workshop presented at the National Boulé of Chi Eta Phi Sorority in Washington, D.C., in 1982, on "The Role of the Black Nurse in Health Care Delivery." She also organized a workshop on "The Effect of Budgetary Constraints on Black Schools of Nursing," given at the National Meeting of the Freedmen's Hospital School of Nursing Alumni in June 1982.

For outstanding leadership in the Health Resources Administration National Research Award Programs for Nurses and for expediting the training of nurse scientists nationwide, Bourgeois received the administration's Distinguished Administrative Award. She has also received the Certificate of Merit for Distinguished Service for her work as a member of the ANF Board of Trustees, and she was made an Honorary Fellow, Academy of Science, Washington, D.C. In 1985, she received the Black Women's Outstanding Special Service Award from the Institute for Urban Affairs and Research, Howard University, Washington, D.C.

The biographical sketches presented speak for themselves of the worthiness of these black nurses, not only in terms of their professional achievements, but also for their many contributions to the profession and to society as a whole. It should be noted that 21 of the 38 black fellows are graduates of 14 historically black nursing schools: Homer G. Phillips, Meharry, and North Carolina A & T—three each; Tuskegee— two; and one each from Dillard, Mercy, Hampton, Lincoln in New York, Kansas City Number 2 in Missouri, Provident in Chicago, Florida A & M, Harlem, Freedmen's, and Mississippi Baptist.

REGIONAL NURSING ORGANIZATIONS

The "Directory of Nursing Organizations," in the April 1990 issue of the *American Journal of Nursing*, lists five regional nursing organizations: the Mid-Atlantic Regional Nursing Association, the Midwest Alliance in Nursing, the New England Organization for Nursing, the Southern Council on Collegiate Education for Nursing (affiliated with the Southern Regional Education Board), and the Western Institute of Nursing. Two of these five, the Southern Regional Education Board (SREB) and the Mid-Atlantic Regional Nursing Association (MARNA), are presented here because they have black chief executive officers—Dr. Eula Aiken with SREB and Dr. Beverly Bonaparte with MARNA.

Southern Regional Education Board

Formal provision for interstate cooperation was built into the Constitution of the United States in 1787 (Article 1, Section 10) by the Founding Fathers. This compact clause permitted the states, with the consent of Congress, to enter into agreements with each other on many matters which, at first, were mostly political in nature—settlement of boundary disputes, apportionment of water, and so forth. It was not until 1948, when the southern states entered into an interstate compact and created the Southern Regional Education Board for the purpose of improving higher education in the South, that nursing began to benefit from this consitutional provision (Carnegie, 1968).

Nursing had been represented on the SREB at the outset with the appointment by the respective state governors of two nurses: Mary Elizabeth Carnegie, Dean, Florida A & M College School of Nursing, Tallahassee, and Frances Helen Ziegler, Dean, Vanderbilt University School of Nursing, Nashville. Through the efforts of these two, along with Alma Gault, Dean, Meharry Medical College School of Nursing, Nashville, nursing became a vital part of SREB in 1950, beginning with a Committee on Graduate Education and Research in Nursing. In 1962, the collegiate nursing programs in the region, which had been focusing mostly on graduate education, began to consider a broad range of issues on nursing education and research. The need for a formal communication network among the institutions and between SREB and the institutions prompted the formation of the SREB Council on Collegiate Education for Nursing (Spector, 1987). By 1975, the council had become an independent, self-supporting organization within the structure of SREB. In affiliation with SREB, the council engages in "cooperative regional planning and activities to strengthen nursing education in colleges and universities in the South" (Reitt, 1987, p. 111).

In 1972, Eula Aiken joined the professional staff of SREB as a project director. In 1990, she succeeded Audrey Spector, who had retired in 1989 as Executive Director, Southern Council on Collegiate Education for Nursing. For five years before then, Aiken had directed SREB's Continuing Nursing Education in Computer Technology project, a Nursing Spiral Project Grant, No. DIONU24198, awarded by the Division of Nursing, U.S. Department of Health and Human Services.

Mid-Atlantic Regional Nursing Association

Funded by the Division of Nursing, HHS, as a special project grant, and established officially in 1981, MARNA is a nonprofit regional nursing association in the Mid-Atlantic area, encompassing the five jurisdictions of Delaware, New Jersey, New York, Pennsylvania, and Washington, D.C. The purpose of MARNA is to improve the quantity and quality for nursing personnel in the region through collaborative endeavors designed to promote education, service, and research in nursing.

From its inception, MARNA has had black nurses as executive officers and on its governing board and staff. In 1990, Dr. Beverly Bonaparte became the chief executive officer.

SELECTED SPECIALTY ORGANIZATIONS

Originally, the plan for this chapter was not only to present the national general nursing organizations, but also to include all the specialty organizations in nursing. Upon review of the large number of specialty organizations included in the *1990 Directory of Nursing Organizations* in the *American Journal of Nursing*, it became prohibitive to try to deal with them all. The organizations to be discussed have thus been limited to the four that have or have had black nurse presidents: the American Association of Nurse Anesthetists, the Association of Operating Room Nurses, the National Federation of Planned Parenthood, and the American Academy of Ambulatory Nursing Administration.

Goldie Brangman (Fig. 4–75), director emerita of the School of Anesthesia at Harlem Hospital, New York, served as president of the American Association of Nurse Anesthetists from 1973 to 1974. **Barba Edwards,**

Figure 4–75   Goldie Brangman, President, American Association of Nurse Anesthetists, 1973–1974.

Director of Surgery, Archbishop Bergan Mercy Hospital, Omaha, Nebraska, served as elected president of the Association of Operating Room Nurses from 1976 to 1977.

The National Federation of Planned Parenthood has had a black president, **Faye Wattleton** (BS, Ohio State University School of Nursing, Columbus; MS, Columbia University, New York [Fig. 4–76]), since 1978. Wattleton, also a certified nurse-midwife, frequently appears on television and speaks before large groups. She constantly travels to keep tabs on the organization's 26,000 staff members at 860 clinics in 49 states (Great Catches, 1990). The Planned Parenthood $300 million nonprofit health care organization was started in 1916 by a nurse, Margaret Sanger. Sanger fought in the early part of the century for revision of archaic legislation that prohibited publication of facts about contraception, and she opened the first birth control clinic in America. She was admitted to the ANA Hall of Fame in 1976. The federation is based on the principle that every individual has the fundamental right to choose when or whether to have a child.

The American Academy of Ambulatory Nursing Administration (AAANA) was founded in 1978 as a voluntary membership, nonprofit, educational forum for nurses with responsibility in ambulatory care. The AAANA serves as a vital resource for nurses who want to develop the highest level of leadership, management, and administrative skills in ambulatory care settings. The academy is committed to the advancement of ambulatory nursing administration and practice and to the promotion

Figure 4–76   Faye Wattleton, President, National Federation of Planned Parenthood.

of educational programs for personal and professional growth. Its goal is to promote health and wellness of mankind by advancing the science and art of ambulatory nursing administration and practice. **Betty Redwine** (AD, Front Range Community College, Denver, Colorado; BS, Regis College of Denver [Fig. 4–77]) is a charter member of AAANA and served as president from 1987 to 1988.

SUMMARY

Black nurses have always taken pride in helping to promote the professionalization of nursing. This chapter has addressed the trials and tribulations of black nurses fighting against the odds for recognition in the key nursing organizations, particualarly the American Nurses' Association. Black organizations have also been included, along with two regional bodies that have black chief executive officers and several specialty organizations that have or have had black nurses in top leadership roles.

REFERENCES

ANA presidency is rigorous, exhilarating. (1982). *American Nurse, 14*, 13.
American Academy of Nursing mission statement. (1990). Kansas City: American
    Academy of Nursing.

Figure 4–77   Betty Redwine.

American Nurses' Association convention proceedings. (1972). New York: American Nurses' Association.

Bourne, S. T. (1989). Mabel K. Staupers Spingarn Medalist dies at 99. *Crisis, 96(10)*, 37, 39.

Carnegie, M. E. (1952). Using the nursing abilities study in curriculum planning. *American Journal of Nursing, 52*, 1482–1486.

Carnegie, M. E. (1968). *Interstate cooperation in nursing. Nursing Outlook, 16*, 48–49.

Christ, E. A. (1957). *Missouri's nurses*. Jefferson City: Missouri Nurses' Association.

Dock, L. A. (1912). *A history of nursing*, (Vol. III). New York: G. P. Putnam, Sons.

First annual report of the American Society of Superintendents of Training Schools for Nurses. (1987). New York: National League for Nursing.

Fitzpatrick, M. L. (1975). *The National Organization for Public Health Nursing, 1912–1952, development of a practice field*. New York: National League for Nursing.

Flanagan, L. (1976). *One strong voice, the story of the American Nurses' Association*. Kansas City: American Nurses' Association.

Fondiller, S. H. (1989). *The vision, the reality: A history of AACN's first 20 years: 1969–1989*. Washington, D.C.: American Association of Colleges of Nursing.

Fondiller, S. H. (1990). Nursing's journal 1900–1990. *American Journal of Nursing, 90(10)*, 18, 22, 33, 40, 42, 46, 50, 56, 60, 68, 74, 80, 84, 94, 96, 98.

Gist, N. P. (1940). *Secret societies: A cultural study of fraternalism in the United States*. University of Missouri: Columbia.

Great catches for the over 40 crowd. (1990). *Ebony.* 45(11), 72.

Hughes, L. (1962). *Fight for freedom*. New York: W.W. Norton & Company.

Jamieson, E. M., & Sewall, M. (1944). *Trends in nursing history*. Philadelphia: W.B. Saunders.

Massey (Osborne), E. (1934). The Negro nurse student. *American Journal of Nursing, 34*, 806–810.

Minor, I., & Shaw, E. (1973), ANA and affirmative action. *American Journal of Nursing, 73*, 1738–1739.

National Student Nurses' Association bylaws. (1972). New York: National Student Nurses' Association.

Nursing research report. (1976). Kansas City: American Nurses' Foundation.

Reitt, B. B. (1987). *The first 25 years of the Southern Council on Collegiate Education for Nursing (SCCEN)*. Atlanta: Southern Council on Collegiate Education for Nursing.

Report of NOPHN council on Negro nursing. (1942). NOPHN Archive Microfilm, No. 17.

Roberts, M. M. (1954). *American nursing: History and Interpretation*. New York: Macmillan.

Seymer, L. B. (1933). *A general history of nursing*. New York: Macmillan.

Spector, A. F. (1987). Preface. *In the first 25 years of Southern Council on Collegiate*

Education for Nursing (SCCEN). Atlanta: Southern Council on Collegiate Education for Nursing.

Staupers, M. K. (1951). Story of the National Association of Colored Graduate Nurses. *American Journal of Nursing, 51,* 222–223.

Staupers, M. K. (1961). *No time for prejudice*. New York: Macmillan.

Summary of proceedings, ANA convention. (1982). Kansas City: American Nurses' Association.

Smith, G. R. (1975). From invisibility to blackness; the story of the National Black Nurses' Association. *American Journal of Nursing, 23,* 225–229.

The evolution of nursing professional organizations: Alternatives for the future. (1987). Kansas City: American Academy of Nursing.

This is ANA. (1975). Kansas City: American Nurses' Association.

Chapter 5

Stony the Road

Brown (1948) in her report, *Nursing for the Future*, pointed out that specialists in clinical nursing would be needed "if the profession is to look forward to a sound, healthy development" (p. 95). It was not until ten years later that the American Nurses' Association set the goal "to establish ways within ANA to provide formal recognition of personal achievement and superior performance." This was the origin of ANA's certification program, which is a part of its credentialing system (Dunkley, 1974).

Credentialing mechanisms serve to provide assurance of quality to the various publics that individuals, programs, or institutions serve. Licensing of individual nurses and state approval of schools of nursing began with the first registration laws in 1903 in North Carolina, New York, New Jersey, and Virginia. The stated purpose of the bill in North Carolina, for example, was "to secure for future nurses better education in theory and such skill in practice that the public will have confidence in the registered nurse" (Wyche, 1938, p. 95). National accreditation of educational programs came later, and the first list of schools accredited by the National League of Nursing Education was published in 1941. Today, diploma, associate degree, baccalaureate, and master's degree programs are accredited by the National League for Nursing. However, certification of nurses who have specialized in a specific area of clinical practice is a recent development, beginning with the certification program of the ANA.

In May 1973, ANA formally announced the initiation of its nationwide certification program to recognize excellence in the clinical practice of nursing. Unlike certification programs that merely acknowledge educational attainments, ANA certification is based on three factors: assessment of knowledge, demonstration of competence in clinical practice, and endorsement by colleagues. With the administration of certification examinations in geriatric nursing and pediatric nursing in ambulatory health care in May 1974, and a psychiatric and mental health nursing examination in September of that year, ANA launched its recognition program. In January 1975, the first nurse-practitioners certified for excellence in clinical practice were honored with a formal ceremony (Flanagan, 1976). As of January 1990, there were over 72,000 registered nurses, including a number of black nurses, certified by the ANA in 19 specialty areas (Markway, 1990). Certification is valid for five years.

The first trained black nurses practiced before the profession had a credentialing system, and many were practicing before all of the states had passed licensing laws for nursing practice. In this chapter, the experiences of four such black nurses—Jessie Sleet Scales, the first black public health nurse; Elizabeth Tyler Barringer, the first black nurse employed at the Henry Street Visiting Nurse Service; and Edith Carter and Emma Wilson, later employed at Henry Street—are reported.

In 1936, the National Association of Colored Graduate Nurses established the Mary Mahoney Award to be given to "a nurse who had made outstanding contributions to the nursing profession and to the community, and who also had worked to improve the professional status of the Negro nurse, thereby helping to improve intergroup and interpersonal relations within the nursing profession" (Staupers, 1961, p. 35). In 1942, an exception was made, and the award was presented to a nonnurse, Ruth Logan Roberts, who had chaired NACGN's National Advisory Council and who had given freely of her time for the improvement of the professional status of the black nurse.

After NACGN dissolved in 1951 and the function of awarding the Mary Mahoney Award was assumed by the ANA, the criteria were changed to "a person, or group of persons, who in addition to making a significant contribution to nursing generally, has been outstandingly instrumental in achieving the opening and advancement of opportunities in nursing on the same basis to members of all races, creeds, colors, and national origins." These criteria do not limit the award to a black nurse(s) and in 1954, 1956, 1962, 1964, 1966, and 1986, the Mary Mahoney Award went to white nurses (see Appendix C).

It seems fitting, also, in this chapter to elaborate on the contributions of the early black nurses who were recipients of the Mary Mahoney Award when it was presented by the NACGN, for it was these pioneers who paved the way for the black nurse of today. References to five of the 13 nurse recipients appear in other chapters—Adah B. Thoms, the first recipient in 1936; Mabel Northcross; Susan Freeman; Estelle Osborne; and Mabel Staupers—so they will not be included in this chapter. The eight presented here are Nancy Lois Kemp, Carrie E. Bullock, Petra A. Pinn, Lula G. Warlick, Ellen Woods Carter, Ludie A. Andrews, Mary E. Merritt, and Eliza F. Pillars.

The origin of organized visiting nursing dates to 1859 in England. William Rathbone, a wealthy man, had employed Mary Robinson to nurse his wife during the last stages of her terminal illness. In his grief, Rathbone pondered the predicament of poor families, bereft of money and comfortable surroundings, who might be faced with long-term illness. He asked Robinson to try an experiment for three months, giving nursing care to families in the poorer quarters of Liverpool. In the United States, Lillian Wald is credited with founding visiting nursing in New York in 1893 with her establishment of the first nurses' settlement house, which developed into the Henry Street Visiting Nurse Service.

Thoms (1929), Roberts (1954), and Staupers (1961) report that **Jessie Sleet Scales** (Fig. 5-1) was the first black public health nurse in the United States. Scales, a native of Stratford, Ontario, Canada, and a graduate of the 1895 class of Provident Hospital School of Nursing in Chicago, had always had a strong desire to become a district nurse, a field of practice that had not been opened to black nurses. When she moved to New York, she applied to many agencies for employment in this area of practice, only to have the doors closed to her because of her race. As Morais (1967) points out in capturing the mood of the times, "That she was a graduate nurse when such nurses were a rarity meant nothing. That her skin was colored meant everything" (p. 71).

After discovering that none of the existing health organizations employed blacks, Scales finally appealed to the Charity Organization Society. The society's tuberculosis committee had become concerned about the high incidence of tuberculosis among the black population of New York City and thought that a black nurse could persuade the victims to seek treatment. With this in mind, Scales was employed on October 3, 1900, for a two-month trial period. She performed her duties so well that after a year she was given a permanent position, which she held for nine years.

The first volume of the *American Journal of Nursing* contains a copy of Scale's report on her work as a district nurse among black people of New York City for a two-month period in 1900. The following is an excerpt, submitted for publication by her superior:

> Visiting 41 sick families, caring for 9 cases of consumption, 4 cases of peritonitis, 2 cases of chicken pox, 2 of cancer, one diphtheria, 2 heart disease, 2 tumor, one gastric catarrh, 2 pneumonia, 4 rheumatism, 2 cases of scalp wound. . . . Other cases might be spoken of, but the above is a specimen of the work. . . . I cannot but feel that this house-to-house visiting, these face-to-face practical talks which I am having with the people, must bring about good results. They have welcomed me to their homes, saying, We don't know you, but we belong to the same race. They have listened to me with attention and respect, and if the advice which I gave was not always accepted, in no case was it readily rejected. [A Successful Experiment, 1901, p. 729]

Figure 5–1   Jessie Sleet Scales, first black public health
nurse.

The editor of the *American Journal of Nursing* described Scales as "a young colored woman and a trained nurse, whose genuine altruism and intelligence in social reform work has impressed with admiration her acquaintances and friends, one of whom ventures, without her knowledge, to make this record of her work."

Many black nurses performed significant roles and made valuable contributions to the development of visiting nurse service. Three who are singled out for their work are Elizabeth Tyler Barringer, Edith Carter, and Emma Wilson.

In 1906, **Elizabeth Tyler Barringer** (Fig. 5-2), a graduate of Freedmen's Hospital School of Nursing in Washington, D.C., was appointed to the staff of the Henry Street Visiting Nurse Service (renamed the Visiting Nurse Service of New York) by Lillian Wald, the founder, who also had become concerned about blacks' high morbidity and mortality rates from tuberculosis and their high maternal and infant death rates. Soon, two more black nurses were employed: **Edith Carter** and **Emma Wilson,** also from Freedmen's. A news item in the September 1906 issue of the *American Journal of Nursing* reported this item:

Figure 5–2 Elizabeth Tyler Barringer, first black nurse on staff of Henry Street Visiting Nurse Service.

From Miss Dock, we learn that the Nurses' Settlement in New York is happy in several important additions to its work. A most gratifying and needed extension in the Visiting Nurse Service had been made in an upper west side region where the colored people live. Salaries have been given for two nurses who are also colored and who have settled in their district in a flat. The work is fortunate indeed in the rare ability and devotion of these two women. Besides being excellent nurses, they are both especially alive to social movements and organized preventive work. [*Nurses' Settlement News*, 1906, p. 832]

Not only did Tyler pioneer in public health nursing in New York City, but also in Philadelphia at the Henry Phipps Institute for Tuberculosis, the State and Welfare Commission of Delaware, and the Essex County Tuberculosis Association in New Jersey, working to solve the health and social problems of blacks and bringing their plight to the attention of health officials.

In 1911, the first county public health agency in the United States was established in Greensboro, North Carolina, at the Guilford County Health Department, which employed a staff of nurses. To serve the black community, black nurses were employed. In 1915, a bill was passed in the legislature requiring public and private hospitals, sanatariums, and such institutions in North Carolina where colored patients were admitted for treatment and where nurses were employed to hire colored nurses for the care of such colored patients (*Consolidated Statutes of North Carolina*, 1915). Such bills were typical all over the country but especially in the South (Fig. 5-3).

The following are biographical sketches of eight recipients of the Mary Mahoney Award when it was being awarded by the NACGN.

In 1937, **Nancy Lois Kemp** (Fig. 5-4) became the second recipient of the Mary Mahoney Award. A charter member of NACGN, Kemp worked with the organization until her retirement to achieve equal opportunity for black nurses. In recognition of her service to NACGN as member, treasurer, and vice president, the organization gave Kemp an honorary life membership.

Kemp was born in Virginia and lived in Washington, D.C., where she attended Howard University for two years before entering Freedmen's Hospital School of Nursing. Immediately after her graduation, Kemp went to Philadelphia, where she practiced private duty nursing, specializing in massage treatment. When World War I began, she joined an active unit of the American Red Cross and became an instructor. She organized first aid classes and supply units.

With the influx of blacks from the South at this time, public health nurses were in great demand in northern cities. Kemp became interested in the field of public health nursing and prepared for this work by studying public health at the University of Pennsylvania. In 1922, she

Figure 5–3   Black nurses on staff of Guilford County Health Department, Greensboro, North Carolina, 1924. The two black nurses in the top row are, left to right, Marian Forney Smith and Louie Booker Benton.

was appointed to the position of staff nurse at the Henry Phipps Institute, which specialized in the study, treatment, and prevention of tuberculosis. The Henry Phipps Institute, the Philadelphia Health Council, and the Whittier Center jointly opened a health clinic in the northwest section of Philadelphia in 1923. Kemp served as supervisor of this dispensary for eight years, and was then transferred back to the Phipps Institute where she remained until retirement in 1940. She died three years later.

Carrie E. Bullock (Fig. 5-5) was graduated from the Scotia Seminary, Concord, North Carolina, before entering the nursing school of Provident Hospital in Chicago in 1909. A few weeks prior to her graduation from Provident, she was asked by its superintendent to join the staff of the Chicago Visiting Nurses' Association. She worked there for 40 years. Beginning as a staff nurse, Bullock became assistant supervisor, and then supervisor of the Chicago Visiting Nurses' Association services to the black people of Chicago. She was the first black nurse to serve in such a capacity. Bullock was thoroughly interested in her profession, reading and studying everything that might serve as a stepping stone toward a higher plane of nursing efficiency. She also took many courses at centers that sponsored extension work for nurses and social workers.

Bullock continued to serve nursing until her death in 1961. During World War II, she served on an NACGN committee created to struggle for the inclusion of the black nurse in the Army Nurse Corps. She was the first black nurse to speak on national leadership at a professional nursing meeting after the "merger" of ANA and NACGN, and she worked for unity within the integrated association.

Among the dedicated northern women who pioneered in nursing in the southern part of the United States was **Petra A. Pinn** (Fig. 5-6). "Pet," as she was known to her friends, was a 1906 graduate of the John Andrew Memorial Hospital School of Nursing at Tuskegee University, Alabama. After graduation, Pinn served as head nurse at Hale Infirmary in Montgomery, Alabama, and later became superintendent of nurses at the Red Cross Sanitarium and Training School in Louisville, Kentucky. She also worked as a metropolitan nurse in the same city.

Because of her preference for institutional work, Pinn accepted an appointment as Superintendent of Nurses, Pine Ridge Hospital, West Palm Beach, Florida. After ten years of dedicated work making friends for the hospital, raising money, and serving without an assistant, she was obliged to retire for a much-needed rest. A year later, she accepted a position as manager of a small hospital in Miami and then worked in a number of small southern communities. Pinn worked at Seaview Hospital in New York City before retiring to live with her family in Wilberforce, Ohio, where she remained until her death in 1958.

Pinn was a charter member of NACGN and served as its president from 1923 to 1926 and as treasurer from 1929 to 1946. While president, she tried to establish a national headquarters for NACGN, and, until this could be accomplished, supported the registry program to help black nurses find jobs.

In 1939, Pinn accepted the Mary Mahoney Award for her contributions and dedicated service in nursing for blacks in the South. At a time when working as a nurse in the South brought problems and dangers as well as challenges, she helped maintain hospitals for blacks in Alabama, Florida, Kentucky, South Carolina, and Virginia. She was not afraid of difficult or unknown situations. She was the answer to those critics at the time who said that nurses reared in the North would not work in the South because of the indignities that black nurses suffered there and the unequal salaries that they were forced to accept. By working in spite of these obstacles, Pinn set an example for other young black nurses who subsequently made contributions to the health and well-being of blacks in the South.

Lula G. Warlick (Fig. 5-7) served the nursing profession in urban areas in the Midwest and East. After graduating from North Carolina's

Figure 5–5   Carrie E. Bullock, third recipient of Mary Mahoney Award, 1938.

Figure 5–4   Nancy Lois Kemp, second recipient of Mary Mahoney Award, 1937.

Figure 5–6   Petra A. Pinn, fourth recipient of Mary Mahoney Award, 1939.

Figure 5–7   Lula G. Warlick, fifth recipient of Mary Mahoney Award, 1940.

Scotia Seminary in 1907, she entered Lincoln School for Nurses in New York. Upon graduating in 1910, she accepted the position as head nurse in the Gynecology Department and Operating Room at Lincoln Hospital. Welcoming the opportunity to work in another part of the country, in 1911 she accepted the position of assistant superintendent of nurses at Provident Hospital in Chicago, holding this position for two years and often acting as superintendent of nurses. From Chicago, she went to Kansas City, Missouri, where she became superintendent of nurses at General Hospital No. 2, which had a bed capacity of 300. According to Christ (1957), this was the "first municipal hospital managed completely by blacks" (p. 203).

In 1920, Warlick returned to the East as superintendent of nurses at Mercy Hospital in Philadelphia. When she arrived, the School of Nursing at Mercy Hospital had only 16 students and was not approved by the State Board of Nursing in Pennsylvania. As a result of her efforts, the school became a Class A school, completely approved by the State Board of Examiners. By 1929, the student enrollment had grown to 40 and the number of faculty had increased from three to nine. Warlick took courses at the University of Iowa and at Columbia University in order to keep her students informed of the latest developments in the nursing profession.

Warlick often spoke of her pride in the development of blacks in the nursing profession, noting that black nurses kept apace of the many changes in nursing education and that they held positions similar to those held by members of other groups. Warlick was awarded the Mary Mahoney Medal in 1940.

Ellen Woods Carter (Fig. 5-8) dedicated her professional life to improving health conditions for blacks in the South. In Virginia, North

Figure 5–8   Ellen Woods Carter,
1941 recipient of Mary Mahoney
Award.

Carolina, South Carolina, and Louisiana, Carter met head-on the double standards that made her work so difficult. In addition to prejudice and the fact that her salary was less than that paid to a white nurse, Carter faced the indifference of blacks to their health problems. She knew that this indifference was born of frustration and neglect, a direct result of the segregation and discrimination that blacks experienced continually. Even their health care facilities were poorer than those for whites. These conditions were a challenge to Carter, and she did all in her power to improve the health care of the black families with whom she worked.

Carter graduated from Dixie Hospital School of Nursing, Hampton, Virginia, in 1895. After graduation, she became head nurse at Good Physicians' Hospital in Columbia, South Carolina. This small institution was the only one in the city where black people could receive medical care. It was operated by white physicians and financed by northern white Episcopalians. Carter devoted herself to this position for six years and then resigned to undertake even more challenging work.

At this time, the Bureau of Child Welfare of the South Carolina State Board of Health was extending its role in a number of counties by forming classes for the instruction of midwives. Special attention was called to the instruction of black midwives, who numbered several thousand in the state. Carter was placed in Beaufort County to do midwife supervision and public health work among her own race. Beaufort County, composed of a series of small islands, had a population of 5,000, of which 4,500 were black. The blacks who inhabited the sea islands were isolated from other people and from medical services. Because communications between them and the mainland were difficult, they had to depend on the midwives for medical treatment as well as obstetric care.

When Carter started her first class in Beaufort County, only three women attended; the others were afraid or did not understand. She reported this to the local registrar, who sent an officer to round them up. After this action she had no further trouble. The women came from miles around to spend the entire day learning from her, to listen to her instruction, and to see her demonstrations. Most of the midwives were unable to read or write, but they learned quickly through Carter's classes.

Another project of this remarkable nurse was her work in persuading families, especially prospective mothers, to accept care by trained physicians. While promoting care by a doctor, she knew that a large number of black babies would be delivered by midwives, and she continued to work hard to improve the services they provided, making house-to-house visits to arouse the interest of each family and spreading the gospel of health through the churches and schools. Both white and black physicians helped her in her efforts to teach health and hygiene to the inhabitants of Beaufort County, where she spent 16 challenging and productive years.

After her service in Beaufort, Carter was given a trip abroad by the Bureau of Hygiene and Public Health Nursing. While in Rome, she spoke through an interpreter to a mother's meeting, telling them about dietary measures and the proper care of infants and demonstrating her important points.

Carter knew that for any health program to be effective, trained personnel would be needed. One of her favorite projects was to encourage bright young women to become nurses, conducting her own recruitment program. In 1941, when she received the Mary Mahoney Award, she could attest to 55 young women who had entered schools of nursing because of her interest and encouragement.

When nurse practice laws became a reality, not all states gave black nurses the opportunity to take the examinations to become licensed to practice nursing. Georgia was one such state. Recognition is given to **Ludie A. Andrews** (Fig. 5-9), a black nurse, who for 10 years fought the battle to gain the right for black nurses to practice nursing within the laws of the state of Georgia.

After completing the nursing course at Spelman College in Atlanta in 1906, Andrews was employed as superintendent of a hospital, connected with the Atlanta School of Medicine, built "to accommodate [sic] 12 Negro patients for the observation and training of medical students (white)" (*Spelman Messenger*, 1913, p. 8). She held the position of superintendent for a number of years, even though she was denied the privilege of holding a license. In 1909, at her own expense, she instituted

Figure 5–9   Ludie A. Andrews, 1943 recipient of Mary Mahoney Award.

legal action against the Georgia State Board of Nurse Examiners. She argued that because black nurses did not have the same certification as white nurses, they would have difficulty being employed in other states. The state of Georgia offered her a license to appease her, but she refused it because other qualified black nurses were not so acknowledged. The time, effort, energy, and monies she contributed to this struggle for the rightful recognition due black nurses in Georgia were rewarded. By 1920, all black nurses who were graduated from Georgia state-approved schools of nursing were permitted to take the same examination as whites for licensure. In 1974, a black nurse, Verdelle Bellamy, a graduate of Grady, was appointed by Governor Jimmy Carter to the Georgia Board of Nursing Education. A black nurse, Mary Long (Fig. 5-10), served as the elected president of the Georgia Nurses' Association from 1981 to 1985. In 1985, Long was elected to the ANA Board of Directors.

It is noteworthy that in 1914, the city of Atlanta appointed Andrews to organize a school of nursing for black students at Grady Hospital. The school became state-approved in 1917. Andrews's administrative and professional capabilities in the development of the Municipal Training School for Colored Nurses were praised by officials of the city of Atlanta. In recognition of her pioneering efforts to secure registration for black nurses in Georgia, Andrews was the recipient of the NACGN Mary Mahoney Award in 1943 and the Grady Nurses Conclave presents a "Ludie Andrews Distinguished Service Award." Nurses in Georgia affectionately refer to her as the "Dean of Black Nurses." On August

Figure 5—10   Mary Long, President, Georgia Nurses Association, 1981–1985.

21, 1987, the Grady Alumnae Associates Conclave in Washington, D.C., unveiled a portrait of Andrews and presented it to Spelman College.

Mary E. Merritt (Fig. 5-11) was born in Berea, Kentucky, and received her education at Berea College. After graduation, she taught for four years in the rural schools of Kentucky.

Merritt had always had an interest in caring for the sick, so when Berea College opened a small hospital for students, she decided to enter the nurses' training program there. The nursing curriculum was composed of one year of theoretical studies and one year of practical work. She and two other black women, Sarah Belle Jerman and Margaret Jones, who completed the program in 1902, were the first and only black graduates of the nursing department, since in 1904 the Kentucky law prohibited interracial education (Peck & Pride, 1982). Blacks would not attend Berea again until the 1950s. The baccalaureate program that is in operation today replaced the diploma one, and the dean is a black nurse, Dr. Cora Newell-Withrow.

Because she desired additional training in a larger hospital, Merritt enrolled at Freedmen's Hospital School of Nursing in Washington, D.C., in 1904. After graduating in 1906, she returned to Kentucky as a private duty nurse for one year, then moved to Leavenworth, Kansas, where she supervised the Protective Home and Mitchell Hospital. While she was in charge, the only class of nurses ever to be graduated from Mitchell Hospital received their diplomas.

In 1911, Merritt became director of the Red Cross Hospital in Louisville, Kentucky. The hospital was founded because of the devoted work of a number of public-spirited black citizens in Louisville. They were not discouraged by a lack of funds, and under Merritt's direction, the Red Cross Hospital grew from a small, frame, rented building to a magnificent brick edifice with a well-equipped training school.

Figure 5–11   Mary E. Merritt, 1949
recipient of Mary Mahoney Award.

In 1949, Merritt received the Mary Mahoney Award from NACGN in recognition of her outstanding 34 years of service as superintendent of nurses at the Louisville Red Cross Hospital.

Eliza Farish Pillars (Fig. 5-12) was born in Jackson, Mississippi, in 1891. She attended public schools in Jackson, then studied at Utica Junior College in Utica, Mississippi. From there she entered the School of Nursing at Meharry Medical College in Nashville. After graduating in 1914, she worked as an office nurse for several doctors and then worked in a number of hospitals.

In 1926, Pillars began a career in public health nursing at the Mississippi State Board of Health. During the 1920s, she was the only "accredited" public health nurse in that state. Pillars traveled into every corner and small town in Mississippi, teaching and training midwives to properly and efficiently deliver babies and take care of mothers. She gave vaccines and inoculations against communicable diseases in schools, churches, and private homes. Wherever the people had health needs, she developed programs to meet them. In cooperation with the Mississippi State Board of Education, Pillars also taught courses in hygiene to girls in Mississippi's black high schools. Through these courses, many young women were inspired to enter the nursing profession.

Pillars played a prominent role after Mississippi's historic 1927 flood, working diligently with the Red Cross in setting up first aid stations in

Figure 5–12   Eliza Farish Pillars, 1951 recipient of Mary Mahoney Award.

Vicksburg and Natchez to take care of the flood refugees as they were brought in by boats down the Mississippi River from the Delta section of the state.

As the years passed, Pillars's eyesight weakened, and although she never became totally blind, she had to give up her work. In 1951, she became the 14th and last recipient of the Mary Mahoney Award given by NACGN. The organization of black registered nurses in Jackson, Mississippi, is named the "Eliza Farish Pillars Club" in her honor. She died June 15, 1970.

SUMMARY

By definition, a pioneer is one who opens new avenues or prepares the way for others to follow. Because of the social and economic climate in the United States, many black nurses have been and still are pioneers in the health care field. In the practice areas referred to in this chapter are those black nurses who paved the way for other black nurses. An excellent example is the story of Ludie Andrews's fight in Georgia to ensure the black nurse the right to practice her profession legally. Another example is that of Jessie Sleet Scales, who paved the way for blacks in public health nursing. More detailed accounts of many more black pioneers appear in *Pathfinders* by Thoms, and references to others are in Staupers's book, *No Time for Prejudice*. They are not repeated here. As Thoms (1929) points out,

It is in the sacrifices of the early pathfinders that we see how real our life work is. Through studying the uphill struggles of the group against prejudices and misgivings the student of today learns to estimate the problems she will meet tomorrow. It is only from such a perspective that we can guide our course in crucial times and show to the world that we are a part of the great army of consecrated women who are working toward the highest standards of nursing efficiency [p. 2].

Black nurses who forged ahead in the early 1900s exemplified courage, commitment, dedication, assertiveness, accountability, and an unwavering belief in the integrity of humankind. Today, because of these pioneers, black nurses are practicing with dignity in all areas of nursing.

REFERENCES

A successful experiment. (1901). *American Journal of Nursing, 1*, 729–731.

Brown, E. L. (1948). *Nursing for the future*. New York: Russell Sage Foundation.

Christ, E. A. (1957). *Missouri's nurses*. Jefferson City: Missouri Nurses' Association.

Consolidated statutes of North Carolina. (1915). Raleigh.

Dunkley, P. (1974). The ANA certification program. *Nursing Clinics of North America, 9*, 485–495.

Flanagan, L. (1976). *One strong voice, the story of the American Nurses' Association*. Kansas City: ANA.

Markway, P. B. (1990). How to become certified in 1990. *The American Nurse, 22*, 2, 23.

Morais, H. (1967). *The history of the Negro in medicine*. New York: Publishers Co.

Nurses' settlement news. (1906). *American Journal of Nursing, 6*, 832–833.

Peck, E. S., & Pride, N. W. (1982). *Nurses in time: Developments in nursing education, 1898–1981*. Berea College, Berea, Kentucky, Appalachian Fund.

Roberts, M. M. (1954). *American nursing: History and interpretation*. New York: Macmillan.

Spelman Messenger. (1913). *29*, 6. Atlanta: Spelman College.

Staupers, M. K. (1961). *No time for prejudice*. New York: Macmillan.

Thoms, A. B. (1929). *Pathfinders, the progress of colored graduate nurses*. New York: Kay Printing House.

Wyche, M. L. (1938). *The history of nursing in North Carolina*. Chapel Hill: University of North Carolina Press.

Chapter 6

✣

So Proudly We Hail

The U.S. federal government is the world's largest employer of professional registered nurses. It also provides consultant services that are helpful in improving the quality and distribution of nursing services throughout the nation. Its principal service agencies are the three military services—the Army Nurse Corps, the Navy Nurse Corps, and the Air Force Nurse Corps—the United States Public Health Service, and the Veterans Administration. In this chapter, black nurses in these agencies are discussed.

THE MILITARY

Army Nurse Corps

Along with their sisters who nursed the soldiers in the Revolutionary and Civil Wars, the contract nurses of the Spanish-American War, under the leadership of Anita Newcomb McGee, a medical doctor, are acknowledged as the forebears of the modern Army Nurse Corps. Formally established on February 2, 1901, as a permanent corps of the Army Medical Department by the Army Reorganization Act of 1901 (31 Stat 753), the Army Nurse Corps is the oldest of the federal nursing services. Although their initial associations with the corps were limited to periods of international conflict when necessity forced the laying aside of racial prejudices, black nurses have served proudly and with distinction since the early days of the corps.

195

Despite their honorable service in the Spanish-American War, when the Army Nurse Corps was formally established in 1901 there were no black nurses among its members. They would not serve again until 1918 when the influenza epidemic, which lasted from September 1918 to August 1919, necessitated tapping all sources of graduate nurses.

The intervening years were not, however, without activity by the black nurses desirous of serving their country. Although not specifically prohibited by regulation from joining the Army Nurse Corps, on inquiry black nurses discovered administrative hurdles. The first was the prerequisite membership in the American Red Cross, which had been designated as the primary source of reserve nurses for the military establishment by President Taft in 1911.

Adah B. Thoms, a black nurse employed in an executive capacity at Lincoln School for Nurses in New York and actively involved in professional and community affairs, set about on her own not only to alert black nurses to enroll in the Red Cross but also, through her lengthy correspondence in 1917 with Jane Delano, chairperson of the American Red Cross Nursing Service, to agitate the Red Cross to remove the limitations that prevented black nurses from enrolling. These efforts led to the eventual removal of the bars. The second hurdle involved Army Nurse Corps policy, which dictated that black nurses not be accepted in the corps because there were no separate quarters for them.

During Thoms's fight to get the color bars removed so that black nurses could serve their country, a massive influenza epidemic erupted without warning in the United States and the world, causing more deaths than did the fighting in the First World War (Kalisch & Kalisch, 1978). "As their doctors and nurses dropped out with the infection, army and civilian hospitals struggled with a dwindling staff until the plight of both the servicemen and their families at home was pitiful" (Dolan et al., 1983, pp. 289–290).

In a memorandum dated February 28, 1918, to Dean F. P. Keppel, Confidential Advisor, Office of the Secretary of War, Emmett J. Scott, a black man who was a special assistant in the War Department, quoted from Surgeon General William C. Gorgas's letter to him of February 14, 1918:

> Referring to your memorandum of February 12th relative to the appointment and training of colored nurses for colored soldiers, *at the present time colored nurses are not being accepted for service in the Army Nurse Corps* as there are no separate quarters available for them, and it is not deemed advisable to assign white and colored nurses to the same posts.

After quoting the surgeon general, Scott continued in his memorandum to Keppel:

From the above, it will be seen that the whole matter of utilizing colored nurses is still very much "up in the air."

The upshot of the whole matter is that—while there are thousands of colored men who have been called to the colors as soldiers,—NO COLORED NURSES HAVE BEEN ADMITTED TO THE SER-VICE, although quite a number have enrolled with the Red Cross organization as suggested, and they, together with many more well-trained, competent, and registered nurses, are ready and willing to look after sick and wounded soldiers who are now and soon will be facing shot and shell upon battlefields abroad.

I would most urgently recommend that some satisfactory way be found that will offer to colored nurses . . . the same opportunity for serving the sick and wounded soldiers, as has been so wisely and timely provided white nurses.

Waiving all discussion as to the matter of assigning white and colored nurses to the same post or quarters, it is difficult for me to understand why some colored nurses have not been given an opportunity to serve.

This vexing question is being put to me almost daily by colored newspaper editors, colored physicians, surgeons, etc., who are constantly bombarding my sector of the War Department, inquiring what has been done, and urging that something should be done in the direction of utilizing professionally trained and efficient colored nurses.

I recognize the 'problems,' but can't they be solved?

[signed] Emmett J. Scott
Special Assistant

Thus, it is noted that pressure had been put on the War Department to use the services of black nurses (Scott, 1918). The pressure of this organized campaign, coupled with the inceasing need for nurses both overseas and at home, worked. In June 1918, it was officially announced that the secretary of war had authorized the calling of colored nurses into the national service. By July 1918, tentative plans were made to send colored nurses in groups of 20 to several posts that had large numbers of colored troops. Delays in the provision of separate quarters and dining facilities resulted in their not being officially assigned to duty until after the armistice.

The black nurses were notified by letter. Aileen Cole's letter from the American Red Cross, dated November 13, 1918, read:

Miss Arleen [sic] Bertha Cole,
918 T. Street, N.W.
Washington, D.C.

Dear Miss Cole:
The Surgeon General has called for a limited number of colored nurses, enrolled in the Red Cross, to be available for service about December 1.

Your name has been selected as one who might be willing to consider an assignment, and if so, would you be good enough to notify us promptly, and also give us a permanent address where transportation may be issued.

Miss Clara A. Rollins has been selected as the one who will be responsible for the group until they reach their posts of assignment.

Anticipating an early reply, I am,

Yours sincerely,

[signed] Clara D. Noyes, Director

Bureau Field Nursing Service

It was followed by a form letter full of admonitions:

It remains with you to justify our selection and to prove that the Red Cross stands for efficient service.

You are likely to find the methods of procedure in a military hospital somewhat more formal than in a civil hospital and authority more absolute. May I urge, however, that you accept conditions without comment or criticism and make every effort to adapt yourself cheerfully and without friction to the environment . . . .

Cole accepted the challenge and formed the first contingent of black nurses along with 17 others: Marion Brown Seymour, Anna Oliver Ramos, Lillian Ball, Pearl Billings, Susie Boulding, Eva Clay, Edna DePriest, Magnolia Diggs, Sophia Hill, Jeanette Minnis, Clara Rollins, Lillian Spears, Virginia Steele, Frances Stewart, Nettie Vick, Jeannette West, and Mabel Williams (Maxwell, 1976).

Nine of the nurses were assigned to Camp Grant, Rockford, Illinois, and nine to Camp Sherman, Chillicothe, Ohio. Their living quarters and recreational facilities were separate, but they were assigned to duties in integrated hospitals.

The written testimonies of the chief nurses at Camps Sherman and Grant attest to the value of the black nurses' contributions (Fig. 6–1). Mary M. Roberts, chief nurse at Camp Sherman, wrote,

I do not mind saying that I was quite sure, when orders came for the colored group, that I was about to meet my Waterloo. My feeling now is that it was a valuable experience for them and for me. They really were a credit to their race, for they did valuable service for our patients and it was a service that patients appreciated. I now find myself deeply interested in the problems of all colored nurses and believe in giving them such opportunities as they can grasp for advancement . . . [Thoms, 1929, p. 164]

Of the Camp Grant group, the chief nurse said,

Since the white and colored patients were not assigned to separate wards, these nurses were assigned to the general wards under the

Figure 6–1   World War I black nurses at Camp Sherman, Illinois. In the front row, left to right, are Ailene Cole, Susan Boulding, Lillian Spears, Jeanette Minnis, Sophia Hill. In the center row, left to right, are Marion Brown Seymour and Jeannette West. In the top row, left to right, are Clara Rollins and Lillian Ball. (Courtesy U.S. Army Center of Military History)

direction of the head nurse. They were serious-minded, quiet, business-like young women . . . [Thoms, 1929, p. 165]

Anna Oliver Ramos, a former assistant executive secretary of NACGN who served at Camp Grant, put it this way: "We came from good schools of nursing and we knew too well that whatever the test, we could measure up to whatever was expected of us" (Staupers, 1961, p. 99).

As they had in previous wars, civilian black nurses aided the military efforts as well. The influenza epidemic so strained the ability of the army to provide nurses that hospital commanders in the United States were granted authority to employ nurses for $75 a month, one ration a day, lodging, laundry, and transportation (*Report of the Surgeon General*, 1918).

Sayres L. Milliken, chief nurse at Camp Sevier, South Carolina, wrote of her black civilian nurses:

> At the peak of the influenza epidemic at Camp Sevier . . . , about fifty percent of the nurses were off duty, sick, and the hospital contained about 3,000 patients. It became necessary to employ locally [although not members of the Army Nurse Corps] every nurse who could be secured. A medical officer on duty . . . who was from the section of the country said that there were several good colored nurses who could be secured in the vicinity of Spartanburg. . . . The idea of securing the services of colored nurses did not immediately meet with enthusiasm, as fully 75 percent of the nurses were women of southern birth and had very positive objections to working with colored nurses. The need was so imperative that it was decided to employ them, furnishing them with quarters and a mess separate from the white nurses.
>
> About 12 reported for duty. They were assigned to the wards in the hospital in subordinate positions and with the exception of one or two who were not young enough to adapt themselves to the trying conditions under which everyone was working, these young women were found to be well-trained, quiet and dignified, and there was never at any time evidence of friction between the white and colored nurses. They served for a period of possibly three weeks . . . I should say that, although these nurses had no opportunity to display executive ability, they did and can fill a valuable place in the nursing profession. [Thoms, 1929, p. 166–167]

Other base hospitals where black nurses were assigned were Camp Funston, Kansas; Camp Dodge, Des Moines, Iowa; Camp Taylor, Louisville, Kentucky; and Camp Dix, Wrightstown, New Jersey. A total of 38,000 colored troops were located at these camps (Dunbar-Nelson, 1919).

With the armistice at hand and the influenza epidemic waning, hospitals began to close in 1919, and the Army Nurse Corps, having reached 21,480 members in November 1918, was correspondingly reduced in size. The peak of demobilization was reached in August 1919, when 2,329 nurses left (*Report of the Surgeon General*, 1919, p. 294). Among them were the 18 black nurses.

By July 1, 1920, only 1,551 nurses remained on active duty with the Army Nurse Corps. During the next 20 years the strength of the corps remained under 1,000 members, and the issue of integration of black nurses in the armed forces again appeared dormant. It was during this period, however, that black nurses began the fight for integration in the professional organization—the American Nurses' Association, and into the mainstream of professional nursing (see Chapter 4).

The international anarchy that characterized the period before the outbreak of World War I reasserted itself shortly after the "War to End Wars" was over. As early as 1922, Mussolini had come to power in Italy, and by 1935 he was seeking to resurrect the Roman Empire by overrunning Ethiopia. These developments gave encouragement and comfort to Adolf Hitler, who was waiting for a chance to use his newly won authority in Germany to extend his control to neighboring nations (Franklin, 1967).

As war clouds gathered, government authorities informed the major nursing organizations—the ANA, the NLNE, and the National Organization for Public Health Nursing—of the need for nurses. At the 1938 biennial convention of these three organizations, it was announced that the "authorized strength of the Army Nurse Corps was increased to 675 on July 1, 1937, and on June 30, 1938, there were 674 on duty" (*Report of the Surgeon General*, 1938, p. 236).

When Europe was plunged into war in September 1939, the policy of isolationism became more and more untenable (Franklin, 1967). Because of the war being waged in Europe, on September 8, 1939, a state of limited emergency was declared. At that time, there were 672 nurses on active duty (*Report of the Surgeon General*, 1939, p. 244). The authorized strength of the corps was immediately increased and by June 30, 1940, there were 942 nurses in the corps (*Report of the Surgeon General*, 1940, p. 257). An additional 15,779 nurses were enrolled in the First Reserve of the American Red Cross Nursing Service, presumably available for service if needed. On May 27, 1941, a state of national emergency was declared because of the threat of global war. Once again, it became necessary to appoint reserve nurses (Shields, 1981). When the attack on Pearl Harbor brought an end to serenity and a state of war, army strength stood at some million and a half men with a Medical Department of over 130,000, including over 6,800 Army Nurse Corps members (Kriedberg & Henry, 1955).

With the Army Nurse Corps expanding its resources and services, black nurses assumed that they would be needed and began writing to the corps for information. The NACGN alerted its members and urged that all eligible nurses enroll in the American Red Cross, the procurement agency for the military. One of the qualifications for enrollment in the American Red Cross was membership in the ANA, which was denied black nurses in the South (see Chapter 4). However, the Red Cross established a special membership category for these nurses, permitting them to enroll if they were members of the NACGN. In answer to their inquiries to the army, however, black nurses were informed: "Your application for appointment to the Army Nurse Corps cannot be given favorable consideration as there are not provisions in the army regulations for the appointment of colored nurses in the corps" (Staupers, 1961, p. 100).

Waging the battle for the inclusion of black nurses in the Army Nurse Corps were the NACGN and other concerned organizations and individuals and by January 1941, a quota of 56 black nurses to serve in the

army had been established, with the stipulation, according to Surgeon
General James C. Magee, that the "Negro nurse . . . would only be called
to serve in hospitals or wards devoted exclusively to the treatment of
Negro soldiers" (Staupers, 1961, p. 102).

With the announcement of the quota for black nurses, NACGN launched
an intensive campaign, using the press and other media, for removal of
the quota and against the practice of segregation and discrimination,
which these young women encountered in their assignments. While the
quota was still in effect, in April 1941 a few black nurses were assigned
to camps. "To date [30 June 1941] 22 colored nurses have been assigned
to Fort Bragg, N.C. and Camp Livingston, La." (*Report of the Surgeon
General*, 1941, p. 245). Later that year, a small group of nurses was
assigned to the Army Flying School for Negro Pilots at Tuskegee, Alabama (Staupers, 1961). Commonly referred to as the Tuskegee Airmen,
the 450-man, all-black unit included the first blacks allowed to serve as
pilots in the Air Corps.

In 1943, the army raised its quota of black nurses to 160, and by the
end of September 1944, there were close to 250 black nurse officers,
including three captains and 30 first lieutenants (*First Indorsement*, 1945).
But it was not until January 20, 1945, because of pressure by NACGN
and others, that nurses were accepted into the Army Nurse Corps without regard to race (Hine, 1982). In fact, the number of Negro nurses
who volunteered and were commissioned in the last year of the war
almost equalled the total in the army in September 1944. In late July
1945, there were some 500 in the corps, including nine captains and
115 first lieutenants. They were serving in four general, three regional,
and 11 station hospitals in the United States as well as in overseas areas
(Groppe, 1945). It is estimated that there were 8,000 black registered
nurses in the country at that time.

In April 1941, Della Raney Jackson (Fig. 6–2) of Suffolk, Virginia,
the first black nurse to be commissioned in the U.S. Army as a lieutenant,
reported for duty at Fort Bragg, North Carolina. In 1942, she became
a chief nurse and was transferred to the station hospital at Tuskegee
Air Field, Alabama. She later served as Chief Nurse, Fort Huachuca,
Arizona, and Camp Beale, California. In 1945, she was promoted to
captain and in 1946, to major. Later she served a tour of duty in Japan.
Jackson was a graduate of Lincoln Hospital School of Nursing in Durham, North Carolina, and continued her studies at Western Michigan
University, Wayne State University, University of Michigan, and Virginia
State University. In 1978, Major Jackson (retired) was honored by the
Tuskegee Airmen for outstanding leadership, service, professionalism,
and for historic achievements that personified the "Tuskegee Spirit." In
1989, Nancy Leftenant Colon, a retired Air Force nurse, was elected
President, Tuskegee Airmen, Inc.

The first group of black nurses to be assigned to the European theater of operations arrived in England in 1944. The unit of 63 nurses, with Captain Mary L. Petty of Chicago as chief nurse, was greeted by Brigadier General Benjamin O. Davis, a black officer ("Army Nurses Tell Us," 1944).

Another one of the 48 black nurses who joined the army in April 1941 was Susan Elizabeth Freeman (Fig. 6–3), a 1926 graduate of Freedmen's Hospital School of Nursing in Washington, D.C., with further study at Columbia University in New York and Howard University and The Catholic University of America in Washington, D.C. Beginning her army career as a second lieutenant assigned to Camp Livingston, Louisiana, Freeman was soon promoted to first lieutenant—the first nurse, black or white, to receive a promotion at Camp Livingston. She later was to become one of the first black nurses in the Army Nurse Corps to be promoted to captain.

In July 1942, 60 black nurses were assigned to Fort Huachuca, Arizona, with Lieutenant Freeman as the chief nurse. She served in Liberia in 1943 as chief nurse of the first overseas unit of 30 black nurses. While there, on November 8, 1943, she and eight other nurses received a unit commendation from the Office of the Commanding General, which stated in part, "During nearly eight months at this foreign service station, and in the face of difficult circumstances, these nurses have clearly demonstrated fidelity to duty, a sense of responsibility, and understanding of their positions as officers that is well above the average." A copy of the commendation was sent to the surgeon general of the U.S. Army in Washington, D.C. The Republic of Liberia honored Freeman by making her a knight official of the Liberian Humane Order of Africa Redemption, a tribute to her success in person-to-person diplomacy with the Liberians (Staupers, 1961).

Captain Freeman retired for medical reasons from the Army Nurse Corps on July 31, 1945, and received the Mary Mahoney Award that year from NACGN for service to the American Red Cross during the Ohio-Mississippi Flood of 1937 and for commanding the first unit of black nurses overseas. Captain Freeman died in 1980 at her home in Stratford, Connecticut.

Two other black nurses who served as chief nurses in the Army Nurse Corps during World War II should be mentioned here—Margaret Bailey and Agnes Glass Pallemon.

Colonel Margaret E. Bailey (Fig. 6–4), was the first black nurse to attain the rank of lieutenant colonel (1964), having joined the army in June 1944. Almost nine of her 27 years of service were spent outside the country—in Germany, Japan, and France. In Germany, she was head nurse on a psychiatric nursing service. In Japan, she was assistant chief nurse of the medical facility at Camp Zama and head nurse on the

Figure 6–2   Della Raney Jackson, first black nurse commissioned in the U.S. Army, 1941.

Figure 6–3   Susan Elizabeth Freeman, Chief Nurse, first overseas unit of black nurses during World War II.

officers' ward. In May 1965, Lieutenant Colonel Bailey received transfer orders for Europe to serve as chief nurse of the 130 general hospitals in Chinon, France.

In 1969, Lieutenant Colonel Bailey was assigned as health manpower training specialist to the Job Corps Health Office, Department of Labor. In January 1970, she was promoted to full colonel, again the first black nurse to hold that rank. Upon her retirement in 1971, Colonel Bailey received the Legion of Merit, the army's second highest noncombat award. In 1972, she was designated as consultant to the surgeon general of the U.S. Army to promote increased participation by minority group members in the Army Nurse Corps recruitment programs.

Colonel Bailey received her basic nursing education at the Fraternal Hospital School of Nursing in Montgomery, Alabama. She earned a certificate in psychiatric nursing at Brooke Army Medical Center, Fort Sam Houston, Texas, and a bachelor's degree from San Francisco State College in California after having accumulated transfer credits from the University of Michigan, Kalamazoo State University in Michigan, and the University of Maryland extension in Germany.

Agnes Beulah Glass Pallemon (Diploma, St. Mary's Infirmary School of Nursing, St. Louis, Missouri [Fig. 6–5]) joined the Army Nurse Corps September 15, 1942, as second lieutenant and was promoted to first lieutenant a year later at Fort Huachuca. On June 3, 1944, she was assigned Principal Chief Nurse, Station Hospital ASF Depot, Ogden, Utah. When the 335th Station Hospital at Tagap, Burma, opened in late

Figure 6–4   Margaret E. Bailey, first black nurse to attain rank of lieutenant colonel, 1964.

Figure 6–5   Agnes Beulah Glass Pallemon, Chief Nurse, 335th Station Hospital, Tagap, Burma, 1944.

December 1944, Lieutenant Pallemon was its chief nurse. In September 1946, she was promoted to captain.

As the United States entered the postwar period, blacks and whites began eradicating segregation and discrimination in the armed forces. This whole matter of blatant discrimination in the armed forces was not eliminated until Executive Order 9981 was issued by President Harry S. Truman on July 26, 1948, the first part of which stated:

> 1. It is hereby declared to be the policy of the President that there shall be equality of treatment and opportunity for all persons in the armed services without regard to race, color, religion, or national origin. This policy shall be put into effect as rapidly as possible, having due regard to the time required to effectuate any necessary changes without impairing efficiency or morale.
>
> 2. There shall be created in the National Military Establishment an advisory committee to be known as the President's Committee on Equality of Treatment and Opportunity in the Armed Services, which shall be composed of seven members designated by the President....

The order was an historic one. For the first time an American president had openly placed the force of his high office on the side of the struggle of the Negro for equal rights (Davis, 1966).

The protests of the 1960s also served as an impetus to further resolve existing inequities. Although male nurses were first admitted to the Army Nurse Corps in 1955, it was not until September 30, 1966, with Public Law 89-609, 89th Congress, that they were commissioned in the regular army (Piemonte & Gurney, 1987). On June 15, 1967, Lawrence C. Washington (Fig. 6–6), who happened to be black, was the first male nurse to receive a regular army commission in the Army Nurse Corps at Walter Reed Army Medical Center, Washington, D.C.

Before Colonel Washington (Diploma, Freedmen's Hospital School of Nursing, Washington, D.C.; MS, The Catholic University of America, Washington, D.C.) entered a school of nursing, he had been an orderly and nursing assistant in civilian and military hospitals. Before retiring, he was Assistant Chief, Department of Nursing, William Beaumont Army Medical Center, Texas.

Ranks of the black nurses have ranged from second lieutenant to brigadier general. Tribute is paid here to Brigadier General Hazel W. Johnson-Brown (Fig. 6–7). In 1979, Johnson-Brown became the first black woman in the Department of Defense to achieve the grade of brigadier general and the first black to be the chief of the Army Nurse Corps. During her administration, the Army Medical Department adopted a document prepared by the corps that recommended education credentials for nursing positions. Johnson-Brown retired from that post August 31, 1983, after 26 years of active commissioned service. Her

Figure 6–6   Lawrence C. Washington, first male nurse to receive a regular commission in the Army Nurse Corps, 1967.

Figure 6–7 Brigadier General Hazel W. Johnson-Brown, first black Chief of Army Nurse Corps, 1979–1983. (Courtesy of U.S. Army, Photograph No. P-190481)

major duty assignments between 1968 and 1979 had been Project Officer, Development Branch, Material Development Division, Surgical Directorate, U.S. Army Medical Research and Development Command, Washington, D.C.; Dean, Walter Reed Army Institute of Nursing, Washington, D.C.; Chief Nurse, U.S. Army Medical Command, Korea; and Special Assistant to the Chief, Army Nurse Corps.

General Johnson-Brown received her basic nursing education at Harlem Hospital School of Nursing in New York and a PhD from The Catholic University of America in Washington, D.C., plus honorary doctorates from Villanova University in Pennsylvania, Morgan State University in Baltimore, Maryland, and the University of Maryland, Baltimore.

Johnson-Brown, the first chief of the Army Nurse Corps to hold an earned doctorate, has been the recipient of numerous awards, among which is the Dr. Anita Newcomb McGee Medal presented by the Daughters of the American Revolution for excellence in the field of nursing and professional performance. Since retiring, Johnson-Brown has been Adjunct Professor, George Washington University, Washington, D.C., and is currently Commonwealth Professor, George Mason University School of Nursing, Fairfax, Virginia.

Clara Adams-Ender was Chief, Army Nurse Corps Division, U.S. Army Recruiting Command in Fort Sheridan, Illinois, from 1981 to 1984. She entered active duty in the army in 1961 after completing her basic nursing education at North Carolina A & T State University School of Nursing in Greensboro. In 1969, she earned a master's degree in medical-surgical nursing from the University of Minnesota, Minneapolis, and in 1976 became the first woman in the army to earn the Master of Military Art and Science degree from the U.S. Army Command and General Staff College, Fort Leavenworth, Kansas. Her other awards include Legion of Merit, the Meritorious Service Medal with Three Oak Leaf Clusters, and the Surgeon General's "A" Professional Designation for Excellence in Nursing Administration.

From June 1984 to August 1987, Colonel Adams-Ender was Chief, Department of Nursing, Walter Reed Army Medical Center, Washington, D.C., the first black nurse to hold this position. She brought to this position a wealth of experience in teaching, clinical practice, administration, research, and consultation. On September 1, 1987, she was promoted to Brigadier General and Chief of the Army Nurse Corps (Fig. 6–8). In 1988, she became the first army nurse officer to be appointed director of personnel for the surgeon general of the army. During her tenure as corps chief, General Adams-Ender has increased the strength of the Army Nurse Corps by 33 percent and has initiated an upward mobility program called the Army Medical Department Enlisted Commissioning Program.

Black nurses also served with distinction during the Korean War and the Vietnam War. Of note was First Lieutenant Diane M. Lindsay (Fig. 6–9), Army Nurse Corps, who received the Soldier's Medal for Heroism in Vietnam in 1970. Lieutenant Lindsay (BS, Hampton University School

Figure 6–8   Brigadier General Clara L. Adams-Ender, 18th Chief of the Army Nurse Corps, 1987. (Courtesy U.S. Army Visual Information Center, Pentagon, Washington, D.C. 20310-4800)

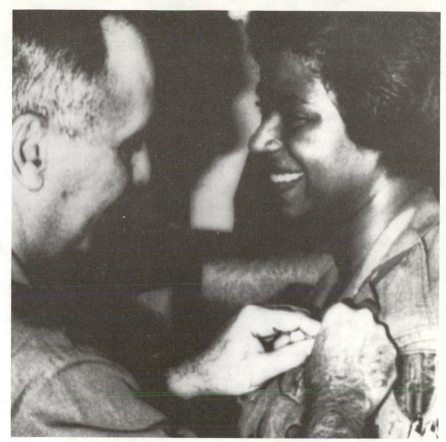

Figure 6–9   Diane M. Lindsay, first lieutenant in the Army Nurse Corps, received the Soldier's Medal for Heroism in Vietnam, 1970. (Courtesy U.S. Army Center of Military History)

of Nursing, Hampton, Virginia), while on duty with the 95th Evacuation Hospital, happened on a berserk soldier who was armed with a grenade. She and a male officer physically restrained the confused soldier and persuaded him to give up the grenade, thus preventing numerous casualties. Lieutenant Lindsay was the second nurse to be honored during the Vietnam War and the first black nurse in history to receive the medal.

Navy Nurse Corps

When President Theodore Roosevelt signed the Naval Appropriations Bill on May 13, 1908, he signed into being the Navy Nurse Corps (Kalisch & Kalisch, 1978). As in the case of the army, the American Red Cross served as the primary source of reserve nurses for the navy. Black nurses, therefore, had the same problem of being discriminated against in terms of serving in the navy as they had with the army. The army had a quota; the navy's reply to black applicants was simply, "Colored nurses are not being assigned to the navy."

The NACGN, along with concerned civic groups and individuals, while fighting to remove the quota for black nurses in the army, fought just as hard to get the navy to reverse its decision of not accepting any black nurses. Finally, in March 1945, after months of prodding, the surgeon general announced that the navy would accept a "reasonable" number of qualified black nurses and was now recruiting for them (MacGregor, 1981). In March 1945, a few months before the cessation of hostilities, Phyllis Daley, a graduate of Lincoln School for Nurses in New York, was sworn into the Navy Nurse Corps as an ensign—the first of the four black nurses who were on active duty in the navy during World War II. (She died in New York on October 31, 1976.)

The three other black nurses commissioned as ensigns were Helen Turner Watson (Fig. 6–10), a Lincoln in New York graduate and now retired professor, University of Connecticut School of Nursing, Storrs; Ella Lucille Stimley of Provident in Chicago who took her oath on May 8, 1945, and was released on June 15 for reasons of physical disability; and Edith DeVoe of Freedmen's. On January 6, 1948, DeVoe was augmented into the regular navy. Approximately 11,000 nurses served in the navy during World War II, but only four of them were black, and this presented a few problems. For example, Watson, who had been

Figure 6–10   Helen Turner Watson, one of the four black nurses commissioned as ensigns in the U.S. Navy, 1945.

assigned to a post in Chicago, had to be housed at a YWCA branch because the navy's policy prohibited her from sharing a room with a white nurse on its facility at Great Lakes.

Joan Bynum was the first black nurse to attain the rank of captain while Assistant Director of Nursing, Naval Regional Medical Center, Yokosuka, Japan, in 1978. A native of Gary, Indiana, Captain Bynum joined the navy shortly after receiving her bachelor of science degree in nursing, serving first at San Diego, then at Great Lakes. While in the navy, she obtained her graduate education in pediatric nursing at Indiana University.

Marcus L. Walker (Diploma, Alexian Brothers' Hospital School of Nursing, Chicago, Illinois; ScD, Johns Hopkins University, Baltimore, Maryland [Fig. 6–11]) served four years in the navy, 1952 to 1956. Walker, the first black man to be graduated from a school of professional nursing in Illinois, enlisted in the navy in 1952, but because of gender, not as a commissioned officer. However, the navy gave him assignments that were beyond the scope of enlisted hospital corpsmen—teaching nursing in the corps school and functioning as clinical supervisor on the psychiatric units and in the operating rooms at the Naval Hospital, Great Lakes, Illinois, during the Korean War.

In 1953, the Korean War ended, and Walker was assigned to the 1st and 3rd Marine Divisions, with the responsibility for establishing and evaluating two infirmaries on the marine bases, as well as supervising the nursing care provided by the hospital corpsmen.

Figure 6–11   Dr. Marcus L. Walker served in the navy before male nurses were commissioned.

In October 1955, Congress passed legislation to allow commissions for male nurses in the armed forces. The Army and Air Force Nurse Corps began commissioning male nurses, but the navy decided not to do so. Walker was given the option of transferring into another branch of the service in order to be commissioned, but, having less than six months left of his four-year enlistment term, he chose to remain as a non-commissioned petty officer until discharge from the navy in 1956. Ten years later, in 1965, the navy began commissioning men in its nurse corps.

With an extensive background in teaching, administration, clinical practice, consultation, and research, Walker, until his death in 1990, had been for 16 years on the graduate faculty of the University of Maryland School of Nursing in Baltimore as associate professor and had been Nurse Consultant, Veterans Administration Medical Center, Loch Raven for four years.

Today, 26 percent of the Navy Nurse Corps are male nurses. Of this 26 percent, 3 percent are black men. Approximately 5 percent of the Navy Nurse Corps are black women. Black nurses—men and women—have continued to attain senior rank and hold high-level positions within nursing administration. Two such nurses are Captain Madeline M. Ancelard (Diploma, Queen of Angels School of Nursing, Los Angeles, California; MS, Naval Postgraduate School, Monterey, California [Fig. 6–12]), Commanding Officer, Naval Medical Clinic, Pearl Harbor, Hawaii; and Captain Hattie Elam, Director, Nursing Services, Naval Hospital, Charleston, South Carolina.

Air Force Nurse Corps

In 1942, the Army Air Forces (AAF) constituted, along with the Army Ground Forces and the Army Service Forces, one of three major commands within the War Department. With the establishment of AAF in June 1941, the official name changed from the Air Corps to the Army Air Forces. Until 1948, officials of the War Department and the AAF reflected society's traditional racist attitude toward the participation of blacks (Osur, 1977).

The U.S. Air Force was created by the National Security Act of 1947. As the newest branch of the service, the Air Force had an open field in which to develop its own sense of purpose and identity (Willenz, 1983). Until then, as a part of the army, the story of the black air force nurse had been incorporated in the story of the army nurse. For example, a few black army nurses, in 1941 and during the war years, were assigned to the station hospital at Tuskegee Air Field (Johnson, 1974). They also served as Army Nurse Corps nurses overseas at AAF stations.

Figure 6–12   Captain Madeline M. Ancelard, Commanding Officer, Naval Medical Center, Pearl Harbor, Hawaii.

In 1948, by Executive Order 9981, President Truman's Human Rights Proclamation directed the integration of the armed forces—the government would not discriminate. The air force decided to integrate immediately and by the time the Air Force Medical Service was established in July 1949, with the Air Force Nurse Corps becoming an integral part of it, integration was policy. At that time, army nurses were permitted to transfer to the air force, and 1,199 transfers were made, of which 307 were from components of the regular army and 892 from the reserve. This group formed the nucleus of the Air Force Nurse Corps (Shields, 1981).

One of the black nurses who transferred from the army to the air force in 1949 was Captain Abbie Sweetwine, who was promoted to her present rank in 1953 after having served at posts in the United States, the United Kingdom, and Korea. Captain Sweetwine was born in Cocoa, Florida, received her basic nursing education at Brewster Hospital School of Nursing in Jacksonville, and worked as a nurse to migrants from the Bahamas and at a VA hospital before joining the army.

Another black nurse, Lieutenant Colonel Ann Lawrence from Chadbourn, North Carolina, was the second highest ranking black woman in the air force in 1976. A graduate of Kate B. Reynolds Hospital School of Nursing in Winston-Salem, North Carolina, Lawrence joined the U.S. Air Force in 1956. Her first assignment was to Wright Patterson Air Force Base in Dayton, OH. From there, she was sent to Japan for two years. After earning her master's degree in public administration from the University of Nebraska in Omaha, she spent tours of duty in Libya, North Africa, the Philippines, and Vietnam before returning to the United States.

There are currently six black nurses with the rank of full colonel: Mary R. Boyd (retired), Clara B. Wallace, Margaret P.C. Nelson, Nora Kendall (retired), Christine Spivey, and Irene Trowell-Harris.

Colonel Mary Rozina Boyd (Diploma, St. Philip Hospital School of Nursing, Richmond, Virginia; MSN, University of California, San Francisco [Fig. 6–13]) a native of Anderson, South Carolina, retired in 1987 as Chairperson, Department of Nursing, Malcolm Grow Medical Center, Andrews Air Force Base, Washington, D.C. She has held various positions—from staff nurse to chief nurse—at many bases in the United States and several foreign countries. She served as Medical Inspector, Headquarters, U.S. Air Force, Inspection and Safety Center. In this role, she evaluated nursing service activities in air force hospitals/medical centers worldwide. During this tour, Colonel Boyd served as interim team

Figure 6–13   Colonel (Ret.) Mary Rozina Boyd, was Chairperson, Department of Nursing, Malcolm Grow USAF Medical Center, Andrews Air Force Base, Washington, D.C.

chief for a period of four months, the first and only time a nurse has served as chief of a medical inspection team.

Colonel Clara B. Wallace (BS, Prairie View A & M University School of Nursing, Prairie View, Texas; MN, University of Washington, Seattle [Fig. 6–14]) is Chief, Nurse Education, Medical Service Education Division, Directorate of Medical Service Officer Programs and Utilization Headquarters, Air Force Military Personnel Center, Randolph Air Force Base, Texas.

Colonel Wallace's military career began in February 1962, when she received a direct commission as a first lieutenant in the U.S. Air Force. Her experiences have not only been in the United States, but also in Japan, Germany, Thailand, Vietnam, and the Philippines. Her decorations include the Meritorious Service Medal, Air Force Commendation Medal, Vietnam Service Medal, Vietnam Gallantry Cross, and Vietnam Campaign Medal.

Colonel Margaret P.C. Nelson (Diploma, St. Philip Hospital School of Nursing, Richmond, Virginia; MA, Teachers College, Columbia University, New York [Fig. 6–15]) is Nurse Staff Development Officer, Keesler Technical Training Center, Medical Center, Keesler Air Force Base, Mississippi. She develops, coordinates, monitors, evaluates, and implements staff development programs which include orientation, skill training, and inservice and continuing education for 306 nurses and 348 medical technicians. She also serves as consultant to Headquarters Air

Figure 6–14   Colonel Clara B. Wallace, Chief, Nursing Education, Randolph Air Force Base, Texas.

Figure 6–15   Colonel Margaret P.C. Nelson, Nurse Corps, Nurse Staff Development Officer, Keesler Air Force Base, Mississippi.

Force Military Personnel Center and Staff Development Officers Air Force-wide.

Colonel Nelson's military experience began in 1963 as charge nurse, Medical Unit, Tinker Air Force Base, Oklahoma. Her prior civilian experience includes nursing education, service, and administration. Among Colonel Nelson's awards are the Bronze Star Medal, and Meritorious Service Medal, and the Air Force Commendation Medal.

Colonel Nora Kendall Noble (Diploma, Lincoln Hospital School of Nursing, Durham, North Carolina; BSN, The Catholic University of America, Washington, D.C.) before retiring was Commander, 2803 Air Force Base Group, Newark Air Force Station, Ohio. In this capacity, she was responsible for managing base support facilities for the 2,600 military and civilians assigned to the Aerospace Guidance and Metrology Center.

Colonel Kendall began her military career in 1960 at Gunter Air Force Base, Alabama. Her experiences have been in the continental United States, Alaska, and Germany. In 1970, she served as clinic chief nurse at McGuire Air Force Base and in 1971 was selected to become the flight nurse reserve advisor at Headquarters, 21st Air Force Base, McGuire, New Jersey. She assumed command of the 2803 Air Base Group on July 16, 1984.

Colonel Kendall's military awards and decorations include the Meritorious Service Medal with Two Oak Leaf Clusters, Air Force Outstanding Unit, Air Force Organizational Excellence Award, Air Force Longevity, Vietnam Service Medal, and the National Defense Service Medal.

Colonel Christine Spivey is stationed at Langley Air Force Base in Virginia.

Colonel Irene Trowell-Harris (Diploma, Columbia Hospital School of Nursing, Columbia, South Carolina; EdD, Teachers College, Columbia University, New York [Fig. 6–16]), stationed at Bolling Air Force Base in Washington, D.C., is Air National Guard Nurse Advisor to the Chief, Air Force Nurse Corps. She began her military career in 1963 with the 102nd Airomedical Evacuation Flight unit in Brooklyn; was appointed commander of the 105th U.S. Air Force Clinic in Newburgh, New York, in 1986; and became the first nurse in Air National Guard history to command a medical unit.

THE U.S. PUBLIC HEALTH SERVICE

The Public Health Service (PHS) came into being July 16, 1798, by an act of Congress. The act, signed by President John Adams, originally identified the PHS as the U.S. Marine Hospital Service, and for over 70 years the primary focus was on the care and relief of sick and injured seamen. In 1870, the Marine Hospital Service was reorganized as a national hospital system with centralized administration under a supervising surgeon given the title of surgeon general. In 1912, the Marine Hospital Service was renamed the U.S. Public Health Service. In later

Figure 6–16 Colonel Irene Trowell-Harris, Air National Guard Nurse Advisor to Chief Air Force Nurse Corps, Bolling Air Force Base, Washington, D.C.

years, its responsibilities increased until, at the time of its transfer from the Treasury Department to the Federal Security Agency in 1939, it was charged with numerous responsibilities relating to the improvement and protection of the public health (Williams, 1951).

The statutory establishment of the PHS Commissioned Corps occurred in 1889. The uniformed corps, set up along military lines with titles and pay corresponding to army and navy ranks, is a mobile force of professionals subject to duty anywhere upon assignment to combat disease and hazards to human health.

In 1918, Congress enacted legislation for a reserve corps, making it possible to recruit professional personnel other than physicians. By 1944, the commissioned corps was expanded to include research scientists, nurses, and other health specialists (Abdellah, 1977). Although nurses were not appointed to the PHS Commissioned Corps until 1944, trained nurses were employed in the hospital nursing services of the PHS as early as 1919. During the influenza epidemic of that year, a black nurse, Charity Collins Miles, a 1906 graduate of Spelman College School of Nursing, Atlanta, Georgia, served in the PHS and received a certificate signed by U.S. Surgeon General Rupert Blue (Thoms, 1929).

Today, a black nurse, Lieutenant Commander Russell L. Green (BSN, Tuskegee University, Tuskegee, Alabama; MSA, Central Michigan University, Mt. Pleasant [Fig. 6–17]), is Commissioned Personnel Program Coordinator, Division of Commissioned Personnel, Personnel Service

Figure 6–17   Lieutenant Commander Russell L. Green, Commissioned Personnel Program Coordinator.

Branch. He is responsible for planning, coordinating, implementing, and evaluating PHS's promotion and assimilation programs.

According to the January 13, 1945, issue of the *People's Voice*, Alma N. Jackson of Richmond, Virginia, was the first black woman to be commissioned by the PHS. At that time (1944), she was serving as assistant sanitarian in the all-Negro PHS Mission to Liberia.

In 1949, the position of chief nurse officer, with the rank of assistant surgeon general, was established (Notter & Spalding, 1965). In response to increasing responsibilities, the PHS has grown from a small nucleus of health professionals to approximately 5,700 commissioned corps officers and 50,000 civil service employees working in a wide variety of health programs. As one of the seven uniformed services (army, navy, air force, Marine Corps, Coast Guard, Public Health Service, National Oceanic and Atmospheric Administration) of the United States, the commissioned corps is a specialized career system designed to attract, retain, and develop health professionals who may be assigned to federal, state, or local agencies or international organizations (Commissioned Officers Handbook, 1990).

Today, the mission of the PHS is:

> to promote the protection and advancement of the Nation's physical and mental health by: Conducting medical and biomedical research; sponsoring and administering comprehensive programs for the development of health resources; preventing and controlling disease and alcohol and drug abuse; providing resources and expertise to the States and other public and private institutions, and to Tribes, Councils and organizations concerned with the health of American Indians and Alaska Natives, in the planning, direction and delivery of physical and mental health care services; enforcing laws to assure the safety and efficacy of drugs and protection against impure and unsafe foods, cosmetics, medical devices and radiation-producing projects; and coordinating with State, local and other Federal agencies to protect the public from exposure to toxic substances; coordinating with the States to set and implement national health policy and pursue effective intergovernmental relations; generating and upholding cooperative international health-related agreements, policies and programs, and cooperating with Commissions and organizations to promote international health activities. [*Organization Manual*, Chap. H, 1990, p. 1]

Initially a part of the Treasury Department, the PHS became a part of the Federal Security Agency in 1939 and remained there until 1953, when it became the health component of the Department of Health, Education, and Welfare, which was established by an act of Congress on April 11. Since the 1960s, PHS has undergone several organizational changes, including a name change from DHEW to the Department of

Health and Human Services. The present structure consists of the Office of the Assistant Secretary for Health (OASH) and eight line agencies.

OASH, under the direction of the assistant secretary for health, is responsible for all programs administered by PHS and provides executive leadership to PHS. The office is charged with the following:

> supports the Assistant Secretary for Health in the discharge of his/her responsibilities for planning and directing the activities of PHS; provides assistance to the States and PHS agencies in the areas of health systems planning, disease prevention and health technology assessment and transfer activities and programs. The OASH responsibilities include: conducting international health affairs; formulating health policy; maintaining relationships with other Federal, State, and local governmental and private agencies concerned with health; providing policy guidance for health-related activities throughout the Department; serving as the principal advisor and assistant to the Secretary on all policies and programs of PHS and health-related policies and activities of the Department for protecting the health of the American public, including environmental; providing leadership in biomedical and health services research; and providing leadership, coordination, and direction of a nationwide program of disease prevention and health promotion. [*Organization Manual*, Chap. HA, 1990, p. 1]

The Office of the Assistant Secretary for Health includes 18 major offices: (1) National AIDS Program; (2) Minority Health; (3) National Vaccine Program; (4) International Health; (5) Health Legislation; (6) President's Council on Physical Fitness and Sports; (7) Scientific Integrity Review; (8) Executive Secretariat; (9) Management; (10) Equal Employment Opportunity; (11) Refugee Health; (12) Emergency Preparedness; (13) Surgeon General; (14) Communications; (15) Population Affairs; (16) Intergovernmental Affairs; (17) Planning and Evaluation; and (18) Disease Prevention and Health Promotion.

In the Office of the Assistant Secretary for Health, from 1978 to 1990, was Dr. Joyce Elmore, who served as director of training in the Office of Population Affairs and Office of Family Planning. Project grants from the Office of Family Planning support the provision of comprehensive voluntary family planning services for all persons who cannot afford such services. Services are provided to women and men through grants to state and local health departments, universities, and a variety of private, nonprofit, and voluntary agencies.

The organization chart of the PHS, dated May 29, 1990, indicates the eight line agencies under the assistant secretary for health as (1) Agency for Toxic Substances and Disease Registry; (2) Alcohol, Drug Abuse, and Mental Health Administration; (3) Centers for Disease Control; (4) Food and Drug Administration; (5) Health Resources and Services Administration; (6) Indian Health Service; (7) National Institutes of Health;

and (8) Agency for Health Care Policy and Research. The PHS also has 10 regional offices located throughout the country.

Black nurses hold or have held key positions in most of the agencies where nurses are employed and in nine of the ten regional offices. Because of the Privacy Act of 1974 (Public Law 93-579), it was not possible to obtain information on individual black nurses from the official files of the PHS. Information presented here was obtained from the literature—books, periodicals, newspapers, and directories—correspondence, personal interviews, and telephone interviews.

Agency for Toxic Substances and Disease Registry

Established in 1983, the mission of the Agency for Toxic Substances and Disease Registry (ATSDR) is to prevent or mitigate the adverse human health effects and diminished quality of life that result from exposure to hazardous substances in the environment. The agency works closely with state, local, and other federal agencies to reduce or eliminate illness, disability, and death that result from exposure of the public and workers to toxic substances at spill and waste disposal sites (*Organization Manual*, Chap. HT, 1989, p. 1). To date, there are no nurses on the ATSDR staff.

Alcohol, Drug Abuse, and Mental Health Administration

The Alcohol, Drug Abuse, and Mental Health Administration (ADAMHA) was established by Congress in 1974 to administer and coordinate national programs to improve understanding and prevention of alcohol, drug abuse, and mental health disorders. The mission of ADAMHA is to:

> provide a national focus for the Federal effort to increase knowledge and promote effective strategies to deal with health problems and issues associated with the use and abuse of alcohol and drugs, and with mental illness and mental health.
>
> To accomplish this mission, the Administration conducts programs of research, training, prevention, information, and education. The Administration provides program expertise and technical assistance in responding to Federal, State, local or private organizations on matters related to their alcohol, drug abuse, and mental health matters. [*Organization Manual*, Chap. HM, 1990, p. 1]

This agency has the major federal responsibilities in the area of mental health. It is charged with helping support and monitor the states' programs, including the development of community mental health centers and programs dealing with alcoholism and drug addiction. ADAMHA also provides specialized care for drug addicts in federal hospitals in Lexington, Kentucky, and Fort Worth, Texas (Grant, 1975).

From 1979 to 1981, a black nurse, Dr. Rhetaugh Dumas, was deputy director of ADAMHA, having previously been Deputy Director, Division of Manpower and Training Programs of the National Institute of Mental Health (NIMH), one of the three institutes within ADAMHA. The other two institutes are the National Institute on Alcohol Abuse and Alcoholism and the National Institute on Drug Abuse. Only NIMH is discussed here.

National Institute of Mental Health

The Division of Mental Hygiene was established as part of the PHS in 1930. With the passage of the National Mental Health Act in 1946, interest and activities in the mental health field increased. In 1949, the Division of Mental Health in the Bureau of Medical Services was abolished, and NIMH was established as a unit of the National Institutes of Health (Williams, 1951). NIMH is now under ADAMHA.

NIMH administers the federal government's major program of support for research in mental health (authorization: Public Health Service Act, Section 301). NIMH conducts and supports research into the etiology, treatment, and prevention of mental and emotional illnesses and research on many public health problems related to mental health. The broad spectrum of biological, genetic, psychological, social, and environmental factors which affect and shape mental health and mental illnesses are studied through NIMH-supported research in hospitals, universities, mental health centers, and community settings.

From 1967 to 1987, St. Elizabeths Hospital, an institution for the mentally ill in Washington, D.C., where some of the earliest nursing research in mental health was conducted, had been under NIMH control. (Eunice Lewis Smith [BS, Florida A & M University, Tallahassee; MS, The Catholic University of America, Washington, D.C.] was the first black director of nursing at St. Elizabeths.) It was then transferred to the government of the District of Columbia, Commission on Mental Health Services. The hospital, however, has some PHS nurses detailed to it. Olive Paylor is one.

Olive Vera Armwood Paylor (Diploma, Harlem Hospital Center School of Nursing, New York; MSN, Howard University, Washington, D.C.), as clinical nurse specialist at St. Elizabeths, provides services to adult chronically ill psychiatric outpatients and conducts individual, group, and family psychotherapy.

The Center for Minority Groups Mental Health Programs was, for a number of years before it closed, a major component of NIMH. The center served as a focal point for institute activities that bore directly on improving the mental health of minority groups (i.e., blacks, Hispanics, Asian Americans, and Native Americans) and on increasing the number of minority group members in mental health research, training, and service fields. Clinical training support was designed to prepare mental health specialists for more effective roles as trainers of, and consultants to, primary health-care providers and to support basic (traditional) mental health personnel needs in research on social problems related to the mental health of minority groups and mental health service research and evaluation.

The center's training activities were designed to train minority group members for professional careers in mental health. In general, this objective was pursued by means of several funding mechanisms: (1) Professional Organization Fellowships for Research Training, (2) Professional Organizational Fellowships for Clinical or Services Training, and (3) Minority Center Postdoctoral Fellowships for Clinical or Services Training.

From 1972 to 1979, Dr. Mary Harper was deputy chief of the center, with the responsibility for the conception, planning, designing, implementation, monitoring, and evaluation of programs in mental health on a national and international level in research, delivery of mental health services, and development of mental health personnel. While in this position in 1974, she was instrumental in the ANA receiving a grant for minority nurses to earn doctorates (see Chapter 3).

From 1979 to 1981, Harper served as Director, Office of Policy Development and Research, 1981 White House Conference on Aging. In 1982, she returned to NIMH as coordinator of Long-Term Care Programs, which included nursing homes, boarding homes, self-care, and home health care. Still on the staff of NIMH, Harper has been again detailed to the White House Conference on Aging.

Centers for Disease Control

The Centers for Disease Control (CDC) serves as the national focus for developing and applying disease prevention and control, environmental health, and health promotion and education activities to improve the health of the people of the United States.

To accomplish its mission, CDC:

> identifies and defines preventable health problems and maintains active surveillance of diseases through epidemiologic and laboratory investigations and data collection, analysis, and distribution; serves as the PHS lead agency in developing and implementing operational programs relating to environmental health problems, and conducts operational research aimed at developing and testing effective disease prevention, control, and health promotion programs; admin-

isters a national program to develop recommended occupational safety and health standards and to conduct research, training, and technical assistance to assure safe and healthful working conditions for every working person; develops and implements a program to sustain a strong national workforce in disease prevention and control; and conducts a national program for improving the performance of clinical laboratories.

CDC is responsible for controlling the introduction and spread of infectious diseases, and provides consultation and assistance to other nations and international agencies to assist in improving their disease prevention and control, environmental health, and health promotion activities. CDC administers the Preventive Health and Health Services Block Grant and specific preventive health categorical grant programs while providing program expertise and assistance in responding to Federal, State, local, and private organizations on matters related to disease prevention and control activities. [*Organization Manual*, Chapter HC, 1982, p. 1]

Two black nurses are on the staff of the CDC: Cheryl Blackmore in the Commissioned Corps and Yvonne Green.

Cheryl Blackmore (BS, State University of New York at Buffalo School of Nursing; MPH, Emory University, Atlanta, Georgia) is Epidemiologist, Division of Reproductive Health. In this position, she conducts epidemiologic surveillance and research and field investigations to evaluate health problems, programs, and policies related to pregnancy and its outcomes. She consults, collaborates with, and provides technical assistance to local, state, other federal agencies, foreign governments, and appropriate nongovernmental organizations on bilateral and multilateral research and demonstration projects, including surveys and assessments of pregnancy-related health problems. Of her many awards is one from CDC for contributions to the advancement of women.

Yvonne Theresa Green (BSN, Dillard University, New Orleans, Louisiana; MSN, Yale University, New Haven, Connecticut) is Assistant Branch Chief for Chronic Disease Prevention and Health Promotion, Division of Reproductive Health, Women's Health and Fertility Branch. She is responsible for management of all operational activities including budget, personnel information systems, contract development and monitoring, and program review and evaluation. Since 1987, she has received three PHS awards.

Food and Drug Administration

The Pure Food and Drug Act of 1906 was administered for a number of years by the Bureau of Chemistry of the Department of Agriculture. Later, the Food and Drug Administration (FDA) was established, and administration of the law was transferred to that organization (Williams, 1951).

The FDA is a scientific regulatory agency whose mission is to:

> protect the public health of the nation as it may be impaired by foods, drugs, biological products, cosmetics, medical devices, ionizing and nonionizing radiation-emitting products and substances, poisons, pesticides, and food additives. FDA's regulatory functions are geared to insure that: Foods are safe, pure, and wholesome; drugs, medical devices, and biological products are safe and effective; cosmetics are harmless; all of the above are honestly and informatively packaged; and that exposure to potentially injurious radiation is minimized. [*Organization Manual*, Chap. HF, 1989, p. 1]

Ernestine W. Murray (BSN, Towson State University School of Nursing, Towson, Maryland; MAS, Johns Hopkins University, Baltimore, Maryland) is Nurse Consultant, Device Technology, Office of Training and Assistance. She is responsible for identifying, on a national scale, problems regarding the safe and efficient use of medical devices by health professionals—with specific emphasis on those used by nurses—and implementing corrective action programs. Since 1982, she has received several PHS awards. She holds the rank of lieutenant commander in the commissioned corps.

Health Resources and Services Administration

The Health Resources and Services Administration (HRSA) provides leadership and direction to programs and activities designed to improve the health services for all people of the United States and to develop health care and maintenance systems that are adequately financed, comprehensive, interrelated, and responsive to the needs of individuals and families in all levels of society. Specifically, HRSA:

> (1) provides leadership and support efforts designed to integrate health services delivery programs with public and private health financing programs, including health maintenance organizations; (2) administers the health services block grants, categorical grants, and formula grant-supported programs; (3) provides or arranges for personal health services, including both hospital and out-patient care to designated beneficiaries; (4) administers programs to improve the utilization of health resources through health planning; (5) provides technical assistance for modernizing or replacing health care facilities; (6) provides leadership to improve the education, training, distribution, supply, use and quality of the Nation's health personnel; and (7) provides advice and support to the Assistant Secretary for

Health in the formulation of health policies. [*Organization Manual*, Chap. HB, 1986, p. 1]

Of the major components of the HRSA, black nurses hold or have held key positions in the following: the Bureau of Health Professions in which are the Division of Nursing, the Division of Medicine, and the Division of Associated and Dental Health Professions; the Bureau of Health Resources Development in which is located the Division of Planning Assistance and Assessment; the Bureau of Health Care Delivery and Assistance with its Division of National Hansen's Disease Programs, Division of National Health Service Corps, Division of Special Populations Program Development, and Division of Federal Occupational and Beneficiary Health Services; and the Maternal and Child Health Bureau.

Bureau of Health Professions.   The Bureau of Health Professions provides national leadership in the development of the personnel required to staff the nation's health care delivery system. This bureau directs resources to areas of high national priority by increasing the supply of primary care practitioners, improving the distribution of health professionals both geographically and by specialty, ensuring the availability of adequately prepared health professionals, and ensuring access to health careers for the disadvantaged.

The bureau's **Division of Nursing** supports programs related to the development, financing, and use of educational resources for the improvement of nurse training. This division supports and conducts programs for the development, use, quality, and distribution of nursing personnel, in order to advance the health status of individuals, families, and communities. It fosters and supports projects to expand the scientific-base of nursing practice and role reformulation and to develop and incorporate new knowledge into practice and education. The division provides consultation and technical assistance on all aspects of nursing to public and private organizations, agencies, and institutions, including international agencies and ministries of health.

Black nurses have held key positions in the Division of Nursing. One such nurse was Dr. Marie Bourgeois who, until her retirement in 1982, was Chief, Research Training Section, Nursing Research Branch. The responsibilities of this position included administering the National Research Service Awards Program; developing policies and programs for research training; interpreting federal policies, developing contract proposals, and providing technical assistance to individuals and to public and private agencies on research projects for nursing and related fields; maintaining source material on research training; and assessing post-training performance, educational trends, and developments.

Other black nurses who have been on the staff of the Division of Nursing as consultants are Camille Alexander, Dr. Martha Lewis Smith,

Dr. Alice Hilfiker, Mabel Morris, Dr. Verna Cook, Mary Whitehurst, and Dr. Doris Mosley. In 1990, Diane Thompkins served as program analyst. Also, Alicia Georges, President, NBNA, was appointed to the National Advisory Council of the division for a two-year term.

The **Division of Medicine** serves as the federal focus for the education, practice, and credentialing of medical personnel, including physician assistants. Doris Mosley (BS, Dillard University Division of Nursing, New Orleans, Louisiana; EdD, Teachers College, Columbia University, New York [Fig. 6–18]) has been with the PHS in various capacities since 1980. Since 1989, she has been a public health analyst/project officer in the AIDS Education and Training Centers (AETC) Program. This program provides grant funds to eligible health professions educational programs to educate/train primary health care providers who are willing and able to care for persons with HIV/AIDS. Current trainee focus is on a multi-disciplinary group of primary caregivers, including physicians, nurses, physician assistants, nurse practitioners, dentists, and dental hygienists. In addition to providing guidance and technical assistance to several of the 15 existing AETC programs, Mosley also serves as a key nursing education resource to the program working collaboratively with the Division of Nursing and other federal agencies and units on issues and activities of mutual interest.

In the **Division of Associated and Dental Health Professions**, Geriatric Education Section, is Camille Alexander. Alexander (BS, Dillard University Division of Nursing, New Orleans, Louisiana; MSN, Boston University, Boston, Massachusetts) is a public health analyst.

Figure 6–18   Dr. Doris Mosley, Public Health Analyst/Project Officer, AIDS Education and Learning Centers Program, Division of Medicine.

Bureau of Health Resources Development. Within the Bureau of Health Resources Development is the **Division of Planning Assistance and Assessment**. From 1981 to 1984, Doris Mosley was program analyst.

Bureau of Health Care Delivery and Assistance. Within the Bureau of Health Care Delivery and Assistance are the Division of National Hansen's Disease Programs, the Division of the National Health Service Corps, the Division of Special Populations Program Development, and the Division of Federal Occupational and Beneficiary Health Services.

In 1953, the PHS Division of Hospitals operated 19 hospitals and approximately 21 outpatient clinics. During the succeeding years, declining demand for hospitalization, created mainly by the reduction in numbers of American seamen, and budgetary necessity led to the closing of some hospitals and the conversion of others to outpatient clinics.

Freedmen's Hospital in Washington, D.C., a black institution that had been operating a school of nursing since 1894, had been under the auspices of several federal agencies until it was placed under the direction of the PHS in 1940 and its functions transferred to the Federal Security Agency by the Reorganization Act of 1939. In 1953, all functions of the abolished Federal Security Agency were transferred to the Department of Health, Education, and Welfare (DHEW). Public Law 87-622, approved September 21, 1961, directed the transfer of Freedmen's Hospital from DHEW to Howard University, although the transfer was not completed until July 1, 1967 (Federal Health Programs, 1971). The name of the hospital was changed to Howard University Hospital.

As of June 30, 1971, the Federal Health Programs Service operated eight general hospitals located in Baltimore, Boston, Galveston, New Orleans, Norfolk, San Francisco, Seattle, Staten Island, and one hospital for the care and treatment of leprosy patients at Carville, Louisiana (Federal Health Programs, 1971). In 1981 the eight general hospitals were closed, leaving only the one at Carville, the facility of the **Division of National Hansen's Disease Programs**.

The hospital at Carville, which has been renamed the Gillis Long Center for Hansen's Disease, is located in Louisiana on the Mississippi River, 25 miles south of Baton Rouge and 75 miles north of New Orleans. Through an act of Congress, the Louisiana Leper Home was purchased by the PHS on January 3, 1921, from the state of Louisiana, which had operated it since 1894 as a home for persons with leprosy within the state. Today, its primary purpose is to afford leprosy patients a facility for complete evaluation and treatment. The hospital also serves as a research and training center for the disease.

Donna Kibble (Diploma, Glendale Adventist School of Nursing, Glendale, California) is the only black professional nurse at Gillis Long, having joined the staff in 1974. Since 1980, she has been clinical nurse supervisor.

The **Division of National Health Service Corps** (NHSC) was authorized under Public Law 91-623, the Emergency Health Personnel Act of 1970, and continued as amended under Public Law 92-585, in order "to improve the delivery of health services to persons living in medically underserved communities and areas of the United States."

The mission of the NHSC is to improve the delivery of health services in areas with shortages of health care workers and to reduce the number of such areas by the appropriate placement of health professionals and health resources. Corps physicians, dentists, nurses, and allied medical personnel assigned to field stations are primarily commissioned personnel of the PHS. Other corps personnel may be part of the civil service system.

In late 1990, Joyce Elmore (Diploma, Freedmen's Hospital School of Nursing, Washington, D.C.; PhD, The Catholic University of America, Washington, D.C. [Fig. 6–19]) was transferred from the office of the Assistant Secretary for Health to the NHSC as area regional nursing consultant. In this position, she assists health professions schools in assigning students for clinical experience or placements in community health centers.

In addition to her 13 years with the PHS, Elmore's experience includes work in private duty and office nursing and as instructor and professor in schools of nursing, dean of Chicago State University School of Nursing, director of the ANA Department of Nursing Education, and consultant to the vice president for health affairs at Howard University, Washington, D.C. Her rank in the PHS Commissioned Corps is that of captain.

In 1990, Mary Long was appointed to a three-year term on the National Advisory Council of NHSC.

Figure 6–19   Dr. Joyce Elmore, Area/Regional Nursing Consultant, Division of National Health Service Corps.

The **Division of Special Populations Program Development** has four black nurses in key positions: Robyn Guerlaine Brown-Douglas, Denise Canton, Deborah Lynnette Parham, and Beverly R. Wright.

Robyn Brown-Douglas (BSN, College of New Rochelle, New York; MA, Barry University, Miami Shores, Florida) serves as nurse consultant. The Air Force Commendation Medal for Meritorious Service is among her many honors and awards.

Denise Canton (BSN, Illinois Wesleyan University, Bloomington, Illinois; DNSc, The Catholic University of America, Washington, D.C.) holds three titles: Federal Program Coordinator in the Division; Senior Staffing Officer, Office of the Surgeon General, USPHS Commissioned Corps; and Nurse Placement Officer, USPHS Commissioned Corps.

Deborah Lynnette Parham (BSN, University of Cincinnati School of Nursing and Health, Cincinnati, Ohio; PhD, University of North Carolina, Chapel Hill) is Chief, Policy and Evaluation Branch. Among her duties is to oversee the management of the Native Hawaiian Health Care Program and Pacific Basin Health Care Initiative.

Beverly R. Wright (Diploma, Long Island College Hospital School of Nursing, Brooklyn, New York; MS, Yale University School of Nursing, New Haven, Connecticut) is Deputy Branch Chief, Prenatal and Child Health Branch.

The **Division of Federal Occupational and Beneficiary Health Services** has two black nurses: Gladys Perkins and Ellen King.

Lieutenant Commander Gladys Perkins (AAS, Bronx Community College, Department of Nursing, Bronx, New York; MS, Hunter College, New York, New York) is a patient care coordinator, responsible for coordinating and evaluating health care services for eligible beneficiaries and ensuring availability and accessibility to adequate resources and continuity and comprehensiveness of care. In 1986 and 1990, she received the PHS Unit Commendation Medal.

Ellen J. King (BS, Columbia Union College School of Nursing, Takoma Park, Maryland) is Senior Clinical Nurse Specialist/Patient Care Coordinator, Health Services Support Branch, with the rank of lieutenant commander, USPHS Regular Corps. In this position, she coordinates medical care for the active duty PHS officers for the National Oceanic and Atmospheric Administration.

Maternal and Child Health Bureau. Lieutenant Commander Melva Tuggle Owens (AD, Community College of Baltimore, Baltimore, Maryland; MPA, University of Baltimore), in her position as nurse consultant, helps states develop emergency medical systems for children and is responsible for block grant programs to children ages five through 12.

Indian Health Service

More than 800,000 American Indians and Alaska Natives depend on the Indian Health Service (IHS) for their total health needs. IHS is the only federal program that provides direct health services to the American Indians, deriving its basic authorities from the Snyder Act of 1921. Before 1955, IHS was under the Bureau of Indian Affairs. In 1955, Congress placed it under the PHS. Having been a component of the Health Resource and Services Administration, in 1988 IHS was made a line agency.

One of the largest federal agencies, IHS:

> provides a comprehensive health services delivery system for American Indians and Alaska Natives with opportunity for maximum tribal involvement in developing and managing programs to meet their health needs. The goal of IHS is to raise the health level of the Indian and Alaska Native people to the highest possible level. [*Organization Manual*, Chap. H.G., 1988, p. 1]

IHS operates 51 hospitals, 99 health centers, and 108 health stations. Three thousand nurses provide the major portion of health care for American Indians and Alaska Natives in 24 states. "The nurses who serve in the Indian Health Service comprise 64 percent of all those RNs in the Public Health Service" (Subcommittee hearings, *American Nurse*, September, 1990, p.2).

Two black nurses hold key positions in the IHS: Carnie Hayes and Glenda Jarrett. Carnie A. Hayes (AA, Merritt College, Oakland, California; MSN, University of California, San Francisco [Fig. 6-20]), a commissioned officer in the PHS, is Senior Nurse Clinician, Phoenix Indian Medical Center, Phoenix, Arizona. Before joining the IHS, Hayes had experience teaching in associate degree and baccalaureate nursing programs and in public health agencies. He was also a contributing author to *Perspectives on Adolescent Health Care* by Ramona T. Mercer, published by J.B. Lippincott Company in 1979.

Glenda O. Jarrett (ASN, Norfolk State University, Norfolk, Virginia; BSN, Hampton University, Hampton, Virginia) is Inpatient Head Nurse, Cherokee Indian Hospital, Cherokee, North Carolina, and serves as an assistant to the director of nursing.

National Institutes of Health

The National Laboratory of Hygiene, established in 1891, was the forerunner of the National Institutes of Health (NIH).

Figure 6–20   Carnie A. Hayes, Senior Nurse Clinician, Phoenix Indian Medical Center, Phoenix, Arizona.

NIH provides leadership and direction to programs designed to improve the health of the people of the United States through the following activities:

> (1) Conducts and supports research in the causes, diagnosis, prevention, and cure of diseases of man, in the processes of human growth and development, in the biological effects of environmental contaminants, and in related sciences, and supports the training of research personnel, the construction of research facilities, and the development of other research resources.
> (2) Directs programs for the collection, dissemination, and exchange of information in medicine and health, including the development and support of medical libraries and the training of medical librarians and other information specialists. [*Organization Manual*, Chap. HN, 1987, p. 1]

Four components of NIH in which black nurses are or have been involved are the following: (1) the Clinical Center; (2) the National Library of Medicine; (3) the National Center for Nursing Research; and (4) the Extramural Associates Program.

Clinical Center.   In 1952, the USPHS established on the grounds of the NIH in Bethesda, Maryland, a research hospital center of 500 beds called the National Clinical Center (Dolan et al., 1983). At the center, research and the clinical care of patients are closely integrated, and the nurse is not only a member of the patient care team, but also of the research team. Nurses at the Clinical Center collaborate with other health professionals to make science consistent with the highest quality of care.

Apart from their roles in research initiated by scientists at the center, nurses are encouraged to use research methods to conduct studies in their own areas of interest.

Two black nurses hold key positions at the Clinical Center: Diane Thompkins and Annette Wright.

Diane Thompkins (BSN, State University of New York at Buffalo; MS, University of Maryland School of Nursing, Baltimore) is nurse consultant, after having served briefly as program analyst with the Division of Nursing.

Annette M. Wright (BSN, Howard University College of Nursing, Washington, D.C.; MA, Central Michigan University, Mt. Pleasant, Michigan) is Chief, Basic Nursing Unit. In this position, she assumes 24-hour responsibility and accountability for patient care and staff activities on the pediatric endocrine/genetic unit in a research setting.

National Library of Medicine. The National Library of Medicine (NLM) was established in 1836 as the Library of the Army Surgeon General's Office and remained in the military until 1956, when it was transferred to the NIH and upgraded to the National Library of Medicine.

NLM is the world's largest research library in a single scientific and professional field. Its holdings include 3.5 million books, journals, technical reports, theses, microfilms, and pictorial and audiovisual materials. Housed in the library is one of the nation's largest medical history collections, with contents dating from the 11th to the mid-19th centuries. NLM also houses historical documents in nursing, including those of the National League for Nursing. The nursing collection includes approximately 174 journals or serial letters and more than 2,000 book titles (Sparks, 1986).

Dorothy L. Moore (Diploma, Lincoln School for Nurses, New York; MS, School of Library Services, Columbia University, New York) is not classified as a nurse by the PHS, but as a technical information specialist. Moore also holds certificates from the NLM Post-Graduate Associate Program in Biomedical Communications and the Health and Human Services Women's Initiate Training Program.

National Center for Nursing Research. On November 20, 1985, the Senate overrode President Reagan's veto of the NIH bill and established the National Center for Nursing Research (NCNR) at NIH. The House had voted to override the veto the week before. Steady lobbying efforts by nurses and nursing groups helped to sway the vote. It was they who convinced Congress of the importance of research to the nursing profession and to the improvement of patient care.

The NCNR was authorized under the Health Research Extension Act of 1985, PL 99-158. On April 18, 1986, Secretary Bowen of the Department of Health and Human Services (HHS) announced the establishment of the NCNR at NIH for the purpose of conducting a program of grants and awards supporting nursing research and research training related to patient care, promotion of health, prevention of disease, and mitigation of the effects of acute and chronic illnesses and disabilities (Merritt, 1986).

According to its director, Dr. Ada Sue Hinshaw, the center provides leadership for a program of support for nurse investigators; works to develop nurse research training programs with investigators and their graduate programs; oversees policy, procedural, and technical matters related to grants and contracts; and supervises negotiations with principal investigators and institutions that receive nursing research grants.

Five initiatives guide the programs of the NCNR: development of the National Nursing Research Agenda identifying national research priorities, creation of a trajectory for research training and career development, facilitation of multidisciplinary research collaboration, implementation of an intramural research program, and initiation of an international research program.

While there are no black nurses on the staff of NCNR, Dr. Ora Strickland, appointed in 1989 to a four-year term by the secretary of HHS, serves on the National Advisory Council. The council advises the secretary, the director of NIH, and the director of NCNR on programs and directions of the center.

Extramural Associates Program. Established in 1978, the Extramural Associates Program (EAP), administered by the Office of Extramural Research at NIH, is designed to promote the entry and participation of underrepresented minorities and women in biomedical and behavioral research. The program is viewed as an investment that will yield multiple benefits to participating individuals and institutions, the NIH, and ultimately, to the vitality of health-related research in the nation. The objectives of the program also coincide with NIH's goals of increasing the pool of minority and women research scientists and supporting research to address disorders which disproportionately affect these special populations.

The NIH selects, on a competitive basis, scientific faculty and academic administrators from institutions which contribute significantly to the pool of minorities and women in science. Those selected become extramural associates and spend five months in residence at the NIH in Bethesda, Maryland. The desired outcome of the program is that, upon return to the home institution, each NIH-trained associate will assume an active role in promoting and expanding opportunities for faculty and students to participate in biomedical and behavioral research. Among the immediate benefits the program offers is the opportunity for NIH staff and associates to work together (NIH Extramural Associates Program, 1990). Since the program's inception, three black nurses have participated. Dr. Johnea Kelley, North Carolina Central University, Durham; Dr. Mamie Montague, Howard University, Washington, D.C., and Dr. Joyce Taylor Harden, University of Texas, San Antonio.

In her final report on her EAP experience, Montague wrote,

> Subsequent to the EAP experience, three new opportunities have become available to me: (1) the challenge of being placed in a new role as coordinator of faculty research and development within the college of nursing at my own institution; (2) the opportunity to be sponsored as a post-doctoral fellow at the University of Pennsylvania Center for Nursing Research by the Minority Fellowship Programs of the American Nurses' Association; and (3) the challenge of redefining my own research status while attempting to orchestrate a beginning research career. [Montague, 1990]

Agency for Health Care Policy and Research

While there are no black nurses on the staff of the Agency for Health Care Policy and Research (AHCPR), Dr. Juanita Fleming and Dr. Linda Burnes-Bolton serve on the 17-member National Advisory Council to advise the secretary of Health and Human Services and the administrator of the agency. The purposes of AHCPR are the following:

> provides national leadership and administration of a program to enhance the quality, appropriateness, and effectiveness of health care services, and access to such services through the establishment of a broad base of scientific research and through the promotion of improvements in clinical practice and in the organization, financing, and delivery of health care services including: (1) The effectiveness, efficiency, and quality of health care services; (2) the outcomes of health care services and procedures; (3) clinical practice, including primary care and practice-oriented research; (4) health care technologies, facilities, and equipment; (5) health care costs productivity, and market forces; (6) health promotion and disease prevention; (7) health statistics and epidemiology; (8) medical liability; (9) delivery of health care services in rural areas; and (10) the health of low-income groups, minority groups, and the elderly. [*Organization Manual*, Chap. HP, 1990, p. 1]

Regional Offices

The PHS Regional Offices support the PHS mission of improving the health of the nation's population by administering regional health programs and activities to ensure a coordinated regional effort in support of national health policies and state and local needs within each region. These responsibilities include the following:

> Assessing regional health requirements, assuring integration of health
> programs, and addressing cross-cutting program issues and initia-
> tives to achieve program goals and meet overall regional health needs;
> providing a PHS focal point for responding to the needs of State
> and local governments, community agencies, and others involved in
> the planning or provision of general health and mental health ser-
> vices; providing a PHS focal point for emergency preparedness and
> emergency medical services in the regions; supporting the Depart-
> ment of Health and Human Services (DHHS) intergovernmental
> relations activities and responding to health issues emanating from
> State and local concerns; and administering health activities and
> programs to provide for prevention of health programs, improved
> systems and capacity for providing health care, and assuring access
> to and quality of general health services. [*Organizational Manual*,
> Chap. HD, 1987, p. 1]

The ten regional offices are I—Boston; II—New York; III—Philadelphia; IV—Atlanta; V—Chicago; VI—Dallas; VII—Kansas City; VIII—
Denver; IX—San Francisco; and X—Seattle. Black nurses hold key positions in nine of these regions.

Region I, Boston.   Shirley A. Smith (Diploma, Boston Hospital School
of Nursing; MS, Boston University School of Nursing, Boston, Massachusetts) has been regional maternal and child health nursing consultant
since 1976. She is responsible for assessment, administration, consultation, and evaluation of federally mandated health care programs for
mothers, children, and families in New England. Prior to this appointment, Smith held positions in hospitals, industry, and public health agencies in the state of Massachusetts in education, service, and administration.

Marva Nathan (Diploma, St. Elizabeth Hospital School of Nursing,
Youngstown, Ohio; MS, Harvard University School of Public Health,
Boston, Massachusetts) is Project Officer, Health Care Financing Administration. In this position, she monitors, directs, and evaluates peer
review organizations in their management of federal contracts to ensure
the quality of health care provided to medical beneficiaries. She also
recommends approval/disapproval of the contract. One of her many
past positions was Instructor, Ahmadu Bello University School of Nursing, Zaria, Nigeria, West Africa.

Region II, New York.   Ramona M. Baptiste (Diploma, Malden Hospital
School of Nursing, Malden, Massachusetts; MA, Johns Hopkins University, Baltimore, Maryland [Fig. 6-21]) is Associate Director, Division
of Federal Occupational Health.

Roberta Annette Holder-Mosley (BAN, Simmons College, Boston,
Massachusetts; MS, Columbia University, New York, New York [Fig. 6-
22]) is Regional Nurse Consultant for Primary Care, Clinical Geographic
Representative for New York City, and Regional Perinatal Coordinator,
Division of Health Services Branch. A certified nurse-midwife, Holder-

Figure 6–21   Ramona M. Baptiste, Associate Director, Division of Federal Occupational Health, Region II, New York.

Mosley provides technical assistance/consultation to migrant and community health centers in relation to maternal and child health/perinatal issues in the region. A commissioned officer in the PHS, she has been the recipient of five awards from the PHS since 1979.

Region III, Philadelphia.   Claudette V. Campbell (MSN, University of Pennsylvania School of Nursing, Philadelphia; MPH, Johns Hopkins University, Baltimore, Maryland) is Chief, Survey and Certification Branch, Division of Health Standards and Quality, Health Care Training Administration, and holds the rank of captain in the PHS Commissioned Corps. She has received many commendations, the latest being the PHS Outstanding Service Medal on December 11, 1990, in recognition of consistent outstanding performance.

Mary L. Flowers (Diploma, Freedmen's Hospital School of Nursing, Washington, D.C.; MEd, Temple University, Philadelphia, Pennsylvania) is Survey and Certification Program Specialist, Division of Health Standards and Quality Survey and Certification Operations Branch. In this position, she assesses the performance of the state survey agency in interpreting and applying administrative procedures in the survey and certification process of all types of medical facilities participating in the Medicare program to ensure compliance with Medicare requirements.

Also in Region III is Barbara Williamson-Hunt (AD, Community College of Philadelphia Department of Nursing; MS, St. Joseph's University,

Figure 6–22   Roberta Annette Holder-Mosley, Regional Nurse Consultant for Primary Care, Region II, New York.

Philadelphia, Pennsylvania) as Medical Review Entity Program Specialist and Nurse Consultant, Health Care Financing Administration. She oversees the Medicare review activities of Medical Review Entities to ensure that medicine recipients receive medically necessary and appropriate care that meets recognized professional standards in the appropriate setting.

Region IV, Atlanta.   Clara Henderson Cobb (BSN, Columbia Union College School of Nursing, Takoma Park, Maryland; MSN, Medical College of Georgia, Augusta [Fig. 6-23]), a commissioned officer in the PHS with the rank of commander, is nurse consultant. In this position, she is responsible for monitoring peer review organizations to ensure protection against potential provider abuses as well as ensure that critically important high quality medical care is provided to Medicare beneficiaries. She is also responsible for complete medical review activities in two of the eight states within the region.

Region V, Chicago.   Dolores Perteet (BSN, Loyola University School of Nursing, Chicago; MPH, Yale University, New Haven, Connecticut), has been medical review specialist with the Health Care Financing Administration, Division of Medicare, since 1987. In this position, she performs duties associated with the development and implementation of Medicare coverage policy and participates in the evaluation of fiscal intermediary medical review operations associated with claims determination. She is also assigned to work on other department initiatives associated with Medicaid-funded maternal/child health services aimed at decreasing maternal and infant morbidity and mortality in the region.

Figure 6–23 Clara L. Henderson Cobb, Nurse Consultant, Region IV, Atlanta.

Region VI, Dallas. Lawanda Prince Gordon (BSN, MSN, University of Cincinnati, Ohio [Fig. 6-24]) is maternal and child health nursing consultant. She functions as the principal regional advisor in planning, organizing, coordinating, and evaluating maternal/child health nursing activities with particular emphasis on children with special health care needs.

Region VII, Kansas City, Missouri. Joyce Goff (BSN, Texas Christian University, Fort Worth; MEd, Georgia State University, Atlanta [Fig. 6-25]) is Director of Operations, Division of Federal Occupational Health, and is responsible for a four-state region of ten occupational health facilities and for supervising all health unit activities. She has served on active duty with the commissioned corps on several occasions during her career. In 1983 and 1989, Goff received the USPHS Unit Accommodation Award.

Region VIII, Denver. Erna S. Sanderson (Diploma, St. Paul's Hospital School of Nursing, Dallas, Texas; BS, Paul Quinn College, Waco, Taxas) is an occupational health nurse.

Region X, Seattle. Vivian O. Lee (BSN, University of Washington, Seattle; MPA, University of Puget Sound [Fig. 6-26]) is regional nursing consultant and the only black nurse employed by Region X, having begun her duties on January 1, 1972, about two and a half years after the region had been formed. From 1972 to 1975, she was program man-

Figure 6–24   Lawanda Prince Gordon, Maternal and Child Health Consultant, Region VI, Dallas, Texas.

agement officer, designing protocols for increasing efficiency and effectivness of programs. While serving as public health advisor from 1975 to 1980, she developed a regional evaluation system, a quality assurance system, a computerized management information system, and a management manual to assist in standardizing services and ensuring high-quality, accessible services to low-income, minority, and other special population groups.

In her 18 years with the Region X office, Lee has received 19 awards and/or promotions from the USPHS for outstanding performance in the family planning program and for special work on behalf of disabled clients and women. Lee has also received one national, one regional, and eight state or local awards from nongovernmental organizations for her leadership in the field of family planning, over the same period.

Other Programs

In addition to assignments to regions, St. Elizabeths Hospital, and the White House Conference on Aging, PHS professionals are frequently detailed from the line agencies to other federal programs, such as the Bureau of Prisons, Immigration Naturalization Service Health Care Program, Health Care Finance Administration, and the District of Columbia Commission on Mental Health Services.

The Federal Bureau of Prisons operates within the Department of Justice in the executive branch of the federal government. Its mission

Figure 6–25   Joyce Goff, Director of Operations, Division of Federal Occupational Health, Region VII, Kansas City, Missouri.

is to provide safekeeping, care, and subsistence for all inmates under the jurisdiction of the U.S. Attorney General. The Bureau of Prisons operates 47 institutions nationwide and Shirley A. Bowman (Diploma, Franklin Square Hospital School of Nursing, Baltimore, Maryland; MA, New York University, New York [Fig. 6-27]) is chief nurse. The Bureau of Prisons has a central office in Washington, D.C.

Norma J. Hatot (BSN, Hampton University, Hampton, Virginia; MA, Central Michigan University, Mt. Pleasant [Fig. 6-28]) is detailed from ADAMHA to the government of the District of Columbia Commission on Mental Health Services, Forensic Inpatient Services, as associate chief nurse.

PHS Programs Overseas

As the influence of the United States in world affairs extended beyond national boundaries, assistance from the PHS was requested for health studies in other countries (Williams, 1951).

During World War II, PHS nurses were assigned to work with the Office of Civilian Defense, the Liberian Mission, the United Nations Relief and Rehabilitation Administration (UNRRA), the Migrant Health Programs of the Department of Agriculture, and the Office of Inter-American Affairs (Williams, 1951). Black nurses of the PHS figured prominently in the Mission to Liberia and with UNRRA in China and South America.

Figure 6–26　　Vivian O. Lee, Regional Nursing Consultant, Region X, Seattle, Washington.

Liberian Mission.　With the location of the United States military installations in Liberia during World War II, our government became extremely interested in the public health conditions there, particularly in the problems of environmental sanitation and malaria control (Williams, 1951).

In January 1944, the president-elect of the Republic of Liberia requested the president of the United States to render such aid as might be available to assist the Liberian government in the solution of many of its major health problems, especially certain preventable diseases that were seriously handicapping the economic and social development of the country.

In a memorandum dated February 4, 1944, President Roosevelt wrote as follows:

> I think we should do everything possible to improve health conditions in Liberia. This should be taken up with the War department and the State department and Lend Lease. I should like to have a report on the progress. [Cooperative Liberia-United States Public Health Program, 1954, p. 1]

In response to the request, on March 28, 1944, the Department of State, with the endorsement of the War Department, requested the PHS to dispatch a mission to Liberia, which was directed as follows:

Figure 6–27   Shirley A. Bowman, Chief Nurse, Federal Bureau of Prisons.

> . . . to perform extra-military sanitation in cooperation with the government of Liberia for the protection of United States military personnel, including such sanitation works as may be necessary in other areas which may affect their health; to render the environs of airports free of exotic mosquito species dangerous to the United States if introduced; to advise the Liberian Government in planning for the sanitation of coastal towns, and to render such aid as may be requested by the Liberian Government in the enlargement of its public health program . . . . [Williams, 1951, p. 466]

In October 1944, the Liberian Mission was organized under the direction of John B. West, who had been active both in appraising the health conditions in Liberia and in preparing preliminary plans and programs for the mission. A group of four persons arrived in Monrovia in November 1944. Shortly thereafter this group was reinforced with the arrival of Surgeon Charles West; Dental Surgeon Louis R. Middleton; Assistant Nurse Officers Theresa Colwell Jordense (Diploma, Lincoln School for Nurses, New York), Virginia Ford (Diploma, Kansas City General No. 2, Kansas City, Missouri), and Hazel Birch (Diploma, Harlem Hospital School of Nursing, New York); and Assistant Sanitarian Alma Jackson.

At about this same time, the Office of Cultural Affairs of the Department of State assigned two nursing arts instructors, Vashti Hall Gilmore and Inez Butler, both graduates of Freedmen's Hospital School

Figure 6–28   Norma Hatot, Associate Chief Nurse, Forensic Inpatient Services, District of Columbia Commission on Mental Health Services.

of Nursing in Washington, D.C., to Liberia for the purpose of assisting the mission in developing a training school for Liberian nurses.

The maximum strength of the mission was reached in 1947, when 21 professional and technical persons were on active duty there (Williams, 1951). Among these were Clara E. Beverly and Lillian Holly, both of Freedmen's Hospital (Beverly, 1947). Captain Beverly served as nursing arts instructor in the school of nursing sponsored by the Liberian government. In 1949, she returned to Freedmen's but was again assigned to the PHS Mission to Liberia in 1952, this time as director of nursing education. In 1956, she returned to Freedmen's but was again assigned to teach practical nursing at the Navajo Medical Center at Fort Defiance, Arizona.

The Mission to Liberia was taken over by the Agency for International Development (AID) in 1954. The pioneer work of the USPHS Mission to Liberia provided a valuable guide in planning health projects in other underdeveloped areas (Williams, 1951).

U.S. Relief and Rehabilitation Administration. The United States Relief and Rehabilitation Administration was established on November 9, 1943, in Washington, D.C., upon the signing of an agreement by 44 nations, including the United States. The administration planned and administered measures for the relief of war victims through the provision of food, fuel, clothing, shelter and other basic necessities, and medical and other services; and presented to the appropriate combined boards the overall requirements for relief (Federal Records, 1950). UNRRA was organized to ameliorate the tragic plight of millions of refugees and displaced persons in liberated countries (Roberts, 1954). China was one of the nations to which nurses from the USPHS were sent, and this mission included two black nurses: Florence M. Hargett and Dorothy Doyle Harrison.

Florence M. Hargett (Diploma, Mercy Hospital School of Nursing, Philadelphia, Pennsylvania; MA, Teachers College, Columbia University, New York [Fig. 6-29]) served as a nursing consultant from 1945 to 1947 with UNRRA Mission to China in Kwangsi, Honan, and Manchuria. During 1950 and 1951, she was Director, National Tubman School of Nursing, Monrovia, Liberia. From 1952 to 1971, she served as educator/consultant for the World Health Organization in Taiwan, Egypt, Sierre Leone, and Iraq, where she was awarded the Silver Seal of the College of Nursing, University of Baghdad. She is now Professor Emerita, Seton Hall University College of Nursing, South Orange, New Jersey, where she had served on the faculty from 1973 to 1983. Included in Hargett's many publications is an article in the July-August 1961 issue of the *International Nursing Review*, entitled "Problems of Communication for International Understanding."

Dorothy Doyle Harrison (Diploma, Mercy Hospital School of Nursing, Philadelphia, Pennsylvania; PhD, The Catholic University of America, Washington, D.C. [Fig. 6-30]) served two years in China, 1945 to 1947, as public health nurse consultant for UNRRA. Later she was appointed public health nurse consultant in the Office of Inter-American Affairs in Brazil, serving the areas of Rio de Janiero and Belem. Her duties included the teaching of nursing and midwifery and setting up public health centers. Harrison is currently on the faculty of Howard University College of Medicine, Washington, D.C., as Associate Professor, Depart-

Figure 6–29 Florence M. Hargett served as a nursing consultant, 1945–1947, with UNRRA Mission to China.

Figure 6–30   Dr. Dorothy Doyle Harrison, Consultant, UNRRA, in China and Brazil.

ment of Community Health and Family Practice, and Director of Biofeedback Program, Howard University Hospital, Departments of Physical Medicine and Psychiatry.

Liquidation of UNRRA began in 1946; it was abolished September 30, 1948, but liquidation activities continued until March 31, 1949, when its remaining funds and records were turned over to the United Nations (*Federal Records*, 1950).

Point Four.   Among the many midcentury international health programs which were outside the direct administrative jurisdiction of the World Health Organization was the Point Four Program, developed by governmental agencies of the United States. The Point Four was so named because it was based on the fourth recommendation in President Truman's inaugural address (1946) of which he said:

> This program will provide means needed to translate our words of friendship into deeds. . . . By patient diligent effort, levels of education can be raised and standards of health improved to enable the people of such areas to make better use of their resources. Their lands can be made to yield better crops . . . . [Aspects of Point Four, 1952]

By 1952, the program was in action in 35 countries, one of which was Liberia, and the USPHS supplied technical support and much of the personnel (Roberts, 1954). Several black nurses participated in this program, particularly in Africa.

Agency for International Development.   The Agency for International Development was established on November 3, 1961, by the State Department Delegation of Authority 104 as an agency within the Department of State. AID carries out nonmilitary U.S. foreign assistance programs and exercises continuous supervision over all assistance programs under the Foreign Assistance Act of 1961, the 1960 act providing for Latin American development and Chilean reconstruction, and the Agricultural Trade Development and Assistance Act of 1954. It provides assistance through development grants and research, investment guarantees and surveys, contributions to international organization, and other activities. Under the Alliance for Progress, AID promotes technical and financial cooperation among the American Republics to strengthen democratic institutions through comprehensive national programs for economic and social development. Under Public Law 480 of 1954, AID administers certain local currency and Food for Peace programs.

Certain programs of AID and its predecessor agencies had their origin in the Economic Cooperation act of 1948, which established the Economic Cooperation Administration (ECA) to administer the European recovery program (the Marshall Plan). The functions of ECA were transferred in 1951 to the Mutual Security Agency (MSA), established to maintain security and provide for the general welfare of the United States by furnishing military, economic, and technical assistance to friendly nations in the interest of international peace and security. Reorganization Plan No. 7 of August 1953, established the Foreign Operations Administration (FOA) to centralize operations, control, and direction of all foreign economic and technical assistance programs and to coordinate mutual security activities. The FOA took over the functions of the MSA, the Office of the Director of Mutual Security in the Executive Office of the President, the Technical Cooperation Administration, the Institute of Inter-African Affairs, and several other foreign assistance activities. The FOA was abolished in 1955 and succeeded by the International Cooperation Administration (ICA), which coordinated foreign assistance operations and conducted all but military mutual security programs. AID replaced ICA in 1961 (*Guide to the National Archives*, 1974).

In 1978, AID employed nurses, among whom were several black nurses, who were assigned to some of the less developed areas of the world. They worked as a team with U.S. physicians, health engineers, and host governments to help develop efficient departments of health and a high standard of health practice. The nurses were particularly concerned with nursing education, nursing service adminstration, and public health. Three such nurses were Jean Martin Pinder, Clemmie Jean Smith, and Mary Mills.

Jean Martin Pinder (Diploma, Highland Hospital School of Nursing, Oakland, California; MPH, Yale University, New Haven, Connecticut [Fig. 6-31]) started her nursing career as a public health nurse with the Department of Health, Education, and Welfare; taught public health and health education at Dillard University School of Nursing in New

Figure 6–31   Jean Martin Pinder, Public Health Advisor, AID, served as advisor and consultant to ministries of health in many African countries.

Orleans; and participated in a pilot multiphasic screening program as health educator for DHEW before going to Africa to develop programs for training assistant health education officers and establishing health education units within ministries of health. At her retirement in 1973, Pinder was public health advisor for the Africa Bureau of AID. While working for AID, she served as advisor and consultant to ministries of health in many foreign countries—Liberia, Ghana, Sierra Leone, Tunisia, Morocco, Botswana and the Ivory Coast—organizing and conducting training programs, developing family planning programs, and assisting ministries of health to plan and develop expanded programs for providing primary health care to rural populations. Subsequent to retirement, from 1973 to 1978, Pinder worked as a consultant to the Africa Bureau and other organizations. Among her many honors was the Superior Honor Award in 1971 from AID Department of State in recognition of exceptional versatility and persuasiveness in gaining acceptance for the implementation of new AID health and population planning programs in the face of considerable adversity.

Clemmie Jean Smith (Diploma, St. Mary's Infirmary School of Nursing, St. Louis, Missouri; MS, St. Louis University [Fig. 6-32]), also a certified nurse-midwife, joined the International Cooperative Administration (now USAID) in 1959 as nursing advisor in medical-surgical nursing at the College of Nursing, Karachi, Pakistan, serving until 1960.

Figure 6–32   Clemmie Jean Smith, nursing advisor with AID in Pakistan and Nepal and WHO nurse educator in Africa.

From 1962 to 1964, she served as senior WHO nurse educator in His Majesty's Government School of Nursing in Kathmandu, Nepal, where she worked with one other WHO nurse, a national counterpart, and four other national nurse faculty members to raise the standards of nursing and nursing education in Nepal.

Between 1966 and 1973, Smith was WHO nurse educator in medical-surgical nursing and senior WHO nurse educator, nursing school administration at the University of Baghdad College of Nursing, a four-year bachelor of science program in nursing. From 1973 to 1980 she was WHO nurse educator in Tanzania, East Africa. In 1983, Smith established the St. Luke's Medical Assistant School of Bulawayo, Zimbabwe, where she is currently located.

Retired in 1976, Captain Mary L. Mills (Fig. 6-33) spent more than 26 years with the USPHS, beginning her career in 1946 with the Office of International Health, PHS, DHEW; later she was detailed to the AID and its predecessor agencies. Twenty of those years were spent abroad, serving the people of Liberia, Chad, Lebanon, Cambodia, and South Vietnam. In these countries, Captain Mills helped set up maternal and child health clinics, schools of nursing, public health sanitation, and small pox and malaria eradication programs. She received several national honors for her humanitarian work in Lebanon, and other citations were awarded her by the governments of Liberia, Chad, and South Vietnam in recognition of her accomplishments in working with people in those nations. She has also represented nursing and midwifery at international

Figure 6–33   Mary L. Mills, retired Captain, U.S. Public Health Service, after having spent more than 26
years of service in the United States
and other countries.

nursing congresses in Mexico, Canada, Germany, Australia, Italy, and
Sweden.

A native of North Carolina, Mills received her nursing diploma from
Lincoln Hospital School of Nursing in Durham and a certificate in public
health nursing from the Medical College of Virginia. At New York University, she earned both the BS and MA degrees, and a certificate in
nurse-midwifery from the Lobenstine School of the Maternity Center
Association of New York. She also completed courses of study in health
care administration, which led to a professional certificate from George
Washington University in Washington, D.C.

Since 1966, Captain Mills has been active on a number of fronts in
the United States. As nursing consultant to the Migrant Health Program,
she was instrumental in shaping health policy to build on the strength
and pride of migrant agricultural workers, frequently members of minority groups. An example of the great esteem in which she is held by
her colleagues is that she was personally asked to go to Detroit after the
1967 riot to help repair communications in the burned-out areas of the
city. She was able to do so with her typical sensitivity and tact.

Mills has received many honors and awards, including an honorary
Doctor of Science from Tuskegee University in Alabama, an honorary
Doctor of Laws from Seton Hall University in South Orange, New Jersey,
and the inclusion of her portrait in the "Exhibit of 33 Outstanding
Americans of Negro Origin" in the Smithsonian Institution in Wash-
ington, D.C. The portrait unveiled January 22, 1953, by Elizabeth K.
Porter, president of ANA, was sponsored by the Harmon Foundation.

The foundation was established by a wealthy philanthropist to encourage blacks to achieve in the arts.

In 1971, Mills received two of the nation's most coveted awards for her outstanding humanitarian service. The USPHS awarded her its Distinguished Service Award, and the Woodrow Wilson School of Public and International Affairs gave her the Rockefeller Public Service Award in the area of Human Resources Development and Protection. She was the first woman ever to be awarded the Rockefeller Award—the highest privately sustained honor for a career civil servant. This award of $10,000 was tax free. In 1972, she was the recipient of the ANA Mary Mahoney Award.

Special Technical and Economic Mission. In 1953, the Foreign Operations Administration, which is now the Agency for International Development, program was called the Special Technical and Economic Mission (STEM) to Southeast Asia. Laura Holloway Yergan (Diploma, Harlem Hospital School of Nursing, New York; MA, Teachers College, Columbia University, New York [Fig. 6-34]) was recruited into the USPHS reserve corps as lieutenant commander and was assigned to FOA and STEM in Indo-China (Vietnam), where she stayed until 1956 as nurse officer, nursing education advisor. Her subsequent USPHS assignments were in Beirut, Lebanon, 1956–1958; Karachi, Pakistan, 1958–1959; and Brooklyn, New York, 1959.

From 1961 to 1968, Yergan was assigned by WHO to the Africa Region (Congo, Brazzaville, Nigeria, Cameroon, and Togo) and Barbados in

Figure 6–34 Laura Holloway Yergan, recruited into U.S. Public Health Service Reserve Corps as lieutenant commander, served in Indochina, Lebanon, Pakistan, Africa, and Barbados.

the Caribbean Region. In 1968, she joined the faculty of the College of the Virgin Islands where she remained until retirement as professor and director of the baccalaureate program.

Before becoming affiliated with USPHS and its foreign missions, Yergan had spent two years as director of nurses at St. Timothy's Hospital in Liberia under the aegis of the National Council of the Protestant Episcopal Church of America. Since 1975, she has been spending three to four months annually in Swaziland and is currently serving as nurse education consultant to Malawi on a project for which Howard University in Washington, D.C., is the contractor.

A Proud History

At the 180th anniversary program of the PHS on July 26, 1978, Julius B. Richmond, MD, assistant secretary for health and surgeon general, DHEW, had this to say:

> The history of the Public Health Service is a testament to our country's enduring commitment to improving the health of its people. Formed when the Nation was young, the service has grown and changed, faced new challenges, new opportunities, and new demands even as the United States evolved from an immature federation of ex-colonies to the most powerful and productive nation on Earth. Yet like the United States, the Public Health Service remains dedicated to the ideas and ideals that gave meaning and urgency to its beginnings, the belief that the vitality of the Nation depends on the health of its people and that government has a continuing responsibility to provide leadership in the effort to protect and promote health. . . .

Black nurses, too, have played and are continuing to play significant roles in the history of the PHS.

THE VETERANS ADMINISTRATION

Shortly after World War I, the federal government began building hospitals throughout the country for disabled veterans. With the exception of some isolated wards, few were available to meet the needs of black veterans (Morais, 1967).

Since more than 400,000 blacks had been enrolled in the armed forces during the war, the problem of providing adequate care and treatment for the disabled black veteran became acute. On August 9, 1920, the Bureau of War Risk Insurance, the Rehabilitation Division of the Federal Board for Vocational Education, and certain hospitals caring for veterans under the direction of the USPHS were transferred and combined into an independent bureau under the president of the United States, to be known as the Veterans Bureau, with a director at its head. During the same year, a committee of experts was appointed to make a survey of the needs of the country for hospital facilities for disabled veterans and to submit appropriate recommendations to the secretary of the treasury.

Included in the recommendations was one that stated that since approximately 300,000 of the blacks who served in the war were natives of southern states, a hospital should be provided specifically for their care and attention and should be located in that section of the country. Tuskegee, Alabama, was selected as the most suitable place for the black hospital, it being in the deep South and near the approximate center of the black population of the United States. Tuskegee, already made famous by Tuskegee University founded by Booker T. Washington, was immediately acclaimed as an ideal location. In addition to the great institution endeavoring to educate black youth, there would be another institution dedicated to the rehabilitation of disabled black world war veterans (Dibble, 1943).

The officials of Tuskegee University welcomed the idea of a hospital for black veterans, but they, along with the National Association for the Advancement of Colored People (NAACP) and the National Medical Association (NMA) demanded the appointment of an all-black staff. In 1921, the Veterans Bureau and Tuskegee University agreed to the construction of a hospital on 300 acres of land owned by the institute. At the cost of $2,500,000, a hospital, consisting of 600 beds in 27 permanent buildings, to treat primarily neurospsychiatric patients, was completed and dedicated on the anniversary of Lincoln's birthday on February 12, 1923. In the meantime, the Veterans Bureau appointed a white physician, Colonel Robert C. Stanley, as superintendent of the hospital despite a promise made to Dr. Robert R. Moton, president of Tuskegee University, that he would be consulted prior to any such appointment. Under Stanley's direction, plans were made to open the hospital "With a full staff of white doctors and white nurses with a colored nursemaid for each white nurse, in order to save them from contact with colored patients" (Morais, 1967, p. 113).

To forestall the execution of Stanley's plans, Moton wrote to President Harding on February 14, 1923, requesting him to give black physicians and nurses an opportunity to qualify for service in the hospital through special civil service examinations. After conferring with Moton, President Harding granted the request. General Frank T. Hines, director of the Veterans Bureau, was sent to Tuskegee to initiate a gradual change in the medical staff from white to black. A committee of the National Medical Association also brought this matter to the attention of the federal government. Several conferences with President Harding and General Hines resulted in agreement on the staffing of the hospital with black personnel. "It was only after a bitter fight that a Negro staff supplanted a white one at the government supported Tuskegee Hospital for Disabled Negro Veterans" (Morais, 1967, p. 98).

Esther Juanita Bullock, a 1920 graduate of Kansas City General Hospital School of Nursing, Kansas City, Missouri, had worked at City Hospital No. 2, St. Louis, Missouri, and South Side Hospital in Chicago before entering the service of the Veterans Bureau in May 1923. In June, she was assigned to the Veterans Hospital in Tuskegee, where she served as night supervisor for four months. In October, Bullock was appointed chief nurse—the first black (Thoms, 1929). Serving as assistant chief nurse was Amelia J. Gears.

Writing in the September 1924 issue of *Crisis*, the official organ of the NAACP, W.E.B. DuBois said, "Our hats are in the air to Tuskegee and Moton. . . . He and the Negro world demanded that the Government Hospital at Tuskegee be under Negro control. Today, at last, it is" (Fig. 6-35).

In 1930, Congress enacted Public Law 536, authorizing the President to consolidate and coordinate government activities affecting war veterans into an agency to be known as the Veterans Administration. The agencies merged by Executive Order were the U.S. Veterans Bureau, the National Homes for Disabled Volunteer Soldiers, and the Bureau of Pensions of the Interior Department (Keough, 1981). On October 25, 1988, President Reagan signed a law which created the Department of Veterans Affairs—a cabinet-level department, which became effective March 15, 1989.

Until 1941, appointments of black nurses to the VA were limited to the all-black facility at Tuskegee. It was around this time that a few black nurses were transferred from Tuskegee to other facilities. However, they were assigned to work on segregated units. For example, the group transferred to the VA Hospital in Kecoughtan, Virginia, in the early 1940s, worked on wards or in buildings reserved for black veterans.

During the post-World War II period, the struggle for equal rights in hospital facilities was part of the wider battle to desegregate medical colleges, nursing schools, and professional bodies. The NMA was in the forefront of the fight to end discriminatory treatment in the country's hospitals. To forestall what happened at the close of the First World War, the NMA's veterans committee, together with representatives from the NACGN, the Medico-Chirurgical Society of the District of Columbia, and the National Negro Publishers Association, met with General Paul R. Harvey, medical director of the VA, in October 1945 to discuss a

Figure 6–35 Edith English (in foreground), first black nurse to arrive at the Tuskegee VA Hospital in 1923.

program for complete integration of the administration's hospital system for both patients and professional personnel. Following the meetings, Dr. Emory I. Robinson, president of the NMA stated that the VA should assist integration just as civilian hospitals were beginning to do. "We fully agree with General Hawley that there is no defense to segregation," Robinson declared. "Our army has changed its policy and our navy has changed its policy. The Veterans Administration cannot look back. It must look forward and must change its policy" (Morais, 1967, p. 142).

To destroy the principal of segregation in the hospital system of the VA was not easy. Despite the fact that veterans were legally entitled to medical care without discrimination, 24 of the 127 veterans hospitals operating in the beginning of November 1947 had separate wards for black patients. Nineteen of them, all located in the South, refused to admit blacks except in cases of medical emergencies. Yet, in spite of such setbacks, the civil rights forces refused to abandon the battle. Finally, in October 1954, the agency ordered the end of segregation in all its hospitals. Thereafter, the order was scrupulously carried out in all veterans hospitals (Morais, 1967, p. 142).

In 1963, Beatrice L. Murray (Diploma, Kansas City General Hospital School of Nursing, Kansas City, Missouri; MSN, Wayne State University School of Nursing, Detroit, Michigan), after having held various positions in governmental agencies such as the U.S. Department of Agriculture, Migratory Labor Health Association, and the VA since 1941, was enrolled as a chief nurse trainee with the VA in 1963. Upon completion of her traineeship in 1964, she was appointed chief nurse at the

VA Hospital in Pittsburgh, Pennsylvania—the first black chief nurse at an integrated facility. Subsequently, from 1966 to her retirement in 1981, Murray served as chief nurse at VA hospitals in Bedford, Massachusetts; Hines, Illinois; and Washington, D.C.

In May 1971, Murray represented the VA Nursing Service at the International Congress for Psychiatry and Social Change in Jerusalem, Israel, as a nurse member of the team. In 1975, she received the Honor Award from the Department of Medicine and Surgery "in recognition of outstanding performance as Chief, Nursing Service in several settings, and for collaborative relationships with the academic and personnel community."

In 1964, Minnie Lee Jones Hartsfield (Diploma, Burwell Hospital School of Nursing, Selma, Alabama; MA, Teachers College, Columbia University, New York) became the first black nurse to be appointed to the staff of the Central Office of the VA in Washington, D.C., having for 25 years held positions in several VA facilities, ranging from staff nurse to instructor to associate chief, nursing education.

As nursing specialist at the VA Central Office, Hartsfield's duties included assisting with gathering and analyzing significant data from VA health facilities in order to identify and justify programs, policies, and procedures needed and/or required; making visits to various health facilities to review and evaluate the standards of nursing care; assisting with recruitment and replacement of nurses in key positions; and serving as consultant as the need arose or when requested. Upon leaving the central office in 1968, Hartsfield served as chief nurse at the VA Westside Hospital in Chicago until 1970, and as chief nurse at the VA Medical Center at Downey, Illinois, from 1970 to 1975.

In 1979, Liz Johnson (BS, Texas Woman's University School of Nursing, Denton; PhD, University of Pennsylvania) was among five applicants selected from a pool of 254 to become a National Veterans Administration Scholar in the Chief Medical Director's Office in Washington, D.C.— a two-year program. Immediately before this recognition, she had been director of nursing at the VA hospital in Baltimore, Maryland, having held other positions in the VA since 1974. Johnson (Fig. 6-36) also holds a certificate in management from the University of Baltimore.

Another black nurse, Pauline V. Skinner, was the 1988 recipient of the VA Award for Excellence in nursing. The award honors VA nursing personnel who stand out above all others in providing high quality medical care to VA patients. Skinner is a member and founder of the Black Nurses Association of Houston, Texas.

Today, there are no barriers, and the national director of nursing services is a black nurse, Vernice Ferguson (Fig. 6-37), who had been chief nurse at several VA hospitals and chief of the nursing department at the Clinical Center, NIH, Bethesda, Maryland. Ferguson, appointed

Figure 6–36   Dr. Liz Johnson, National VA Scholar, 1979.

Figure 6–37   Vernice Ferguson, first nurse appointed Deputy Assistant Chief Medical Director for Nursing Programs, VA, 1980.

director of nursing service July 1980, has brought outstanding professional knowledge and an enthusiastic spirit to lead the VA Nursing Service forward. In October 1980, Ferguson became the first nurse appointed deputy assistant chief medical director for nursing programs (Keough, 1981).

Today, there are 172 medical centers (formerly called hospitals), 356 outpatient clinics and community outreach clinics, 126 nursing home care units, and 35 domiciliaries. As of December 31, 1990, the number of nursing personnel in the system totaled 62,310 and was made up of 36,726 registered nurses; 10,724 licensed practical nurses; and 14,860 nursing assistants. The VA Nursing Service employs nurses with educational preparation reflecting every type of academic nursing education available in America today. More than 40 percent of the VA professional nurses hold baccalaureate or higher degrees. About 30,000 RN and LPN nursing students affiliate with VA medical centers for nursing experience each year.

SUMMARY

As indicated in this chapter, black nurses fought for the right to participate as nurses and as citizens during World War I and World War II.

Solely because of the color of their skin, they were not accepted in the Army Nurse Corps until after the armistice was signed, signaling the end of World War I. With persistence and cooperation of many white and black Americans, black nurses gained acceptance in the Army Nurse Corps on a quota basis in 1941, and more than 500 served during World War II, although assigned mostly to segregated units. Four black nurses were finally accepted in the Navy Nurse Corps during the last months of World War II. Today, black nurses are virtually completely integrated in all branches of the armed services, being assigned without discrimination.

Black nurses can be found in the Public Health Service at practically all levels of positions, holding commissioned ranks from the equivalent of ensign in the navy and second lieutenant in the army to captain in the navy and brigadier general in the army in this and other countries.

The Veterans Administration, the last of the federal agencies to integrate its professional staff, has done so completely, with a black nurse holding the highest nursing office—deputy assistant chief medical director for nursing programs.

REFERENCES

Abdellah, F. G. (1977). U.S. Public Health Service's contribution to nursing research—Past, present, future. *Nursing Research, 26,* 244–249.

Army nurses tell us. (1944). *American Journal of Nursing, 44,* 998.

Aspects of Point Four Program. (1952). Department of State Bulletin, September 22.

Beverly, C. E. (1947). Nursing schools in Liberia. *American Journal of Nursing, 47,* 530–531.

Commissioned officer's handbook 1990, CCPM Pamphlet No. 62. (1990). Washington, D.C.: Public Health Service, U.S. Department of Health and Human Services.

Cooperative Liberia-United States Public Health Program Under the Joint Liberian-United States Commission for Economic Development. (1954). Republic of Liberia, National Public Health Service.

Davis, J. P. (Ed.). (1966). *The American Negro reference book.* Englewood Cliffs: Prentice-Hall.

Dibble, E. H. (1943, September). Care and treatment of Negro veterans at Tuskegee. *Journal of the National Medical Association,* 166–170.

Dolan, J., Fitzpatrick, M. L., & Herrmann, E. K. (1983). *Nursing in society; A historical perspective* (15th ed.). Philadelphia: Saunders.

Dunbar-Nelson, A. (1919). Negro women in war work. In E. J. Scott (Ed.), *The American Negro in the world war.* Washington, D.C.: Author.

Federal health programs service operations manual. (1971). Transmittal Letter No. 45, September 23. Washington, D.C.

Federal records of World War II, Vol. I, civilian agencies. (1950). U.S. Government Printing Office, National Archives, Pub. No. 51-7. Washington, D.C.

First indorsement. (1945). Memorandum from the Surgeon General to Office of Secretary of War, Attention: Mr. Truman Gibson, Jr., Civilian Aide to the Secretary of War, Washington, D.C., National Archives, Jul 26.

Franklin, J. H. (1967). *From slavery to freedom*, 3rd ed. New York: Alfred Knopf.

Grant, M. (1975). *Handbook of community health.* Philadelphia: Lea & Febiger.

Groppe, E. (1945). Memorandum to Truman Gibson, Civilian Aide to the Secretary of War, Jul 26, Washington, D.C.: National Archives.

Guide to the National Archives of the United States. (1974). Washington, D.C.: National Archives and Records Service, General Services Administration.

Hine, D. C. (1982). Mabel K. Staupers and the integration of black nurses in the armed forces. In J. H. Franklin and A. Meier (Eds.), *Black leaders of the twentieth century.* Chicago: University of Illinois Press.

Johnson, J. J. (1974). *Black women in the armed forces, 1942–1974.* Hampton: Author.

Kalisch, P., & Kalisch, B. (1978). *The advance of American nursing.* Boston: Little, Brown & Co.

Keough, G. (1981). *History and heritage of the Veterans Administration nursing service, 1930–1980.* New York: National League for Nursing.

Kreidberg, M. A., & Henry, M. G. (1955). History of military mobilization in the United States Army, 1775–1945. Washington, D.C.: Government Printing Office.

MacGregor, M. J., Jr. (1981). *Integration in the armed forces.* Washington, D.C.: U.S. Army Center of Military History.

Maxwell, P. E. (1976). *History of the Army Nurse Corps, 1775–1948.* Unpublished Manuscript. Maintained by the Army Nurse Corps Historian, U.S. Army Center of Military History, Washington, D.C.

Merritt, D. H. (1986). The National Center for Nursing Research, *Image: Journal of Nursing Scholarship, 18*(3), 84–85.

Montague, M. C. (1990). *Final report of the EA experience.* Bethesda: National Institutes of Health.

Morais, H. (1967). *The history of the Negro in medicine.* New York: Publishers Co.

NIH extramural associates program. (1990). U.S. Department of Health and Human Services, National Institutes of Health.

Notter, L., & Spalding, E. (1965). *Professional nursing: Foundations, perspectives, and relationships.* Philadelphia: J. B. Lippincott.

Organization manual. (1990). PHS Chapter H. Washington, D.C.: Public Health Service.

Organization manual. (1990). PHS Chapter HA. Washington, D.C.: Public Health Service.

Organization manual. (1990). PHS Chapter HM. Washington, D.C.: Public Health Service.

Organization manual. (1990). PHS Chapter HP. Washington, D.C.: Public Health Service.

Organization manual. (1989). PHS Chapter HF. Washington, D.C.: Public Health Service.

Organization manual. (1989). PHS Chapter HT. Washington, D.C.: Public Health Service.

Organization manual. (1988). PHS Chapter HG. Washington, D.C.: Public Health Service.

Organization manual. (1987). PHS Chapter HD. Washington, D.C.: Public Health Service.

Organization manual. (1987). PHS Chapter HN. Washington, D.C.: Public Health Service.

Organization manual. (1986). PHS Chapter HB. Washington, D.C.: Public Health Service.

Organization manual. (1982). PHS Chapter HC. Washington, D.C.: Public Health Service.

Osur, A. M. (1977). *Blacks in the army air force during World War II.* Washington, D.C.: Office of Air Force History.

Piemonte, R., & Gurney, C. (1987). *Highlights in the history of the Army Nurse Corps.* Washington, D.C.: U.S. Army Center of Military History.

Report of the surgeon general. (1918). U.S. Army to the Secretary of War. Washington, D.C.: Government Printing Office.

Report of the surgeon general. (1919). U.S. Army to the Secretary of War. Washington, D.C.: Government Printing Office.

Report of the surgeon general. (1938). U.S. Army to the Secretary of War. Washington, D.C.: Government Printing Office.

Report of the surgeon general. (1939). U.S. Army to the Secretary of War. Washington, D.C.: Government Printing Office.

Report of the surgeon general. (1940). U.S. Army to the Secretary of War. Washington, D.C.: Government Printing Office.

Report of the surgeon general. (1941). U.S. Army to the Secretary of War. Washington, D.C.: Government Printing Office.

Roberts, M. M. (1954). *American nursing: History and interpretation.* New York: Macmillan.

Scott, E. J. (1918). *Memorandum to Dean F. P. Keppel, Confidential Advisor, Office of the Secretary of War.* Record Group 407, Washington, D.C.: National Archives, Feb. 28.

Shields, E. A. (Ed.). (1981). *Highlights in the history of the Army Nurse Corps.* Washington, D.C.: Government Printing Office.

Sparks, S. M. (1986, March–April). The U.S. National Library of Medicine: A worldwide nursing resource. *International Nursing Review*, 47–49.

Staupers, M. K. (1961). *No time for prejudice.* New York: Macmillan.

Subcommittee hearing brings praise to IHS nurse. (1990, September). *American Nurse*, 2.

Thoms, A. B. (1929). *Pathfinders, the progress of colored graduate nurses.* New York: Kay Printing House.

Willenz, J. A. (1983). *Women veterans: America's forgotten heroines.* New York: Continuum.

Williams, R. C. (1951). *The United States Public Health Service 1790–1950*. Bethesda: Commissioned Officers Administration, USPHS.

Bibliography

Allen, M. E., Nunley, J. C., & Scott-Warner, M. (1988). Recruitment and retention of black students in baccalaureate nursing programs. *Journal of Nursing Education, 27*(3), 107–116.

American Nurses' Association Hall of Fame. (1976). Kansas City: ANA.

Banks, J. (1986). Stress management for black nurses. *Jornal of the National Black Nurses' Association, 1*(1), 61–65.

Bennett, L. (1964). *Before the Mayflower: A history of the Negro in America, 1619–1964*. Chicago: Johnson Publishing Co.

Bessent, H. (1987). Doctorally prepared nurses in mental health. *Journal of the National Black Nurses' Association, 1*, 36–40.

Blaustein, A. P., & Zangrando, R. L. (Eds.). (1968). Civil rights and the American Negro: A documentary history. New York: Washington Square Press.

Buckley, J. (1980). Faculty commitment to retention and recruitment of black students. *Nursing Outlook, 28*, 46–50.

Bullough, B., & Bullough, V. (1981). Educational problems in a woman's profession. *Journal of Nursing Education, 20*, 6–17.

Burke, S. (1983). The nurse training act: A history of support. *American Journal of Nursing, 83*, 47–52.

CIS annual legislative history of U.S. public laws. (1986). Bethesda: Congressional Information Service.

Campinka-Bacote, J. (1988). The black nurses' struggle toward equality: An historical account of the National Association of Colored Graduate Nurses. *Journal of the National Black Nurses' Association, 2*, 15–25.

Capers, C. F. (1985). Nursing and the Afro-American client. *Top Clinical Nursing, 7*(3), 11–17.

Carnegie, M. E. (1962). The path we tread. *International Nursing Review, 9*, 25–33.

Carnegie, M. E. (1965). The impact of integration on the nursing profession. *Negro History Bulletin, 28*, 154–155.

Carnegie, M. E. (1974). The minority practitioner in nursing. *Current Issues in Nursing Education* (39–42). New York: National League for Nursing.

Carnegie, M. E. (1984). Black nurses at the front. *American Journal of Nursing, 84*, 1250–1252.

Carnegie, M. E. (1987, March–April). Blacks in nursing. *The Black Collegian, 17*(4), 109–114.

Carnegie, M. E. (1988). M. Elizabeth Carnegie in T. M. Schorr & A. Zimmerman (Eds.), *Making choices, taking chances: Nurse leaders tell their stories* (pp. 28–42). St. Louis, MO: C. V. Mosby.

Carnegie, M. E. (1990). Blacks in nursing: An update. *American Nurse, 22*(2), 6.

Chambers, L. A. (1957). *America's tenth man.* New York: Twayne Pub.

Cofer, A. B. (1974). Autobiography of a black nurse. *American Journal of Nursing, 74,* 1836–1838.

Coles, A. B. (1969). The Howard University School of Nursing in historical perspective. *Journal of the National Medical Association, 61,* 105–118.

Coles, A. B. (1972). The status of black nurse power. *Urban Health, 1,* 32–33.

Cornely, P. B. (1934). A study of Negro nursing. *Public Health Nurse, 34,* 449–451.

Cousar, R. (1984). Minorities in professional nursing, where are they? *Pennsylvania Nurse, 39*(2), 6, 13.

Dannett, S. (1966). *Profiles of Negro womanhood,* 1619–1900 (Vol. 1). Philadelphia: Goodway.

Dannett, S. (1966). *Profiles of Negro womanhood, twentieth century,* (Vol. II). Philadelphia: Goodway.

Davis, A. (1987). Architects for integration and equality: Early black American leaders in nursing. New York: Teachers College, Columbia University, Unpublished doctoral dissertation.

Davis, L. (1974). The minority practitioner in nursing. In *Current Issues in Nursing Education* (43–45). New York: National League for Nursing.

Davis, M. (1982). *Contributions of black women to America.* Columbia, SC: Kenday Press.

Dell, M. A., & Halpin, G. (1984). Predictors of success in nursing school and on state board examinations in a predominately black baccalaureate nursing program. *Journal of Nursing Education, 23*(4), 147–150.

DeYoung, L. (1976). *The foundations of nursing.* St. Louis: C. V. Mosby.

Diploma schools. (1973). For Negro schools, nearly a century. *RN, 36,* 67–68.

Dodson, D. W. (1953). No place for race prejudice. *American Journal of Nursing, 53,* 164–166.

Doona, M. E. (1986). Glimpses of Mary Eliza Mahoney. *Journal of Nursing History, 1,* 20–34.

Doswell, W. M. (1989). Nursing research needs of black Americans: 1989 and beyond. *Journal of the National Black Nurses' Association, 3*(1), 45–53.

Elmore, J. A. (1976). Black nurses: Their service and their struggle. *American Journal of Nursing, 76,* 435–437.

Fauset, A. H. (1938). *Sojourner Truth: God's Faithful Pilgrim.* Chapel Hill, NC: University of North Carolina Press.

Feldbaum, E. A. (1980). *The nursing profession and black nurses.* College Park, MD, University of Maryland.

Francis, G. M. (1967). A minority of one. *Nursing Outlook, 15,* 36–38.

Freedmen's school administered by U.S. Public Health Service. (1941). *American Journal of Nursing, 41,* 102.

Gaskin, F. C. (1986). Detection of cyanosis in the person with dark skin. *Journal of the National Black Nurses' Association, 1*(1), 52–60.

Gunter, L. M. (1961). The effects of segregation on nursing students. *Nursing Outlook, 9,* 74–76.

Hagans, I. R. (1986). The black nurse as advocate. *California Nurse, 84*(7), 3.

Harris, L. (1986). Has affirmative action in nursing been successful in North Carolina? *Journal of the National Black Nurses' Association, 1*(2), 71–78.

Harris, L. O. (1972). Where is the black nurse? *American Journal of Nursing, 72,* 282–284.

Harvey, L. H. (1970). Educational problems in minority group nurses. *Nursing Outlook, 18,* 48–55.

Haupt, A. C. (1935). A pioneer in Negro nursing. *American Journal of Nursing, 35,* 857–859.

Heisler, A., & Marr, G. (1954). Intergroup relations. *American Journal of Nursing, 72,* 1341–1343.

Heisler, A. (1956). Promoting the intergroup relations program. *American Journal of Nursing, 56,* 588–589.

Highlights in Nursing in North Carolina, 1935–1976. (1977). Raleigh: North Carolina Nurses' Association.

Hine, D. C. (1982). The Ethel Johns Report: Black women in the nursing profession, 1925. *Journal of Negro Education, 67,* 212–228.

Hine, D. C. (1982). From hospital to college: Black nurse leaders and the rise of collegiate nursing schools. *Journal of Negro Education, 51,* 222–237.

Hine, D. C. (Ed.). (1985). *Black women in the nursing profession, a documentary history.* New York: Garland.

Hine, D. C. (1988). They shall mount up with wings as eagles: Historical images of black nurses, 1890–1950. In A. H. Jones (Ed.), *Images of nurses: Perspectives from history, art, and literature* (pp. 177–196). Philadelphia: University of Pennsylvania Press.

Hine, D. C. (1989). *Black women in white: Racial conflict and cooperation in the nursing profession, 1890–1950.* Bloomington & Indianapolis: Indiana University Press.

Hine, D. C. (1989). Black women in the nursing profession, A documentary history. In S. Reverby (Ed.), *The history of American nursing.* New York: Garland Publishing.

Holt, R. (1944). The Negro nurse: A study in professional relations. *RN, 7,* 39–40, 72–80.

Iveson, J. (1984). A pin to see a peep show . . . Mary Seacole. *Nursing Mirror, 158,* 13, 36.

Kalisch, B. J., Kalisch, P. A., & Clinton, J. (1981). Minority nurses in the news. *Nursing Outlook, 29,* 49–54.

Kenny, J. A. (1919). Some facts concerning Negro nurse training schools and their graduates. *Journal of the National Medical Association, 11,* 53–68.

Kupperschmidt, B. (1988). Culturally sensitive nursing care for black clients. *Oklahoma Nurse, 33*(5), 9, 18.

Leone, L. P. (1987, February–March). The U.S. Cadet Nurse Corps: Nursing's answer to World War II demands. *Imprint,* 46–48.

Lerner, G. (Ed.). (1973). *Black Women in white America: A documented history.* New York: Vintage Books.

Lewis, M. C. (1981). A black perspective: Afro-American men in nursing. *Nursing Leadership, 4,* 31–33.

Long, O., & Bolton, L. B. (1986). The National Black Nurses' Association's response to the Secretary's Task Force Report. *Journal of the National Black Nurses' Association*, *1*(2), 24–26.

Luckraft, D. (Ed.). (1976). *Black Americans: Implications for black patient care.* New York: American Journal of Nursing Co.

Matula, H. (1987). Mary Elizabeth Carnegie's research on black history and black nurses. *Society of Nursing History Gazette*, *7*(2), 1–2.

McCarthy, R. T. (1985). *History of the American Academy of Nursing, 1973–1982.* Kansas City, MO: The Academy.

McPherson, J. M. (1975). *The abolitionist legacy: From reconstruction to the NAACP.* Princeton, NJ: Princeton University Press.

Memorial for first black nurse unveiled. (1973). *Missouri Nurse*, *42*, 4.

Miller, H. S. (1968). *The history of Chi Eta Phi Sorority, Inc.* Washington, D.C.: The Association for the Study of Negro Life and History.

Miller, H. S. (1986). *America's first black professional nurse: A historical perspective.* Atlanta: Wright Publishing Co.

Miller, H. S. (1988). *Mary Mahoney.* Chi Eta Phi Sorority: Washington, D.C.

Miller, H. S., & Mason, E. D. (Eds.). (1983). *Contemporary minority leaders in nursing: Afro-American, Hispanic, Native American perspectives.* Kansas City: ANA.

Miller, M. H. (1972). On blacks entering nursing. *Nurses Forum*, *11*, 248–263.

Montag, M. (1957). *Community college education for nurses.* New York: McGraw-Hill.

Negro nurses in Liberia commended. (1946). *American Journal of Nursing*, *46*, 799.

Nichols, L. (1954). *Breakthrough on the color front.* New York: Random House.

Northrup, H. R. (1950). The ANA and the Negro nurse. *American Journal of Nursing*, *50*, 207–208.

Newell, H. (1951). *The history of the National Nursing Council.* New York: The Council.

Osborne, E. M. (1949). Status and contribution of the Negro nurse. *J. Negro Ed.*, *18*, 364–369.

Piero, P. (1974). Black-white crises. *American Journal of Nursing*, *74*, 280–281.

Prestwidge, K. J. (1989). *Bibliography of African-Americans, Native Americans, Hispanics in engineering, science and the health professions.* Flushing, NY: Huespin Publication.

Prestwidge, K. J. (1990). *Women in science, engineering, and the health professions: A bibliography.* Flushing, NY: Huespin Publication.

Rann, E. L. (1916). The Good Samaritan Hospital of Charlotte, North Carolina. *Journal of the National Medical Association*, *56*, 223–225.

Riddle, E. (1984). What price quotas. *Public Health Nursing*, *36*, 389–393.

Robinson, A. M. (1972). Black nurses tell you: Why so few blacks in nursing. *RN*, *35*, 35–40; 73–76.

Rowland, H. S. (1978). *The Nurse's Almanac.* Germantown, MD: Aspen.

Ruffin, J. E. (1974). Issues for the black nurse today: Competence and commitment. *Current Issues in Nursing Education.* New York: National League for Nursing.

Rutledge, A. L., & Gass, G. Z. (1967). *Nineteen Negro men: Personality and manpower retraining*. San Francisco: Sage.

Sands, R. F. (1988). Enhancing cultural sensitivity in clinical practice. *Journal of the National Black Nurses' Association, 2*, 54–63.

Schorr, T. M., & Zimmerman, A. (Eds.). (1988). *Making choices, taking chances: Nurse leaders tell their stories*. St. Louis: C. V. Mosby.

Scott, E. J. (1919). *The American Negro in the world war*. Washington, D.C.: Author.

Seacole, M. (1857). *Wonderful adventures of Mrs. Seacole in many lands*. WJS (Ed.). London: James Blackwood.

Shapiro, C. (1948). The Negro nurse in the U.S. *RN, 12*, 32–35.

Sloan, P. E. (1978). A history of the establishment and early development of selected nurse training schools for Afro-Americans, 1886–1906. Unpublished doctoral dissertation, Columbia University Teachers College.

Sloan, P. E. (1985). Early black nursing schools and responses of black nurses to their educational programs. *Western Journal of Black Studies, 9*, 158–172.

Smith, G. R. (1979). *Liberation through a professional association: A case study of the National Black Nurses' Association*. Unpublished doctoral dissertation, University Graduate School—Midwest, University for the Experimenting Colleges and University, Cincinnati, OH.

Staupers, M. K. (1970). The black nurse and nursing goals. *Journal of the National Medical Association, 62*, 304–305.

Tate, B. L., & Carnegie, M. E. (1965). Negro admissions, enrollments, and graduations—1963. *Nursing Outlook, 13*, 61–63.

The ANA and you. (1941). New York: ANA.

The Negro public health nurse. *Public Health Nurse, 34*, 452–454.

Tomes, E., & Nicholson, A. D. (1979). *Black nursing pioneers, leaders, organizers (1770–1980)*. Washington, D.C.: The Association for the Study of Afro-American Life and History.

Tomes, E. K., & Shaw-Nickerson, E. (1986). Predecessors of modern black nurses: An honored role. *Journal of the National Black Nurses' Association, 1*, 72–78.

Vernon, C. (1969). The Florence Nightingale of Jamaica; the story of Mary Seacole. *Jamaica Nurse, 9*, 19, 22.

Vreeland, E. M. (1950). Fifty years of nursing in the federal government services. *American Journal of Nursing, 50*, 626–631.

Watson, C. (1984). Hidden from history: Mary Seacole, the black nurse famous in her day for her work in the Crimea. *Nursing Times, 80*, 16–17.

Williams, B. S. (1976). Historical review of ethnic nurse associations. In M. F. Branch & P. P. Paxton (Eds.), *Providing safe nursing care for ethnic people of color*. New York: Appleton-Century-Crofts.

Williams, B. S. (1986). Guest editorial: The challenge to black nurses. *Journal of the National Black Nurses' Association, 1*(2), 11–15.

Wilson, E. H. (1943). *Hope and dignity*. Philadelphia: Temple University Press.

Winder, A. E. (1971). Why young black women don't enter nursing. *Nursing Forum, 10*, 56–63.

Yearwood, A. C. (1983). The effective and ineffective behaviors of black and white nurse leaders: An executive development program. Unpublished dissertation, Teachers College, Columbia University, NY.

Yergan, L. (1956). Mission in Liberia. *Nursing Outlook*, 4, 564–566.

Yergan, L. (1956). The new look in Vietnamese nursing. *American Journal of Nursing*, 56, 1132–1134.

Appendix A

Black Deans and Directors of Baccalaureate and Higher Degree Programs in Nursing, December 31, 1990

Alabama

Dr. Margie N. Johnson, Tuskegee University, Tuskegee
Dr. Roberta O. Watts, Jacksonville State University, Jacksonville

Arkansas

Dr. C. DaCosta Hunte, University of Arkansas at Pine Bluff,
    Pine Bluff

California

Dr. Juanita Lee (Interim), University of Southern California,
    Los Angeles

Delaware

Dr. Marcella A. Copes, Delaware State College, Dover

District of Columbia

Dr. Ivy Nelson, University of the District of Columbia
Dr. Dorothy Powell, Howard University

Florida

Dr. Linda Gale Hawkins, Bethune-Cookman College, Daytona Beach
Dr. Margaret W. Lewis, Florida A & M University, Tallahassee
Dr. Joanette Pete McGadney, University of West Florida, Pensacola

Georgia

Dr. Joyce Newman Giger, Columbus College, Columbus
Dr. Frederick A. Moore (Interim), Morris Brown College, Atlanta
Dr. Lucille B. Wilson, Albany State College, Albany

Illinois

Dr. Marguerite Dixon (Interim), Chicago State University, Chicago
Dr. Annie L. Lawrence, Governors State University, University Park

Iowa

Dr. Geraldene Felton, University of Iowa, Iowa City

Kentucky

Dr. Cora Newell-Withrow, Berea College, Berea

Louisiana

Janet Rami, Southern University-Baton Rouge, Baton Rouge
Marguerite H. Rucker (Interim), Dillard University, New Orleans

Maryland

Dr. Joyce G. Bowles, Bowie State University, Bowie
Dr. Loretta M. Richardson, Coppin State College, Baltimore

Massachusetts

Dr. Brenda S. Cherry, University of Massachusetts, Boston

Michigan

Dr. Rhetaugh G. Dumas, University of Michigan, Ann Arbor
Dr. Gloria R. Smith, Wayne State University, Detroit
Dr. Regina Williams, Eastern Michigan University, Ypsilanti

Mississippi

Dr. Frances Henderson, Alcorn State University, Natchez

Missouri

Dr. Pearl H. Dunkley, Central Missouri State University, Warrensburg
Dr. Euphemia G. Williams, Southwest Missouri State University, Springfield

New Jersey

Dr. Gloria Boseman, Jersey City State College, Jersey City
Dr. Dolores Brown-Hall, Thomas Edison State College, Trenton
Dr. Rosetta Sands, William Paterson College, Wayne

New York

Dr. Pearl Skeete Bailey, York College, Jamaica
Dr. Bertie M. Gilmore, Medgar Evers College, Brooklyn
Dr. Geraldine B. Mosley, Dominican College of Blauvelt, Orangeburg

North Carolina

Dr. Marion F. Gooding, North Carolina Central University, Durham
Dr. Beverly Malone, North Carolina A & T State University, Greensboro
Sadie B. Webster, Winston-Salem State University, Winston-Salem

Ohio

Dr. Valerie D. George, Cleveland State University, Cleveland

Oklahoma

Dr. Ira Trail Adams, University of Tulsa, Tulsa
Dr. Carolyn Kornegay, Langston University, Langston

Pennsylvania

Dr. Jean H. Woods (Interim), Temple University, Philadelphia

South Carolina

Dr. Debra L. Austin, South Carolina State College, Orangeburg

Texas

Darimell Waugh (Interim), Prairie View A & M University, Houston

Virginia

Dr. Elnora D. Daniel, Hampton University, Hampton

Wisconsin

Dr. Sallie Tucker-Allen, University of Wisconsin, Green Bay

Appendix B

Charter Members, National Association of Colored Graduate Nurses

Dara Yarborough Allen	Georgia
Sadie Poole Bomar	New York
Edith Carter	New York
Eva Davis Felton	District of Columbia
Martha Franklin	Connecticut
Mary I. Grant	New York
Clara M. Harris	New York
Pattie Reeves Holmes	Georgia
Margaret A. Johnson	Florida
Nancy Lois Kemp	Pennsylvania
Minnie B. Kelly Lee	Virginia
Mary Clark Lemus	Virginia
Annie L. Marin	New York
Jane Hammond Nelson	New York
Frances Robinson Quinn	Virginia
Charlotte A. Rhone	North Carolina
Eleanor Christie Selah	Pennsylvania
Mrs. Theodore B. Strickland	New Jersey
Viola Symons	Ohio
Adah B. Thoms	New York
Mary Tucker	Pennsylvania
Viola Ford Turner	South Carolina
Louise Walters	New York
Octavia Walters	New York
Effie Brooks Watkins	New York
Rosa Williams-Brown	Florida

Source: Staupers, M. K. (1961). *No Time for Prejudice*. New York: Macmillan.

Appendix C

Mary Mahoney Award Recipients, 1936–1990

Mary Mahoney Medal.

1936 Adah B. Thoms
1937 Nancy Lois Kemp
1938 Carrie E. Bullock
1939 Petra A. Pinn
1940 Lula G. Warlick
1941 Ellen Woods Carter
1942 Ruth Logan Roberts
1943 Ludie A. Andrews

1944   Mable C. Northcross
1945   Susan E. Freeman
1946   Estelle M. Riddle Osborne
1947   Mabel Keaton Staupers
1949   Mary E. Merritt
1951   Eliza F. Pillars
1952   Marguerette Creth Jackson
1954   May Maloney (white)
1956   Mildred Ann Vogel (white)
1958   Fay O. Wilson
1960   Marie Mink
1962   Mildred Adams (white)
1964   M. Elizabeth Pickens (white)
1964   Alice M. Sundberg (white)
1966   Katharine Ellen Faville (white)
1968   Helen S. Miller
1970   Vernice D. Ferguson
1972   Mary Mills
1974   Fostine G. Riddick Roach
1976   Carolyn McCraw Carter
1978   Mary S. Harper
1980   Mary Elizabeth Carnegie
1982   Lillian Holland Harvey
1984   Verdelle Bellamy
1986   Elnora Daniel
1986   Mary Malone (white)
1988   Hattie Bessent
1990   Ethelrine Shaw-Nickerson

Appendix D

Charter Members, Chi Eta Phi Sorority

Chi Eta Phi logo.

Aliene C. Ewell
Clara Beverly
Gladys Catching
Bessie Cephas
Henrietta S. Chisolm
Susan Freeman

Ruth Garrett
Olivia Howard
Mildred Lucas
Lillian Mosely
Clara Royster
Katherine Turner

Source: Directory, Chi Eta Phi Sorority. Washington, D.C., The Sorority, 1983.

Appendix E

Honorary Members, Chi Eta Phi Sorority

Ella W. Allison
Ludie Andrews
Hattie Bessent
Hazle W. Blakeney
Amanda C. Blount
Rose Lee Brady
Delores F. Brisbon
Edith P. Brocker
Mary Elizabeth Carnegie
Lillian Carter
Olivette Kalfa Caulke
Anna B. Coles
Alida C. Dailey
Blythe Davis
Anne Davis Drice
Rhetaugh G. Dumas
Vernice Ferguson
Lula P. Foster
Florence Gipe
Ann Papino Glenn
Hazel A. Goff
Camille Masco Goldsmith
Charles E. Hargett
Mary S. Harper
Ruth W. Harper
Paula C. Hollinger
Theoria Houston
Virginia Hunter

Jennie Jergenson
Alma Vessells John
Hazel W. Johnson
Alleah B. King
Lena Lavette
Katherine Lepper
Mary Eliza Mahoney
Grace Sata Matsunaga White
Charlotte K. May
Mary Mills
Barbara Nichols
Estelle Massey Osborne
Betty Phillips
Edith V. Plump
Isabelle Ryer
Marion B. Seymour
Gloria R. Smith
Myrtis Snowden
Reva Speaks
Mabel K. Staupers
Ivy Tinkler
Sharon McBride Valente
Lula Warlick
Bessie Whitman
Betty Smith Williams
Marian Willingham
Margaret A. Wilson

Appendix F

Charter Members,
National Black Nurses' Association

NBNA logo.

Betty Jo Davison
Mary Harper
Florrie Jefferson
Phyllis Jenkins
Mattie Kelly
Geneva Norman

Winifred Riddle
Gloria Rookard
Janice Ruffin
Lauranne Sams
Ethelrine Shaw-Nickerson
Betty Williams

Source: Smith, G. R. (1979). Liberation Through a Professional Association: A Case Study of the National Black Nurses Association. Unpublished doctoral dissertation, Union Graduate School, Cincinnati, Ohio.

Chronology

1854–1856—Mary Seacole, a black woman, nursed in the Crimean War with Florence Nightingale

1861–1865—Black women nursed in the Civil War—Sojourner Truth, Harriet Tubman, Susie King Taylor, to name a few

1865 —Freedmen's Bureau established by Congress, March 3

1879 —Mary Mahoney, America's first black trained nurse, graduated from New England Hospital for Women & Children, Boston, Massachusetts

1883 —Sojourner Truth, abolitionist and Civil War nurse, died September 26, Battle Creek, Michigan

1886 —Spelman Seminary (renamed Spelman College), Atlanta, Georgia, started first nursing program for blacks. Led to a diploma

1893 —Nursing program (diploma) established at Howard University, Washington, D.C.; first in the country in a university setting

1896 —American Nurses' Association founded; membership derived from alumnae associations, hence blacks eligible then

—Supreme Court decision, *Plessy* v. *Ferguson*, established the "separate but equal" doctrine

1898 —Namahyoke Curtis, a black untrained nurse, assigned by War Department as a contract nurse in Spanish-American War

—Anita Newcomb McGee, MD, organized army nursing service

1900   —Jessie Sleet Scales, first black public health nurse

1901   —Army Nurse Corps established under Army Reorganization Act, with a nurse in charge

1903   —Nurse Practice Acts secured by the state nurses' associations in New York, New Jersey, North Carolina, and Virginia

1906   —Elizabeth Tyler Barringer, first black public health nurse on staff of the Henry Street Visiting Nurse Service, founded in New York by Lillian Wald

1908   —National Association of Colored Graduate Nurses founded by Martha Franklin

      —Navy Nurse Corps authorized by Navy Appropriations Act of 1908

1909   —First convention of NACGN held in Boston

      —Lillian Wald was among the 60 persons who signed the call to conference, which led to the establishment of the National Association for the Advancement of Colored People, February 12

      —Ludie Andrews, at her own expense, sued the Georgia State Board of Nurse Examiners to secure black nurses the right to take the state board examination and become licensed; succeeded in 1920

1912   —At the invitation of Lavinia Dock, NACGN sent a representative to International Congress of Nurses in Cologne, Germany—Rosa Williams Brown; Adah B. Thoms and Ada Senhouse represented Lincoln School for Nurses

1913   —Harriet Tubman, Civil War nurse, died in Auburn, New York, March 10

1914   —Booker T. Washington, founder of Tuskegee University, initiated National Negro Health Week to inspire public and private agencies to join forces to improve the health of the Negro people. Black nurses in all areas of work and education participated in projects to call attention to the many health needs of black people

1916   —Membership in ANA derived from state nurses' associations; some states barred black nurses, hence barred from ANA

1918   —Eighteen black nurses admitted to the Army Nurse Corps after armistice of World War I; assigned to Camp Sherman, Ohio, and Camp Grant, Illinois

—Frances Reed Elliott Davis, first black nurse accepted in the American Red Cross Nursing Service; her pin read "1-A," with the letter "A" designating "Negro"

—NACGN organized a nursing registry to place black nurses for private duty, staff nursing, and as directors of nursing

1920 —NACGN incorporated in New York state

1921 —Nursing Service, Veterans Bureau, established

1923 —The newly constructed Veterans Hospital at Tuskegee, Alabama, dedicated. Until 1941, this was the only Veterans Administration facility where blacks were assigned

1926 —Mary Mahoney, America's first black trained nurse, died January 4; buried in Everett, Massachusetts

—Annual observation of Negro History Week (now Black History Month) initiated by Carter G. Woodson to raise consciousness of African-Americans regarding their worth and to draw attention of others to what they have contributed to American culture

1928 —NACGN began publishing *National News Bulletin* as its official organ

1929 —Adah B. Thoms published *Pathfinders*, the first historical account of black nurses

1931 —Estelle M. Osborne, first black nurse in the United States to earn a master's degree—Teachers College, Columbia University, New York

1932 —Chi Eta Phi Sorority, Inc., a national sorority, composed of black registered nurses, organized in Washington, D.C., by Aliene Carrington Ewell, October 16

1934 —First regional conference by NACGN convened at Lincoln School for Nurses, New York

—Headquarters for NACGN established at 50 West 50th Street, New York City, in the same building with the three major national organizations—ANA, National League of Nursing Education, and National Organization for Public Health Nursing

1935 —NACGN organized the National Citizens Committee for Nursing Education and Service

1936 —St. Philip Hospital School of Nursing, a segregated unit of the Medical College of Virginia at Richmond, inaugurated a new course in public health nursing for Negro graduate nurses—one year in length, leading to a certificate

1939   —Biracial National Advisory Council of NACGN established.
              Ruth Logan Roberts, first chairperson

1940   —NACGN invited by the three major nursing organizations
              to become a member of the Nursing Council on National
              Defense, which in 1942 became the National Nursing
              Council for War Service

1941   —U.S. Army established a quota of 56 black nurses for ad-
              mission to the Army Nurse Corps, January

              —Florida State Nurses Association voted to delete the word
              "white" from its constitution

              —NACGN began campaigning in March for the removal of
              the quota of 56 that had been established for black nurses
              in the army. By the end of World War II, 512 black nurses
              had been commissioned in the army, and three units had
              served overseas

              —First black nurse to enter the military service during World
              War II—Lt. Della Raney Jackson, April. She was promoted
              in 1942 to chief nurse and then major, Army Nurse Corps

              —Midwifery School for Negro nurses inaugurated at Tus-
              kegee Institute, Alabama

1943   —Estelle Massey Riddle Osborne appointed consultant,
              NNCWS

              —Adah B. Thoms died at Lincoln Hospital in New York,
              February 21

              —The Honorable Frances Payne Bolton, Congresswoman
              from Ohio, introduced in Congress a new amendment to
              the Nurse Training Bill that barred racial bias, June. With
              this new amendment a legal fact, more than 2,000 black
              students were enrolled in the U.S. Cadet Nurse Corps;
              black specialists were appointed to U.S. Public Health Ser-
              vice, Children's Bureau of the Department of Labor, and
              the Federal Security Agency as consultants, advisors, and
              staff members

              —Susan E. Freeman, chief nurse of first black overseas unit,
              Liberia

1944   —A telegram from Truman Gibson of the War Department
              in July read: "Negro nurses will be accepted without regard
              to any quota. They will be used both in this country and
              abroad should they apply for commissions in the regular
              manner"

1945   —The U.S. Navy dropped the color bar against black nurses, January 25

—Frances F. Gaines, president, NACGN, appointed to the ANA Postwar Planning Committee—the first black nurse to serve on an ANA committee

—NACGN invited by the Joint Board of Directors of ANA, NLNE, and NOPHN in February to join these organizations in a proposed study of the structure of the national nursing organizations

—First black nurse commissioned in the U.S. Navy as ensign, Phyllis Daley, March

1946   —Mabel K. Staupers elected to board of directors of the National Nursing Council, March 1

—ANA House of Delegates in convention adopted unanimous resolution for the elimination of discrimination against racial groups

—Alma Vessells John appointed Executive Secretary, NACGN, June 27, succeeding Mabel K. Staupers, who resigned after 12 years of service

—President Truman created the landmark Committee on Civil Rights, December 5

1947   —Alma Vessells John appointed to the National Commission on Children and Youth, Children's Bureau, Department of Labor, February

—Grace Higgs, president of the Florida Association of Colored Graduate Nurses, named to the board of the Florida State Nurses Association as a courtesy member without voice or vote

1948   —Ensign Edith DeVoe, one of the four black nurses commissioned in the U.S. Navy during World War II, sworn into the regular navy (Nurse Corps), January 6

—First Lt. Nancy C. Leftenant, first black to become a member of the Regular Army Nurse Corps, March. She had joined the Reserve Corps in February 1945

—Estelle M. Osborne, first black to be elected to the ANA Board of Directors. Nominated by the Oregon delegation, she received the second highest number of votes cast; served a four-year term

—House of Delegates at ANA convention voted individual membership to all black nurses excluded from any state association with the proviso that when a state admitted black members, they would give up individual membership

—Georgia Brown McKenzie appointed auxiliary instructor, VA hospital, Castle Point, New York. First black nurse promoted beyond staff level at any integrated VA facility

—President Truman issued two executive orders mandating an end to racial discrimination in federal employment and equal treatment in the armed services, July 26

1949   —Estelle M. Osborne represented ANA as delegate to the ICN, Stockholm, Sweden, June

—NACGN members in convention in Louisville, Kentucky, August, voted to dissolve the organization

—ANA-NACGN Liaison Committee suggested that functions and responsibilities of NACGN be absorbed by ANA

—Mary Elizabeth Carnegie, first black nurse elected to the board of directors of a state nurses association. The state was Florida, and she received the highest number of votes of any candidate for that office. Reelected in 1950 for a three-year term

1950   —ANA House of Delegates adopted an intergroup relations program to work for full integration of nurses of all racial groups in all aspects of nursing

—Esther McCready instituted legal proceedings to gain admission to the University of Maryland School of Nursing

—First issue of the annual *Glowing Lamp*, official organ of Chi Eta Phi

1951   —Estelle M. Osborne elected to the board of directors of the American Journal of Nursing Company—first black. At that time, she was on the faculty of New York University

—NACGN dissolved, January

—Mabel K. Staupers received the NAACP's Spingarn Medal for "spearheading the successful movement to integrate Negro nurses into American life as equals." The medal was given at the 42nd convention of the NAACP in Atlanta, Georgia. Staupers was the fourth woman to receive it. The other three were: Mary Talbert, Mary McLeod Bethune, and Marian Anderson

1952   —ANA assumed from NACGN the presentation of the Mary Mahoney Award. That year, it went to Marguerette Creth Jackson

—First black nurse elected to the National League for Nursing Board—Willie Mae Johnson Jones, Montclair, New Jersey Public Health Nursing Service

—Governor Pyle of Arizona appointed Muriel Cheesman Island to the State Board of Nurse Examiners; first for a black in any state

1953　—Rita E. Miller Dargan, first black nurse to serve on the Basic Board of Review of the NLN Accrediting Service

—NLN Board voted unanimously to reaffirm its position that all activities of NLN, including visual aids and radio spot announcements, shall include all groups regardless of race, color, religion, and sex

—Mary Elizabeth Carnegie, first black nurse appointed to editorial staff of the *American Journal of Nursing*, July 23

1954　—Estelle M. Osborne appointed Assistant Director for General Administration of the NLN February 1. She retired in 1966 as associate general director

—Supreme Court decision, *Brown* v. *Board of Education*, asserted that "separate educational facilities were inherently unequal," thus nullifying the *Plessy* v. *Ferguson* decision, May 17

1955　—Norfolk Division, Virginia State University, only black school to participate in experimental study to establish associate degree programs. Hazle Blakeney, director of Norfolk Program

—Elizabeth Lipford Kent, first black nurse to earn a PhD

1956　—Larcie Levi Davis from New York, first black nurse to receive NLN Fellowship Award for doctoral study. The fellowships, administered by NLN until 1963, were made available through a grant from the Commonwealth Foundation

—Mary Elizabeth Carnegie joined the editorial staff of *Nursing Outlook* as associate editor, September, after having served three years with the *American Journal of Nursing* as assistant editor

—Estelle M. Osborne, assistant director for General Administration of the NLN, was one of 150 delegates to the fourth annual conference of the National Women's Advisory Committee of the Federal Civil Defense Administration, October

1961   —Mabel K. Stauper's book, *No Time for Prejudice*, published—
            history of NACGN

1962   —Lillian Harvey began a two-year term on the 12-member
            Expert Advisory Committee for the Professional Trainee-
            ship Program of the USPHS

1964   —Margaret E. Bailey, first black nurse to be promoted to
            lieutenant colonel, U.S. Army, July 15

            —Medical Committee for Human Rights, which included
            nurses, sent a team to Mississippi to provide medical as-
            sistance to civil rights workers, July

            —On July 2, President Lyndon B. Johnson signed the Civil
            Rights Act of 1964. Title VI prohibits discrimination in
            federally supported programs and institutions. Black nurses
            and students benefited

            —President Lyndon B. Johnson signed into law, September
            1, the Nurse Training Act of 1964, thereby making it pos-
            sible for many black nurses to get federal funding for their
            education

1966   —First grants awarded by the Sealantic Fund to selected
            nursing programs to reach out for Negro and other dis-
            advantaged youth to prepare them for entering and com-
            pleting baccalaureate programs in nursing

1967   —Warren Hatcher, first black male nurse to earn a PhD. A
            graduate of Mills School for Men at Bellevue Hospital in
            New York, his doctorate from New York University was
            in public administration

            —Lawrence Washington, first man (who happened to be black)
            to receive a regular army commission in the Army Nurse
            Corps. This was the result of PL 89-609 passed September
            30, 1966, by the 89th Congress, which authorized com-
            missions in the regular army for male nurses

1968   —Chi Eta Phi Sorority, Inc., organized and chartered a chap-
            ter in Monrovia, Liberia, West Africa. Twenty-one neo-
            phytes were pledged under Supreme Basileus Leota Brown

            —Helen Miller wrote and published *History of Chi Eta Phi*

1970   —Mary Harper and Lauranne Sams on ANA Commission
            on Nursing Research

1971   —National Student Nurses' Association received its first con-
            tract of $100,000 from the Division of Nursing, Depart-
            ment of Health, Education and Welfare, to employ a
            program director and staff for its Breakthrough to Nurs-

ing Project for the recruitment of minority students and men to schools of nursing, June

1972 —Ethelrine Shaw-Nickerson was elected third vice president of ANA. ANA developed a strong affirmative action program with Shaw-Nickerson as chairperson of the task force. She also served as first chairperson of the Commission (now Cabinet) on Human Rights—1976-1980

—Juanita Fleming elected to Executive Committee, ANA Council of Nurse Researchers

—National Black Nurses' Association incorporated

—Colonel Hazel W. Johnson-Brown received the Anita Newcomb McGee Award, given by the Daughters of the American Revolution to the nurse chosen by the surgeon general as the U.S. Army Nurse of the Year

1973 —American Nurses' Foundation published the *International Directory of Nurses With Doctoral Degrees*, January. Forty-six blacks identified

—Of the 36 charter fellows named by the ANA Board of Directors to the American Academy of Nursing, January 31, two were black—Rhetaugh Dumas and Geraldene Felton

—Mabel K. Staupers received the NLN Linda Richards Award at convention, Minneapolis

—Chi Eta Phi, in cooperation with ANA, restored the gravesite of Mary Mahoney, first black graduate nurse

—Mary Elizabeth Carnegie appointed editor, *Nursing Research*, September 4

1974 —ANA received a grant in July from the National Institute of Mental Health to initiate a fellowship program to help minorities earn PhDs. Dr. Ruth Gordon was appointed project director

1975 —Eleanor Acham Lynch appointed director, Department of Test Construction, NLN, January

—Lillian G. Stokes received the NLN Lucile Petry Leone Award for excellence in teaching. She had achieved recognition by her peers at Indiana University School of Nursing as an innovator of teaching techniques. She was the first black to earn this award

—First Distinguished Ludie Andrews Award presented by the National Grady Nurses Conclave, held in New York August 11, to Theresa Dixon of Detroit. The award, which was presented by Mabel K. Staupers, was initiated by Pecola Rodriquez

1976   —Cleophus Doster from California elected president of the NSNA. First black and first man

—Clara L. Adams-Ender, first woman in the U.S. Army to be granted the Master of Military Art and Science degree, June 10

—Evelyn K. Tomes received one of six grants from the ANF to collect information on black nurses. Her research project was "Black Nurses—An Investigation of Their Contributions to Health Services and Health Education"

—Three Black nurses inducted into ANA Hall of Fame: Mary Mahoney, Martha Franklin, and Adah B. Thoms

1977   —Dedication of the M. Elizabeth Carnegie Nursing Archives at Hampton University, Hampton, Virginia, October 7. Patricia Sloan, historiographer, is director of the archives

—ANA received a grant from NIMH, July 1, to help minority nurses pursue doctoral study in the area of psychiatric/ mental health nursing

1978   —Charles Hargett, first male nurse to receive the Mabel K. Staupers Award; presented by Omicron Chapter, Chi Eta Phi Sorority, New York

—The original art work of the U.S. commemorative postage stamp honoring Harriet Tubman, Civil War nurse and freedom fighter, was presented to Hampton University, April 15, for placement in the M. Elizabeth Carnegie Archives

—Barbara Nichols was first black nurse to be elected president of the ANA; re-elected in 1980

—Estelle M. Osborne, first black nurse to be inducted as an honorary fellow in the American Academy of Nursing

—Master's program in nursing at Hampton University accredited by the NLN; first master's program at an historically black institution

—Mary Elizabeth Carnegie, first black elected president, American Academy of Nursing

1979   —Brigadier General Hazel Johnson-Brown became the first black chief of the Army Nurse Corps

—Barbara Sabol appointed by Governor John Carlin of Kansas as secretary, Department on Aging—a cabinet-level post

1980   —Vernice Ferguson appointed Deputy Assistant Chief Medical Director for Nursing Programs of the VA. Her prior position was Chief, Clinical Center, Nursing Department, National Institutes of Health

—Nita Barrow knighted Dame of St. Andrew by order of Her Majesty, Queen Elizabeth II

—Patricia Sloan appointed ombudsman and consultant to executive director, ANA

1981   —Estelle M. Osborne died, December 12, in California

1982   —Cleophus Doster, past president, NSNA, elected to honorary membership

—Irmatrude Grant was first black nurse to receive the Ann Magnussen Award for Volunteer Service to the Red Cross, May 26

—Fostine Riddick Roach was the first black nurse to be appointed to the board of trustees of a major academic institution—Tuskegee University, Alabama

—Freddie Johnson, first graduate of the ANA Registered Nurse Fellowship Program, died, November 3. Johnson was an associate professor and assistant director of research at the University of Nebraska College of Nursing in Omaha

1983   —Barbara Nichols appointed secretary of Wisconsin's Department of Regulation and Licensing, a cabinet-level post

—Barbara Sabol appointed secretary, Department of Health and Environment of Kansas—a cabinet-level post

—Gloria Smith appointed Director, Michigan Department of Public Health, March 1, by Governor Jim Blanchard—the first for a nurse. For ten years, Smith had been dean of the College of Nursing, University of Oklahoma, Oklahoma City

—Three black nurses were honored by the University of Pennsylvania School of Nursing May 7 for national contributions to the profession—Mabel K. Staupers, Mary Harper, and Mary Elizabeth Carnegie

—Colonel Clara Adams-Ender, U.S. Army Nurse Corps, received the Roy Wilkins Meritorious Award for her service in seeking and achieving new milestones as a professional and a role model, July 14. The award was presented at the annual convention of the NAACP in New Orleans

—Lieutenant Colonel Joyce Johnson Bowles received the Anita Newcomb McGee Award

1984 —Estelle M. Osborne inducted into the ANA Hall of Fame

—Vernice Ferguson elected honorary fellow, Royal College of Nursing of the United Kingdom, September 12

—Ora Strickland, first black chairperson of the Board of Directors of the American Journal of Nursing Company

1985 —Mary Elizabeth Carnegie honored by Nurses' House with the first Emily Howland Bourne Award for her achievements as a leader, educator, consultant, editor, and author

—Vernice Ferguson elected President, Sigma Theta Tau International, the Honor Society of Nursing

—Ethelrine Shaw-Nickerson elected President, ANF

1986 —Nita Barrow, Permanent Mission of Barbados to the United Nations

1987 —Honorary Doctor of Laws bestowed upon Mary Elizabeth Carnegie by Hunter College, City University of New York

—Recognition Award to Mary Elizabeth Carnegie from Mugar Library Associates, Boston University, Boston, Massachusetts

—Barbara Sabol appointed New York State's Executive Deputy Commissioner of Social Services

1988 —Juanita Hunter, recipient of ANA Honorary Human Rights Award

1989 —NBNA initiated annual celebration of Black Nurses Day, February 1

—Mabel K. Staupers died, September 30, at age 99

—Gloria Smith appointed by Secretary Louis Sullivan of Health and Human Services as chairperson, National Commission on the Nursing Shortage

—Nancy Leftenant Colon (retired Air Force nurse) elected National President, Tuskegee Airmen, Inc., August, at 18th annual convention, Washington, D.C.

1990 —Congress proclaimed March 10 as Harriet Tubman Day, honoring her as the brave black woman freedom fighter

—Nita Barrow, public health nurse educator and stateswoman, appointed Governor General of Barbados, West Indies

—Geraldene Felton named to four-year term as commissioner-at-large by the Commission on Institutes of Higher Education, North Central Association of Colleges and Schools

—Geraldene Felton appointed to the VA Special Medical Advisory group—the only nurse on the 22-member panel

—Barbara Sabol named by Mayor David Dinkins to head New York City's Human Resources Administration—the first nurse to run the giant agency

—Dr. Juanita Fleming and Dr. Linda Burnes-Bolton named to the 17-member National Advisory Council for Health Care Policy, Research and Evaluation. The council advises the secretary of the HHS and the administrator of the Agency for Health Care Policy and Research

—Nita Barrow received the R. Louise McManus Award for Distinguished Service to Nursing by the Department of Nursing Education Alumni, Teachers College, Columbia University, New York, June

Index

Adams-Ender, Clara, 160–161, 207–208, 286, 287

Agency for International Development, 246–251

Agency for Toxic Substances and Disease Registry, 221

Aiken, Eula, 170, 171

Aiken, Linda, 125

Air Force Nurse Corps, 212–217

Albany State College, Georgia, 36, 44

Alcorn State University, Mississippi, 35, 36, 116

Alexander, Camille, 226, 227

American Academy of Nursing, 124–170

  honorary fellows in, 166–170

  regular fellows in, 125–166

American Association for the History of Nursing, 119–121

American Association of Colleges of Nursing, 115–116

American Association of Nurse Anesthetists, 172

American Journal of Nursing Company, 110–111, 283, 288

American Nurses' Association, 74–92, 277

  affirmative action program of, 82–84, 284

  certification program of, 177–178

  commemoration of Harriet Tubman, 10

  Commission on Organizational Assessment and Renewal, 91

  Council on Cultural Diversity in Nursing Practice, 85

  Directory of Nurses with Doctoral Degrees, 61–62

  Hall of Fame, 85, 286, 288

  limited recognition of blacks in, 75–76, 117–119, 278

  Mary Mahoney Award presented by, 21, 80, 81–82, 117

  membership for black nurses, 75–78

  Minority Fellowship Program of, 61–68

American Nurses' Foundation, 113–115, 284, 285

  International Directory of Nurses with Doctoral Degrees, 61, 285

American Public Health Association, 105

American Red Cross Nursing Service, 100–103, 279

  qualifications for enrollment in, 196, 201, 209–210

Ancelard, Madeline M., 212

Anderson, Marian, 282

Andrews, Ludie A., 188–190, 278

  Ludie Andrews Award, 287

Army Nurse Corps, 195–209, 278, 279, 284

  quota for black nurses, 97, 202, 279

Associate degree nursing programs, 36–38

Association of Black Nursing Faculty in Higher Education, 122–124

Association of Operating Room Nurses, 172

Baccalaureate nursing programs, 32–36
Bailey, Margaret, 203–204, 205, 284
Ball, Lillian, 198, 199
Baptiste, Ramona M., 236
Barnes, Alberta, 54
Barringer, Elizabeth Tyler, 178, 181, 278
Barrow, Nita, 287, 288, 289
Barton, Clara, 10, 14, 102
Battle Creek Sanitarium, Michigan, 27
Bayne, Laura Morrison, 20
Bell, Peggy, 120
Bellamy, Verdelle, 80, 85, 109, 189
Bellevue Hospital Training School, 75
Bello, Teresa, 83
Benedict College, South Carolina, 28
Berea College, 22
Bessent, Hattie, 64, 65, 80, 112, 123
Bethune, Mary McLeod, 22, 282
Bethune-Cookman College, Florida, 34, 36
Beverly, Clara E., 244
Billings, Pearl, 198
Birch, Hazel, 243
Bischoff, Lillian, 38, 58
Blackmore, Cheryl, 224
Blakeney, Hazle W., 37, 63, 283
Blockley Hospital Training School, 22
Blount, Betty Martin, 73
Bluefield State College, West Virginia, 35, 38
Bohannon, Beth, 53
Bolton, Frances Payne, bill of 1943, 48, 49, 96, 280
Bonaparte, Beverly, 73, 112, 155–156, 170, 172
Boston University School of Nursing, 58, 61
Boulding, Susie, 198, 199
Bourgeois, Marie, 168–170, 226
Bowie State University, Maryland, 44, 116
Bowles, Joyce, 44
Bowman, Shirley A., 241, 243
Boyd, Mary Rozina, 214–215

Brangman, Goldie, 172
Braxton, Josephine, 20
Breakthrough Project of National Student Nurses' Association, 53–57, 284–285
Brewster Hospital, Florida, 26
Brooks, Sarah Jane Ennies, 14
Brown v. the Board of Education of Topeka, 30, 283
Brown Hospital, West Virginia, 28
Brown, Leota, 85, 284
Brown, Rosa Williams, 278
Brown-Douglas, Robyn, 230
Bryan, Edith, 61
Bullock, Carrie E., 183–184, 185
Bullock, Esther Juanita, 254
Bureau of Health Care Delivery and Assistance, 228–230
  Division of Federal Employee Occupational Health, 230
  Division of Maternal and Child Health, Genetics, 230
  Division of National Hansen's Disease Programs, 228
  Division of National Health Service Corps, 229
  Division of Special Population Program Development, 230
Bureau of Health Professions, 226–230
  Division of Associated and Dental Health Professions, 227
  Division of Medicine, 227
  Division of Nursing, 226–227
Bureau of Health Resources Development, 228
Burgess, Eunice Johnson, 33
Burnes-Bolton, M. Linda, 161, 162, 235, 289
Burrell Hospital, Virginia, 28
Burwell Hospital, Alabama, 26
Bush Memorial (Royal Circle) School, Arkansas, 26
Butler, Inez, 243–244
Bynum, Joan, 211

Cadet Nurse Corps, 47, 48–53
Campbell, Claudette V., 237
Canton, Denise, 230
Carnegie, Mary Elizabeth, 63, 72, 80, 106, 112, 114, 119, 122, 123, 171, 285, 286, 287, 288

and American Academy of Nursing, 124–125, 133–134
and American Journal of Nursing Company, 111, 283
and Florida State Nurses Association, 77–78, 282
and Hampton University nursing program, 42, 43
and Sealantic fund, 58
Carnegie Nursing Archives, 10, 154, 286
Carnegie Scholarship, 112–113
Carter, Carolyn McCraw, 157–158
Carter, Edith, 178, 181
Carter, Ellen Woods, 186–188
Carter, Lillian, 109
Carville Facility for Hansen's Disease, 228
Center for Minority Groups Mental Health Programs, 222–223
Centers for Disease Control, 223–224
Charity Hospital, Georgia, 27
Cheesman, Muriel, 283
Chi Eta Phi Sorority, 108–110, 279, 284
  charter members of, 273
  commemoration of Mary Mahoney, 21, 285
  honorary members of, 274
Chicago State University, 116
Chow, Effie Poy Yew, 63
Christie, Teresa, 119
Chronology of blacks in nursing, 277–289
City Hospital, Georgia, 27
City of Memphis Hospitals, Tennessee, 28
Civil Rights Act of 1964, 284
Civil War, 5–12, 277
Clay, Eva, 198
Cobb, Clara L. Henderson, 238–239
Cole, Ailene, 197–198, 199
Coles, Anna B., 43–44
Collier (Duncan), Elouise, 79
Collins, Orieanna, 51, 52
Columbia Hospital, South Carolina, 28
Columbia University, Teachers College, 32, 36, 38, 42, 102, 279
Colwell (Jordense), Theresa, 243
Community colleges, associate degree programs in, 36

Community Health Project, Inc., 21
Community Hospital, North Carolina, 28
Cook, Verna, 227
Cooper, Signe, 63
Coppin State College, Maryland, 35, 116
Cornell University–New York Hospital, 58
Crimean War, 1–4, 227
Crownsville State Hospital, Maryland, 27
Cuello, Carolyn, 73
Curtis, Namahyoke, 13–15, 277

Dagrosa, Terry Williams, 43
Dailey, Alida, 98
Daley, Phyllis, 210, 281
Daniel, Elnora, 145–146
Dargan, Rita E. Miller, 29–30, 49, 50, 76, 79, 283
Daughters of the American Revolution Hospital Corps, 13
Davis, Althea, 120
Davis, Benjamin O., 203
Davis, Frances Reed Elliott, 102, 103, 107, 279
Davis, Larcie Levi, 283
Davis, Lucille, 131
Daytona Hospital, Florida, 26
Delano, Jane, 102, 196
Delaware State College, 34
Densford, Katharine, 76
DePriest, Edna, 198
Derham, James, 1
DeVoe, Edith, 210, 281
Diggs, Magnolia, 198
Dillard University, Louisiana, 34, 42, 49
Dillit, Ann, 20
Diploma programs for blacks, 23–32
Directory of Nurse Researchers, 107
Dix, Dorothea Lynde, 5
Dixie Hospital, Virginia, 28
Dixon, Alma Yearwood, 73
Dixon, Theresa, 285
Dock, Lavinia, 94, 278
Doctoral programs, 61–68
Doster, Cleophus, 112, 113, 286, 287
Doswell, Willa, 114
Douglass Hospital, Kansas City, 25, 27

Douglass Hospital, Philadelphia, 25, 28
Doyle (Harrison), Dorothy, 41, 245–246
Dreves, Katherine Densford, 76
DuBois, W.E.B., 254
Dumas, Rhetaugh, 124, 125–127, 222, 285
Dunant, Henri, 100
Dunbar Memorial Hospital, Michigan, 27
Duncan, Elouise Collier, 79
Durham, Claudia, 41, 73

Edge, Sylvia C., 73
Educational programs. See Schools of nursing
Edwards, Barba, 172–173
Edwards, Elizabeth Ann, 76
Elam, Hattie, 212, 213
Elliott (Davis), Frances Reed, 102–107, 279
Elmore, Joyce, 10, 220, 229
English, Edith, 255
Evans, Bette, 64
Ewell, Aliene Carrington, 108, 279

Federal Bureau of Prisons, 240–241
Felton, Geraldene, 116, 124, 127–128, 285, 289
Ferguson, Vernice, 73, 80, 106, 256–257, 287, 288
    and American Academy of Nursing, 125, 132–133
Fleming, Juanita, 114, 115, 128–130, 235, 285, 289
Flint-Goodridge Hospital, Louisiana, 27, 42
Florida A & M College, 26, 30, 33–34, 116
Flowers, Mary L., 237
Food and Drug Administration, 224–225
Ford, Virginia, 134–135, 243
Franklin, Martha M., 22, 85, 92–94, 120, 286
Fraternal Hospital, Alabama, 26
Freedmen's Hospital, 24, 26, 32, 43, 108, 228
Freeman, Susan Elizabeth, 203, 204, 286
Futtrell, Ronaldo, 112

Gage, Nina D., 29, 104
Gaines, Frances F., 281
Gault, Alma, 171
Gears, Amelia J., 254
Georges, Alicia, 119, 120, 227
Gibson, Truman, 280
Giles, Harriet E., 23
Gillis Long Center for Hansen's Disease, 228
Gilmore, Vashti Hall, 243–244
Glass (Pallemon), Agnes Beulah, 203, 204–205
Glowing Lamp, 109, 282
Goff, Joyce, 239, 241
Good Samaritan Hospital, North Carolina, 28
Good Samaritan Waverly Hospital, South Carolina, 28
Gordon, Lawanda Price, 239, 240
Gordon, Ruth, 63, 285
Goshen College, Indiana, 58
Grace, Helen, 123
Grady Hospital, Georgia, 27
Grambling University, Louisiana, 34, 116
Grant, Irmatrude, 103, 287
Great Southern Fraternal School, Arkansas, 26
Green, Russell L., 218–219
Green, Yvonne Theresa, 224
Gunter, Laurie, 146–147

Hale Infirmary, Alabama, 26
Hall (Gilmore), Vashti, 243–244
Hampton University School of Nursing, 10, 35, 42, 43, 116, 286
Hannah, John, 120
Hansen's Disease Center, 228
Harden, Joyce Taylor, 235
Harding, Warren G., 94, 253
Hargett, Charles, 113, 114, 286
Hargett, Florence M., 245
Harlem Hospital, 25, 27
Harper, Mary S., 82, 117, 139–141, 223, 284, 287
Harris, Faye Gary, 147–148
Harrison, Dorothy Doyle, 41, 245–246
Hartsfield, Minnie Lee Jones, 256
Harvey, Lillian, 73, 87–88, 284
Harvey, Paul R., 254
Hastie, William H., 99

Hatcher, Warren, 284
Hatot, Norma J., 241, 244
Haupt, Alma C., 29, 104
Hayes, Carnie, 231, 232
Health Resources and Services Administration, 225–230
Heisler, Anna, 76
Henderson, Clara L., 238–239
Henry Street Visiting Nurse Service, 80, 103, 178, 179, 181–182
Higgs, Grace, 77, 281
Hilfiker, Alica Sonja, 227
Hill, Sophia, 198, 199
Hine, Darlene Clark, 120, 121
Hines, Frank T., 253–254
Hines-Martin, Vicki, 113
Hinshaw, Ada Sue, 234
Holder, Barbara, 113, 114
Holder-Mosley, Roberta Annette, 236–237, 238
Holland, Jerome, 103
Holloway, Lavinia, 20
Holly, Lillian, 244
Homer G. Phillips Hospital, Missouri, 27
Ho Sang, Pamela E., 122
Hospital Training School, South Carolina, 28
Houston Negro Hospital, Texas, 28
Howard University, 26, 32, 34, 42, 43–44, 116
    first nursing program of, 23–25, 277
Hunter, Juanita K., 161–163, 288
Hunter College, New York, 58

Illinois Training School, 75
Image: Journal of Nursing Scholarship, 107
Indian Health Service, 231
Indiana University School of Nursing, 106–107, 285
Influenza epidemic in 1918, 196, 199
International programs of Public Health Service, 241–252

Jackson, Alma N., 219, 243
Jackson, Della Raney, 202, 280
Jackson, Herlinda Q., 63
Jackson, Julia Kelly, 73
Jackson, Marguerette Creth, 80, 85, 109, 282

Jackson, Rosalie, 64
Janosov, Carmen D., 63
Jefferson Polyclinic, Chicago, 22
Jerman, Sarah Belle, 22
John, Alma Vessells, 49, 85, 97, 281
John D. Archbold School, Georgia, 27
Johns Hopkins, 22, 61, 75
Johnson, Edith Ramsey, 73
Johnson, Freddie, 287
Johnson, Hazel W., 90, 156–157, 206–207
Johnson, Liz, 256, 257
Johnson, Lyndon B., 285
Johnson, Ruth W., 73, 74
Johnson, Salina L., 41
Johnson, Willie Mae, 73, 283
Johnson-Bowles, Joyce, 288
Johnson-Brown, Hazel W., 90, 156–157, 206–207
Jones, Margaret, 22
Jones, Willie Mae Johnson, 73, 283
Jordense, Theresa Colwell, 243

Kansas City General Hospital, Missouri, 27, 186
Kate Bitting Reynolds School of Nursing, North Carolina, 28
Kellogg Foundation Fund, 66, 67
Kelly, Johnea, 234–235
Kemp, Nancy Lois, 182–183, 185
Kendall, Nora, 216
Kent, Elizabeth Lipford, 61, 283
Kentucky State University, 34, 38
Kibble, Donna, 228
Kiereini, Eunice Muringo, 88, 89
King, Ellen J., 230
Knight, Frances, 56

Lacey, Bernardine M., 163
Laird, Linnie, 76
LaMar Wing, University Hospital, Georgia, 27
Lancaster (Carnegie), Mary Elizabeth. *See* Carnegie, Mary Elizabeth
Langston University, Oklahoma, 35
Lavinia Dock Award, 120
Lawrence, Ann, 213
Lee, Vivian O., 239–240, 242
Leftenant, Nancy C., 281, 285

Legislative internship for minorities, 65–66
Leone, Lucile Petry, 49, 58
Leprosy patients, care for, 228
Levine, Myra E., 63
Lewis, Irene D., 151–152
Lewis, Martha, 226
Liberian mission of Public Health Service, 242–244
Lincoln, Abraham, 7–8
Lincoln Hospital, North Carolina, 28
Lincoln School for Nurses, New York, 25, 27, 93, 196
Lincoln University, Missouri, 35, 38
Linda Richards Award, 73, 285
Lindsay, Diane M., 208–209
Logan, Barbara, 152–153
Long, Mary, 109, 115, 189, 190, 229
Louie, Kem, 63
Lowenstein, Bernadine M., 163
Loyola University, Chicago, 58
Lucile Petry Leone Award, 73, 285
Ludie Andrews Award, 285–286
Lula Grove Hospital, Georgia, 27
Lynch, Eleanor Acham, 73, 285

MacVicar Hospital, Georgia, 23
Magnussen Award, 103, 287
Mahoney, Mary Eliza, 19–20, 85, 120, 277, 279, 285, 286 See also Mary Mahoney Award
  and National Association of Colored Graduate Nurses, 178
Male nurses, 284, 286. See also specific names
  in the military, 206, 284
Malone, Beverly, 115, 159–160
Mary Mahoney Award
  awarded by ANA, 20, 80, 81, 272
  established by NACGN, 96, 178
  recipients of, 271–272. See also specific recipients
Maryland Tuberculosis Sanatorium, 27
Massachusetts General Hospital, 22, 75
Massey, Estelle. See Osborne, Estelle Massey Riddle
Master's degree programs, 42–44
Maternity Center Association, New York, 40
Matheson, Don, 64

Mathwig, Gean, 83
McArthur, Barbara Martin, 141–142
McCready, Esther, 31, 282
McGee, Anita Newcomb, 13, 195, 277
  Anita Newcomb McGee Award, 285, 288
McKane Hospital, Georgia, 27
McKenzie, Georgia Brown, 282
McLean Hospital, 22
Meharry Medical College, 19, 28, 30, 34, 43
Mental health services, 186–189
Mercy-Douglass Hospital School of Nursing, Philadelphia, 25, 28
Mercy Hospital, Philadelphia, 25, 28, 41, 186
Merritt, Mary Eliza, 22, 190–191
Mid-Atlantic Regional Nursing Association, 171–172
Middleton, Louis R., 243
Midwifery, educational programs in, 40–42, 280
Miles, Charity Collins, 218
Military Service, 195–217, 278, 280–281, 286
  Air Force Nurse Corps, 212–217
  Army Nurse Corps, 195–209, 278, 279, 284
  Navy Nurse Corps, 209–212, 278
  quota systems in, 97, 202, 280
  Veterans Administration, 252–257, 279
  in wartime. See Wartime activities
Miller, Etta Mae Forte, 42
Miller, Helen S., 40, 109, 284
Miller (Dargan), Rita E., 29–30, 49, 50, 76, 79, 283
Millie Hale Hospital, Tennessee, 28
Milliken, Sayres L., 200
Mills, Mary L., 80, 247, 249–251
Minnis, Jeanette, 198, 199
Minor, Irene, 83
Mississippi Baptist Hospital, 27
Mississippi Valley College, 38
Montag, Mildred, 36
Montague, Mamie, 235
Moore, Dorothy L., 233
Morris Brown College, Georgia, 27, 34
Morris, Mabel, 227
Moton, Robert R., 253
Mosley, Doris, 227, 228

Murray, Beatrice L., 255–256
Murray, Ernestine W., 225

Nakagawa, Helen, 64
Nathan, Marva, 236
National Association of Colored
  Graduate Nurses, 92–100, 178,
  278, 279
  and ANA, 75, 76
  charter members of, 270
  dissolution of, 77, 79–80, 282
  and military nursing, 202, 210
  and recruitment of blacks into
    nursing, 47
  registry of, 94, 279
National Black Nurses' Association,
  117–119, 285
  charter members of, 275
National Clinical Center, 232–233
National Council of Negro Women,
  19
National Federation of Planned Par-
  enthood, 173
National Health Service Corps, 229
National Institute of Mental Health,
  222, 285
  grant from, 61–62, 63
National Institutes of Health, 231–
  235, 283
  Clinical Center, 232–233
  Extramural Associates Program,
    234
  National Center for Nursing Re-
    search, 233–234
  National Library of Medicine, 233
National League for Nursing, 71–74
  fellowships of, 71–74, 283
National League of Nursing Educa-
  tion, 72–73
National Library of Medicine, 233
National News Bulletin of NACGN, 279
National Nursing Council for War
  Service, 48–49, 51, 280
National Organization for Public
  Health Nursing 103–105
National Student Nurses' Associa-
  tion, 111–112, 284
  Breakthrough Project of, 53–57,
    284–285
Navy Nurse Corps, 209–212, 278
Negro Baptist Hospital, Texas, 28

Negro Division, State Sanatorium,
  North Carolina, 28
Nelson, Margaret P. C., 215–216
New England Hospital for Women
  and Children, 19, 22, 277
New Home Sanatorium, Illinois, 27
New York Infirmary, 2
Newell-Withrow, Cora, 163–164
Nichols, Barbara, 84, 86–87, 89–90,
  158, 286, 287
Nickerson, Ethelrine Shaw, 63, 80, 82–
  83, 84, 115, 150–151, 285, 288
Nightingale, Florence, 2, 3, 4, 100,
  277
No Time For Prejudice, 284
Noble, Nora Kendell, 216
Noel, Nancy, 121
Norfolk Division, Virginia State Col-
  lege, 35, 36, 116, 283
North Carolina A & T State Univer-
  sity, 32, 36, 116
North Carolina Central University,
  35, 39, 119
Northcross, Mabel C., 85, 94, 95
Nurse Practice Acts, 287
Nurse Training Act of 1964, 284
Nurses' Educational Funds, 112–113
Nursing Outlook, 110–111, 283
Nursing Research, 61, 62, 110–111, 285
Nutting, Adelaide, 102–103

ODWIN Project, in Massachusetts, 58
Ohlson, Agnes, 79
Osborne, Estelle Massey Riddle, 49,
  72–73, 97, 104, 279, 280, 286,
  288
  and American Journal of Nursing
    Company, 110, 282, 283
  and American Nurses' Association,
    76–77, 81, 85, 99, 281, 282
  master's degree education and, 42
  in memoriam, 166–168
  and National Association of Col-
    ored Graduate Nurses, 85, 94–
    95
  and National League for Nursing,
    72–73
  and National Nursing Council for
    War Service, 279, 280
  nursing school recommendations
    of, 29, 30
Osborne Memorial Scholarship, 113

Osborne, Oliver, 64, 142–143
Owens, Melva Tuggle, 230

Packard, Sophia B., 23
Pallemon, Agnes Beulah Glass, 203, 204–205
Parham, Deborah, 230
Pathfinders, 85, 279
Paylor, Olive Vera Armwood, 222
Pennington, Helen S., 41
People's Hospital, Missouri, 27
Perkins, Gladys, 230
Perteet, Delores, 238
Petry, Lucile, 49, 58. *See* Leone, Lucile Petry
  Lucile Petry Award, 73, 285
Petty, Mary L., 203
Philadelphia General Hospital, 23
Piedmont Sanatarium, Virginia, 28
Pillars, Eliza Farish, 191–192
Pinder, Jean Martin, 247–248
Pinn, Petra A., 183–184, 185
Plessy vs. Ferguson, 26, 277, 283
Poindexter, Jeanette O'Neal, 164, 165
Point Four Program, of Public Health Service, 246
Prairie View A & M University, Texas, 28, 30, 35, 116
Prentice, Fannye M., 41
Primeaux, Martha, 63
Primus-Heath, Bobbie Jean, 113
Provident Hospital School of Nursing
 in Baltimore, 27
 in Chicago, 25, 27
 in St. Louis, 27
Public health nursing
 educational programs in, 38–40
 national organization for, 103–105
Public Health Service, 217–252
 Agency of International Development, 246–251
 Agency for Toxic Substances and Disease Registry, 221
 Alcohol, Drug Abuse and Mental Health Administration, 221–222
 Bureau of Health Care Delivery and Assistance, 228–230
 Bureau of Health Professions, 226–230
 Bureau of Health Resources Development, 228

 Center for Minority Groups Mental Health Programs, 222–223
 Centers for Disease Control, 223–224
 Food and Drug Administration, 191, 224–225
 Health Resources and Services Administration, 225–231
 international programs of, 241–252
 Liberian mission of, 242–244
 National Institute of Mental Health, 222, 285
 National Institutes of Health, 222–223
 Point Four Program, 246
 regional offices of, 235–241
 St. Elizabeths Hospital, 222
 Special Technical and Economic Mission, 251–252
 United States Relief and Rehabilitation Administration, 244–246

Quota systems
 in military service, 97, 202, 280
 in schools of nursing, 19

Ramos, Anna Oliver, 198, 199
Ramsey, Dorothy E., 165–166
Raney (Jackson), Della, 202, 280
Rathbone, William, 179
Recruitment programs
 in Breakthrough Project, 53–59, 284–285
 in Sealantic Project, 57–60, 277, 284
Red Cross Hospital, Louisville, 27, 190
Redwine, Betty, 174
Reeves, Anne, 22
Reynolds, Emma, 25
Richards, Hilda, 118–119
Richards Award, 73, 285
Richardson, Donna Rae, 90–91
Richardson Memorial Hospital, North Carolina, 28
Richmond Medical College, Virginia, 28, 35, 38, 39
Riddick, Fostine, *See* Roach, Fostine G. Riddick
Riddle, Estelle Massey. *See* Osborne, Estelle Massey Riddle
Roach, Fostine G. Riddick, 43, 109, 135–137, 287
Roberts, Mary M., 198
Roberts, Ruth Logan, 178, 280

Robinson, Emory I., 254
Robinson, Mary, 179
Rodriguez, Pecola, 286
Roosevelt, Franklin D., 242
Rollins, Clara, 198–199
Rosenwald, Julius, 29
Ruffin, Janice E., 83
Rusk, Benjamin, 1

Sabol, Barbara, 286, 287, 288, 289
St. Agnes School of Nursing, North
    Carolina, 28
St. Elizabeths Hospital, D.C., 222
St. Louis Protestant Hospital, 75
St. Mary's Infirmary, Missouri, 27
St. Philip Hospital, Virginia, 28, 38,
    279
Sams, Lauranne, 82, 83, 117, 118, 284
Sanderson, Erna S., 239
Sanger, Margaret, 173
Scales, Jessie Sleet, 178, 179–181, 278
Scholarship funds, 113–115
Schools of nursing
    advanced programs in, 38–44
        deans and directors of, 267–269
        doctoral, 61–68
        master's degree, 42–44
        in midwifery, 40–42
        in public health, 38–40
    associate degree programs in, 36–
        38
    baccalaureate programs in, 32–36
    characteristics of, 31–32
    diploma programs for blacks, 23–
        32
    integration of, 31
    quota systems in, 19
    recruitment for
        in Breakthrough Project, 53–57,
            284–285
        in Sealantic Project, 57–60, 284
    segregation of, 23–32
    surveys of, 29–30
Scott, Emmett J., 196–197
Seacole, Mary, 2–5
Sealantic Project, 57–60, 277, 284
Senhouse, Ada, 278
Seymour, Marion Brown, 198, 199
Shannon, Iris, 105, 106, 137
Shaw-Nickerson, Ethelrine, 63, 80, 82–
        83, 84, 115, 150–151, 285
Sigma Theta Tau Society, 106–108
Singleton, Nellie, 14

Skinner, Pauline V., 256
Slattery, Jim, 53
Sleet (Scales), Jessie, 178, 179–181,
    278
Sloan, Patricia E., 153–155, 286, 287
Smalls, Sadie, 113, 114
Smith, Clemmie Jean, 247, 248–249
Smith, Eunice Lewis, 222
Smith, Gloria, 63, 115, 138–139, 287,
    288
Smith, Martha Lewis, 226
Smith, Roxie Dentz, 20
Smith, Shirley, 236
Snowden, Myrtis J., 130–131
Snowden, Rose, 22
Society for Nursing History, 121–122
Sojourner Truth, 6–8, 22, 277
Southern Regional Education Board,
    174
Southern University, Louisiana, 34,
    116
Spalding College, Kentucky, 58
Spanish–American War, 12–15, 196
Spears, Lillian, 198, 199
Special Technical and Economic Mis-
    sion, of Public Health Service,
    251–252
Spector, Audrey, 171
Spelman College, Georgia, 23, 24, 277
Spivey, Christine, 217
Stanley, Robert C., 253
Staupers, Mabel K., 281, 282, 285,
    286, 287, 288
    awards presented to, 73, 100, 101,
        284
    and National Association of Col-
        ored Graduate Nurses, 79–80,
        85, 95–96, 97, 98, 104
Steele, Virginia, 198
Stewart, Frances, 198
Stillman College, Alabama, 26
Stimley, Ella Lucille, 210
Stokes, Lillian, 73, 74, 285
Stowall, Sarah, 14, 22
Strickland, Ora, 110, 143–145, 234,
    288
Sumley, Lillian May, 14
Sweetwine, Abbie, 213
Syphax, Orieanna Collins, 51, 52

Talbert, Mary, 282
Taylor, Susie King, 10–12, 277

Tennessee Coal & Iron School, Alabama, 26
Tennessee State University, 35, 38, 116
Thomas, Margaret, 41
Thompkins, Diane, 227, 233
Thoms, Adah B., 21, 93, 96, 120, 278, 279, 280
  ANA and, 85, 286
  and the military, 85, 196
Toliver, Kittie, 20
Tomes, Evelyn K., 114–115, 243, 286
Trowell-Harris, Irene, 217
Truman, Harry S., 205, 282
Tubman, Harriet, 8–10, 277, 278, 286, 288
Tucker-Allen, Sallie, 122–123
Tuggle Institute, Alabama, 27
Turner, Eunice, 91
Turner (Watson), Helen, 210–211
Tuskegee Institute, 26, 30, 34, 116, 278
  association with Veterans Hospital, 253–254, 279
  Nurse–Midwifery School, 41–42
Tyler (Barringer), Elizabeth, 178, 181, 278

United Friends School, Arkansas, 26
United States Public Health Service. See Public Health Service
United States Relief and Rehabilitation Administration, 244–246
University of Arizona, 58
University of Arkansas at Pine Bluff, 34, 116
University of Cincinnati, 32, 58
University of Maryland School of Nursing, 31
University Medical College, Missouri, 27
University of North Carolina at Chapel Hill, 39–40
University of Pennsylvania School of Nursing, 287
University of Portland, Oregon, 58
University of the District of Columbia, 116
University of West Tennessee, 28

Veterans Administration, 252–257, 279

segregation in hospital system, 253–255
Vick, Nettie, 198
Vietnam War, 208–209
Virginia State College, Norfolk Division, 35, 36
Virginia Union University, 38
Visiting nurse services
  development of, 179–181
  Henry Street, 80, 103, 178, 179, 181–182
Voorhees, Gertrude, 22

Wagner College, New York, 38
Wald, Lillian, 94, 102, 103, 104, 179, 181, 278
Walker, Marcus L., 211–212
Wallace, Clara B., 215
Warlick, Lula G., 184–186
Wartime activities. See also Military service
  and Cadet Nurse Corps, 47, 48–53
  in Civil War, 5–12, 277
  in Crimean War, 2–5, 277
  in Spanish–American War, 12–15, 277
  in Vietnam War, 208–209
  in World War I, 196–200
  in World War II, 97, 201–205
Washington, Booker T., 253, 278
Washington General Hospital, 22
Washington, Lawrence C., 206, 284
Watson, Helen Turner, 210–211
Wattleton, Faye, 173
Waverly Fraternal Hospital, South Carolina, 28
Wells, Marcia, 113
West, Charles, 243
West, Jeanette, 198–199
West, John B., 243
Wheatley Provident School of Nursing, Missouri, 27
White, Walter, 99
Whitehurst, Mary, 227
Whiteside, Marian Davis, 84–85
Whittaker Memorial Hospital, Virginia, 28
Williams, Betty Smith, 83, 148–150
Williams, Daniel Hale, 25
Williams, Mabel, 198
Williams, May, 15
Williamson-Hunt, Barbara, 237–238

Wilson, Emma, 178, 181
Wilson, Fay, 81, 82, 109
Wilson, Janie, 64
Wilson, Juanita Franklin, 31
Wilson, Lucille B., 44
Winston-Salem State University, North Carolina, 35, 116
Women's Hospital, Philadelphia, 22
Wood, Rosemary, 83

World War I, 196–200
World War II, 97, 201–205
Wright, Annette, 233
Wykle, May Louise, 159

Yergan, Laura Holloway, 251–252
Young, Janice Barnes, 120

Ziegler, Frances Helen, 171